THE COMPLETE HANDBOOK OF
FRONT WHEEL DRIVE CARS

BY JAN P. NORBYE

62527

TAB BOOKS

BLUE RIDGE SUMMIT, PA. 17214

FIRST EDITION

FIRST PRINTING—DECEMBER 1979

Library of Congress Cataloging in Publication Data

Norbye, Jan P.

The complete handbook of front wheel drive cars.

Includes index.
1. Automobiles—Front-wheel drive. I. Title.
TL260.N67   629.22'22   79-14368
ISBN 0-8306-97777-2
ISBN 0-8306-2052-4 pbk.

Contents

Foreword

Front wheel drive has fascinated me ever since I first found out it was possible to make a car go by other means than a rear axle. But at first I thought it was a dumb idea. As a boy I saw f-w-d DKWs and Adlers struggling on the hillsides, often slippery, of southeastern Norway, and was inclined to prefer more conventional machinery. But in 1937 I had my first ride in a Citroen, and that changed my whole outlook. Its wide stance and surefootedness made up for any apparent deficiency in traction. I was instinctively on the side of f-w-d from that moment on. But when I reached driving age I did not get much f-w-d experience at first, and my first cars had rear axle drive (Model A Ford and Peugeot 203). My first extended experience of f-w-d came with the 2 CV—Citroen again—on Norwegian roads.

While living and working in America, I remember applauding Oldsmobile for launching the Toronado and some aspects of the car remain impressive even in hindsight; but its original brake system was worse than worthless and steered me towards Fiat's idea that f-w-d is OK only for cars up to a certain size and weight. The Citroen DS-23 from 1973 has satisfied me that no such limits exist if steps are taken to design against the problems.

As a road tester for *Car and Driver*, I vociferously condemned the Hillman Imp in comparison with the equally powerful Austin Mini, and lauded the virtues of the MG-1100 while berating the Volkswagen Beetle.

Citroen DS-21 (1970 model) at speed on the French Autoroute. The car could cruise all day at 100 mph.

Icy Personal Experience

When Bridgehampton race circuit was frozen over I had an opportunity to show myself the difference between f-w-d and other cars under very difficult conditions. Jim Dunne and I once tested a group of cars for *Popular Science* made up of the Ford Cortina and Opel Kadett plus the f-w-d Simca 1100. The Ford and the Opel could not go straight anywhere and you were afraid to gain too much speed downhill. Roughly, I would say my lap times about doubled from what those cars could do under dry conditions. But the Simca was under control at nearly normal speed and my lap times were only 30 percent slower.

We found the same thing with the Citroen SM some years later, also out at Bridgehampton, comparing it with the V-12 Jaguar and the Mercedes-Benz 450 SLC. The SM gave traction, braking, and balance on glare ice that was completely lacking in the other two. The difference is so vast you have to experience it to believe it.

When I moved back to Europe, I became the owner of my first f-w-d car, an Alfasud L sedan. And I don't want to exchange it for anything.

Writing this book has been a labor of love, though not blind love. I am well aware of the drawbacks of f-w-d and owe particular thanks to my friends Paul Frere, engineer and journalist, former racing driver and LeMans winner, and Nick Valery, motor industry correspondent for *The Economist* in London, for discussing their objections to f-w-d with me.

On the positive side, no man has helped me more than Jean-Albert Gregoire, whose contributions to f-w-d technology I greatly admire. I have had his factory, his private car collection, his library,

The R-15 is a sports coupe with its own special body on the R-12 chassis.

his incredible memory and his friendly companionship at my full disposal whenever asked.

Many other engineers have given me personal interviews and revealed their thoughts on f-w-d and I am particularly grateful for the observations made by Stuart M. Frey of Ford, Howard Kehrl of General Motors, Rudolf Hruska of Alfa Romeo, Friedrich Goes of Volkswagen, Hubert Seznec and Pierre Tiberghien of Renault, Kenichi Yamamoto of Toyo Kogyo, and Hans Scherenberg of Mercedes-Benz.

Special mention must be made of Erik Carlsson, former rally driver and Monte Carlo winner, who has taken me for wild rides in Saabs to demonstrate the lack of constraints that f-w-d puts on your speed or driving style, while explaining what he was doing and why it worked.

Prof. Mihailo Borisavljevic of Belgrade, head of the Yugoslav society of auto engineers, pulled one historical treasure after another out of his files for my use. Dr. Wiersch of Volkswagen's central archives has also been of invaluable assistance. Al Bloemker of the Indianapolis Motor Speedway Museum kindly provided pictures and artist John Peckham allowed me to use his exquisite Cord

Gamma coupe, built on shorter wheelbase, is aimed at VHW/Mercedes-Benz customers, if they are ready to try f-w-d.

Citroen GS Birotor was good for 115 mph but had very poor fuel economy. Wankel engine was combined with C-Matic drive.

L-29 drawing. Tom Jakobowski of Chrysler was able to supply new data on the corporation's early f-w-d experiments, with photographs. Illustrations of some of the oldest f-w-d vehicles have been placed at my disposal by W. Hofr and R. Niederhuemer of the Technisches Museum Wien and Daniel Chevalier of Renault Industrial Vehicles.

For information and technical drawings, photographs, etc. of modern f-w-d cars, I am indebted to Jacques Wolgensinger and Jean-Paul Cardinal of Citroen, Jean Broncard of Peugeot, Jean-Claude Maroselli and Michel Rolland of Renault, Alain-Serge Delaitte of Chrysler-France, Lennart Lonnegren and Peter Salzer of Saab-Scania, Giuseppe Giraudi and Etienne Cornil of Fiat, Paolo Astore and Giusto Doneux of Lancia, Dietmar Fritsche and Rudolf Maletz of Volkswagen, Arno W. Holand of Audi-NSU, Thomas L. Pond of Buick and Fritz Bennetts of Oldsmobile. Precious material has also been furnished by Takanori Sonoda and Toshio Ashizawa of Honda, M. Goto and T. Etoh of Nissan Motor Co. International Division, and D. Hosoki of Fuji Heavy Industries.

Karl E. Ludvigsen, Oddone Camerana, and Etienne Cornil of Fiat produced the four-color cover, featuring the Ritmo. My gratitude also goes out to Dorothy Greenberg who had the perspicacity to seize my idea for an f-w-d book when I brought it up during her visit at our place in France, to my wife Margaret who turned my scribblings into a proper script, and to Dic Van der Feen who edited and supervised the production of the book.

Jan P. Norbye

Chapter 1
Everybody's Doing It

Front wheel drive is happening all over. Production of front wheel drive cars has more than doubled in the past ten years, and will probably double again in the next decade. About 8.7 million front wheel drive cars were built in 1978. That's equivalent to 28 percent of an estimated worldwide output of 31 million cars of all types.

Western Europe has led the trend, and now builds more than five million front wheel drive cars a year. Yet there is one country where front wheel drive completely dominates: France, with 94 percent of production. The f-w-d percentage for all of Western Europe is about 45. That compares with 16 percent in Japan, 10 percent in the Communist bloc, and less than 1 percent in the United States.

Big U.S. Switch to Front Wheel Drive

The American scene is about to change dramatically. Chrysler became the first domestic mass-producer of front wheel drive cars with the introduction of the Plymouth Horizon and Dodge Omni at the start of 1978.

After adapting front wheel drive to the 1979 Buick Riviera, General Motors will switch to front wheel drive for its 1980-model X-body compacts (new cars that will replace the Chevrolet Nova, Pontiac Phoenix, Oldsmobile Omega, and Buick Skylark—possibly continuing the same model names). At that time, Cadillac's Seville will also switch to front wheel drive, using the Eldorado engine and drive train. Overseas, GM has an f-w-d replacement for the rear-axle-drive Opel Ascona, Opel Manta, and Vauxhall Cavalier ready

Versatility of hatchback body and folding rear seat is possible with r-w-d but results are better with f-w-d, as exemplified by the Saab-99.

for production, and is experimenting with an f-w-d minicar, to replace the Chevette and other T-body models. "Pete" Estes has said that by 1982 perhaps 40 percent of all GM cars will use front wheel drive.

Ford is not far behind. The f-w-d Fiesta has been in production in Europe since 1976 and the car that will replace the Pinto (code name, Erica) for 1981 has front wheel drive. Volkswagen's total

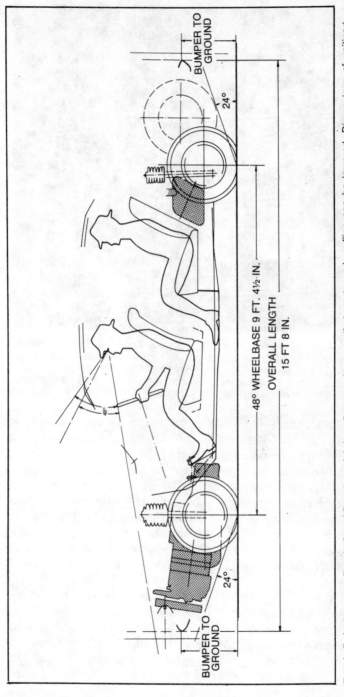

48° WHEELBASE 9 FT. 4½ IN.

OVERALL LENGTH
15 FT 8 IN.

BUMPER TO
GROUND

24°

F-w-d eliminates propeller shaft and floor tunnel, brings floor pan lower so that seats and roofline can be lowered. Dimensions of unitized power package determine length of hood and its weight sets limits for vehicle design in terms of weight distribution.

Cargo platform below bumper height is made possible on the Citroen CX station wagon by a combination of f-w-d and independent rear suspension. Minimal rear overhang minimizes changes in weight distribution between unladen and fully-loaded conditions. Since rear wheels have no traction duties, they can be moved wherever they give the best ride and handling.

U.S. production at the Westmoreland plant in Pennsylvania is made up of front wheel drive vehicles and American Motors will switch to front wheel drive as soon as it begins to assemble Renault cars (under an agreement signed in the spring of 1978).

The Japanese automobile industry was quite slow in developing front wheel drive but now it is clear that a large-scale switch is coming. Honda has made nothing but f-w-d cars since 1967. Nissan (Datsun) now has two f-w-d models in the lineup and Toyota has just introduced its first one. Toyo Kogyo (Mazda) is preparing f-w-d cars. Subaru, Daihatsu and Mitsubishi are already in production with f-w-d models.

In Europe, several manufacturers produce f-w-d cars exclusively. That includes Citroen, Renault, Audi, Autobianchi, Lancia, Saab, and Volkswagen. In addition, the most popular Austin-Morris, Fiat, and Simca models have front wheel drive, though these companies also produce various types of conventional layout with front-mounted engines and rear wheel drive. Peugeot makes more f-w-d cars than any other type and Alfa Romeo has one plant assigned to f-w-d models exclusively. Few makes that have tried f-w-d have gone back. One such case is Triumph which introduced its 1300 in 1965. The car retained f-w-d when being renamed 1500 in 1971 but was converted to rear-axle drive in 1974.

The number of front wheel drive models built around the world is growing at an accelerated pace. Their importance can be readily grasped by a study of this list:

Current Front Wheel Drive Cars

Make	Model	Country of origin	Start of production	Estimated 1978 output
Alfa Romeo	Alfasud	Italy	1972	100,000
Audi	50	W. Germany	1974	60,000
Audi	80 (Fox)	W. Germany	1972	140,000
Audi	100(5000)	W. Germany	1969	100,000
Austin	Mini	U.K.	1959	125,000
Austin	Allegro	U.K.	1973	45,000
Autobianchi	A-112	Italy	1969	55,000
Buick	Riviera	U.S.A.	1978	10,000
Cadillac	Eldorado	U.S.A.	1966	30,000
Citroen	2 CV	France	1948	130,000
Citroen	Dyane	France	1967	120,000
Citroen	Mehari	France	1969	10,000
Citroen	LN	France	1976	60,000
Citroen	Visa	France	1978	15,000
Citroen	GS	France	1970	250,000
Citroen	CX	France	1974	125,000
Daihatsu	Fellow Max	Japan	1970	35,000
Daihatsu	Charade	Japan	1977	75,000
Datsun	Cherry	Japan	1975	160,000
Dodge	Omni	U.S.A.	1978	120,000
Fiat	127	Italy	1971	350,000
Fiat	128	Italy	1969	250,000
Fiat	138 Ritmo	Italy	1978	200,000
Fiat	147	Brazil	1976	160,000
Ford	Fiesta	Spain	1976	400,000
Ford	Corcel	Brazil	1969	75,000
Honda	Civic	Japan	1972	250,000
Honda	Accord	Japan	1976	400,000
Lancia	Beta	Italy	1973	75,000
Lancia	Gamma	Italy	1976	25,000
Mitsubishi	Mirage	Japan	1978	80,000
Nissan	Pulsar	Japan	1978	100,000
Nuova Innocenti	Mini	Italy	1977	45,000
Oldsmobile	Toronado	U.S.A.	1965	15,000
Peugeot	104	France	1972	200,000
Peugeot	304	France	1969	150,000
Peugeot	305	France	1977	150,000
Plymouth	Horizon	U.S.A.	1978	150,000
Princess	1800	U.K.	1975	30,000
Princess	2200	U.K.	1975	20,000

Make	Model	Country of origin	Start of production	Estimated 1978 output
Renault	4	France	1961	225,000
Renault	Rodeo	France	1971	5,000
Renault	5 (Le Car)	France	1972	350,000
Renault	6	France	1968	100,000
Renault	7	Spain	1975	75,000
Renault	12	France	1969	350,000
Renault	14	France	1976	200,000
Renault	15/17	France	1971	20,000
Renualt	16	France	1965	80,000
Renault	18	France	1978	125,000
Renault	20	France	1975	90,000
Renault	30	France	1975	25,000
Saab	96	Finland	1959	40,000
Saab	99	Sweden	1968	100,000
Saab	900	Sweden	1978	20,000
Seat	127	Spain	1973	90,000
Seat	1200 Sport	Spain	1975	15,000
Simca	1100	France	1967	200,000
Simca	1307/1308	France	1975	250,000
Simca	Horizon	France	1978	150,000
Subaru	Leone	Japan	1971	110,000
Trabant		E. Germany	1958	90,000
Volkswagen	Polo	W. Germany	1975	100,000
Volkswagen	Derby	W. Germany	1977	125,000
Volkswagen	Golf	W. Germany	1974	350,000
Volkswagen	Rabbit	U.S.A.	1978	140,000
Volkswagen	Scirocco	W. Germany	1974	75,000
Volkswagen	Passat	W. Germany	1973	200,000
Wartburg	353	E. Germany	1968	60,000
Zastava	101	Yugoslavia	1971	125,000
			Total	8,775,000

FWD Not Sole Answer

These are impressive numbers, and there is no telling how far it will go. Yet, a word of caution may be needed here. Front wheel drive cannot be the ideal solution for *all* cars. Some cars that have f-w-d would have been better with an ordinary live rear axle. The conventional car will survive, at least in the upper weight classes, and there must be room for cars with rear-mounted engines, too.

Perhaps one day the majority of all cars built will use f-w-d. But I do not believe that all cars will go that way, and I think it would be a great pity if that were to happen. There is a threat of too much sameness in our cars even today and it's more variety, not more conformity, that is needed. People are different and have different tastes in cars. Drivers have different driving styles and want their cars to suit their own habits and preferences. They want their cars to be different. Let's hope the industry will understand this and make

Fastback sedan with low trunk floor and folding rear seat shows capacity for bulky loads and convenient liftover height. This car is a subcompact Citroen GS Club.

use of f-w-d to add new and different products, and not to realign all its cars into a new straitjacket.

When an automobile manufacturer brings out a front wheel drive model, it must not be misinterpreted as a signal that the whole car line will switch to f-w-d. The company may have reasons to choose f-w-d for a certain size vehicle while preferring rear wheel drive for other models. This is the case with Fiat, for instance, whose model lineup includes cars with rear engines and rear wheel drive as well as cars with front-mounted engines and rear wheel drive.

Mercedes-Benz has never put a front wheel drive car in production but that must not be taken to mean its engineers are opposed to f-w-d. "We have made serious, large-scale tests with front wheel drive on our cars," technical director Hans Scherenberg told me in September 1977, "and it has many advantages as well as certain drawbacks. My engineers know how to minimize the drawbacks and we were quite interested in getting a front wheel drive car into production. But the main reason we have not done it is because of our modular construction system with a number of interchangeable power trains suitable for two different basic body shells. Therefore,

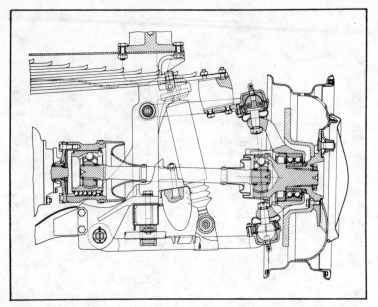

Major cost of f-w-d design lies in the front drive shafts and their constant-velocity universal joints. But it is not true that driving the front wheels necessitates reinforcement of the wheels, steering, or suspension.

we would have had to go to front wheel drive across the board, and this we are not ready to do." New product planning at Mercedes-Benz is evolutionary with the kind of continuity that builds and conserves customer loyalty. A total switch to front wheel drive would be too controversial for the marque's clientele and would not have a chance of being approved by the management board.

Only one company has a "clean" record of having built nothing but f-w-d cars throughout its existence, and that's Saab. Its traditions in car-making are not very ancient, however, and there are other firms that have been in continuous production with f-w-d cars (except for wartime interruptions) much longer. This list includes only makes of cars that are still active producers of f-w-d cars and forms a chronology for their models that introduced front wheel drive to the respective makes.

Roster of Continuous Producers

Model Year	Make	Model	Remarks
1933	Audi	Front UW	6-cyl. Wanderer engine
1934	Citroen	7 CV	Presaged complete switch to f-w-d in 5-year period
1949	Saab	92	2-cyl. 2-cycle engine

Year	Make	Model	Remarks
1956	Wartburg	P-311	Based on pre-war DKW design
1958	Renault	Estafette	Compact van
1958	Sachsenring	Trabant	Derived from AWZ P-70 Zwickau
1959	Austin	Mini	Transverse 4-cyl. engine
1959	Morris	Mini-Minor	Transverse 4-cyl. engine
1960	Lancia	Flavia	Flat-four engine
1962	Ford	Taunus 12-M	'Cardinal' project
1965	Oldsmobile	Toronado	V-8 7-liter engine
1965	Autobianchi	Primula	Fiat design
1965	Peugeot	204	Diesel engine optional since 1972
1967	NSU	Ro-80	Wankel engine
1967	Simca	1100	Fiat design
1967	Honda	N-360 Life	2-cyl. air-cooled engine
1967	Subaru	FF-1	Flat-four engine
1967	Cadillac	Eldorado	Based on Toronado
1969	Fiat	128	Transverse 4-cyl engine
1970	Datsun	A-100 Cherry	Transverse 4-cyl. engine
1970	Daihatsu	Fellow Max	2-cyl. 2-cycle engine
1972	Alfa Romeo	Alfasud	Flat-four engine
1973	Volkswagen	Passat	Based on Audi 80
1977	Nuova Innocenti	Mini	Based on Mini-Minor
1978	Plymouth	Horizon	Based on Simca design
1978	Dodge	Omni	Based on Simca design
1978	Mitsubishi	Mirage	8-speed transmission
1979	Buick	Riviera	All-independent transmission

Adaptable to Design Demands

You don't have to look very far for the reason why more and more automobile manufacturers are turning to f-w-d. We live in an era when ceaseless cost pressures are forcing the industry to maximize rationalization and standardization. That means designing groups or families of cars with modular construction. With a few basic elements, a large number of variations become possible. And front wheel drive lends itself much more easily to modular construction than the conventional layout with front engine and rear wheel drive.

The same f-w-d power train and rear suspension system can form the basis for vehicles of widely different character and purpose, starting with the basic sedan. It takes little extra to make a station wagon. A long-wheelbase wagon or taxicab? It can be built without changing any drive train parts—extra sheet metal is inserted and reinforcements added, exhaust pipe is lengthened, longer hand-brake cable and hydraulic brake lines are fitted, and a longer fuel line from the tank goes in. That's all.

Conversely, the wheelbase can just as easily be shortened to build a sports coupe or convertible with their own, specific sheet metal. A further possible variation is the sports-wagon. With a new

Conventional drive train of the Fiat 124 shows encumberment of propeller shaft and rear axle. Both need generous clearance from body shell to permit wheel travel and spring deflections on bumps, etc.

chassis platform, the steering column can be raised and seats moved forward to create a line of light commercial vehicles of the compact-van type, with a short hood or without a hood. Van, minibus, pickup, ambulance, hearse, plus cab-and-chassis only for a multitude of special-purpose vehicles. There's a basis for recreational vehicles of many types, too.

Because standard components can be used to such a large extent, it can become profitable to build small series of vehicles that differ in body type, styling, equipment and carrying capacity. Allied with this body style versatility is the promise that f-w-d gives more useful space within a given package size.

Ramifications of Lower, Flatter Floor

A conventional car with its propeller shaft has either a high floor or a central tunnel from dashboard to back seat. Both rob interior space. A high floor also tends to push up the roofline, adding frontal area, which means greater air drag. The f-w-d car makes a lower-flatter floor possible, with more useful space. Not all f-w-d designs exploit these possibilities to the full but the VW Polo and the Citroen CX2400 are outstanding examples of what can be done on widely different scales

Without the need for a drive line to the rear, f-w-d cars don't care which way you put the engine. It can go sideways, it can be installed lengthwise but offcenter, or packaged in any way that saves space, lowers the center of gravity, facilitates assembly and improves accessibility. The low floor is especially important for station wagons and hatchback sports cars with folding seats, adding considerably to their versatility.

Cars with rear-mounted engines are not suited for station wagon layouts, for instance. And even cars with front engines and rear axle drive waste a lot of space to provide room for the axle to bounce around in. Most f-w-d cars have independent rear suspension which offers greater freedom to move the back seat further to the rear without ruining the ride comfort and simultaneously frees up more space for fuel tanks, spare wheel, and luggage.

Huge Variety of Power Trains

Among current f-w-d models there is an amazing variety of engine types and drive train configurations. They can be divided into five basically different families. There is no agreement among the constructors as to which is best for any given type of size of car. One

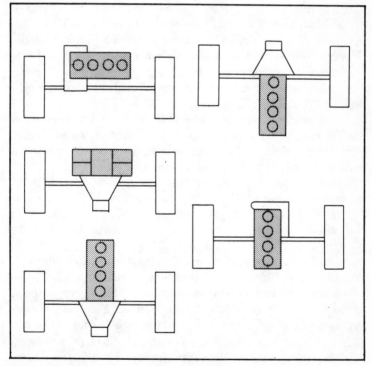

Families of f-w-d layouts are shown schematically. Left, top to bottom: Transverse engine, overhanging flat-four and overhanging in-line four. Top right: Longitudinal engine inside wheelbase, and below: Longitudinal engine centered on front wheel axis.

manufacturer even builds cars of three different families: Renault. The 4, 5, 6 and 16 have four-cylinder in-line engines standing vertically behind the front wheel axis, with the final drive and gearbox in front. The 12, 15, 17, 18 and 20 have the exact opposite layout: the engines are placed ahead of the front wheel axis, with the transmision behind. The 30 even has a V-6 in this overhanging position. Another model, the 14, has a transversely mounted slant-four. This one is the easiest to explain, for it's a Peugeot engine, as used in the 304, with the same drive train. And Peugeot had adopted the transverse engine installation for its first f-w-d car, and sticks with it.

Transverse mounting (east-west engines, as some call them) has gained great popularity for four-cylinder engines, and even some sixes are installed crossways. Leyland's Princess comes with either an 1800 cc four or a 2200 cc six, both mounted transversely. Other cars in this family are Audi 50, Austin Allegro, Austin Maxi, Autobianchi A-112, Citroen LN, Citroen CX, Datsun F-11, Fiat 127 and 128, Ford Fiesta, Honda Civic, Lancia Beta, Leyland Mini, Peugeot 104 and 304, Seat 127, Seat 1200-Sport, Simca 1100 and 1307/1308 (Chrysler Alpine in the UK), Volkswagen Polo, Derby, Golf and Scirocco, and Zastava 101. All have four-cylinder engines. Some stand straight up, some slant forwards and others backwards. Some have offset final drive units, and some of those have unequal-length drive shafts (notably Fiat).

Oldsmobile engineers wanted to install the V-8 tranversely in the Toronado, but the corporation ordered them to place it in line. Why? At that time Cadillac was preparing the Eldorado, and also a V-12 engine. And the V-12 was too long to fit sideways. Olds later said it was because of engine rocking, due to torque reactions but those are the same whichever way the engine is installed. The GM V-8 installation puts the engine partly on top of, partly alongside the transmission. Four-cylinder engines in this family include the Saab 99 and the now defunct Triumph 1300/1500.

Only Renault persists in using the straight-back method, which both Citroen and Audi adopted when they began production of f-w-d cars in the early 1930s. But the in-line overhanging layout has been adopted by several important makers: Audi 80, 100, and Volkswagen Passat, with their slant-fours, and the Saab 96 with its German Ford V-4. There's the Ford Ckorcel with its in/line four (developed from the same base as the Renault 12), and the NSU Ro 80 with its twin-rotor Wankel engine (discontinued in 1977). Finally, there's the three-cylinder in-line two-stroke engine of the Wartburg 353, also overhanging, in the nose of the car.

The fifth family ranges from the most primitive to the most advanced. This category includes cars with horizontally opposed engines (flat-twins and "quadrazontals") positioned ahead of the front wheel axis. This configuration provides a short engine, many not protruding in front of the wheels, with a low center of gravity. Horizontally opposed four-cylinder engines are also better balanced than in-line fours. Citroen builds a group of cars with air-cooled flat-twin engines: 2 CV, Dyane, Mehari, and Visa. A more modern design, the GS, has a four-cylinder version of the same basic engine. Two years ago, about 1,000 GS Birotor cars were built, with a twin-rotor Wankel engine placed transversely. Water-cooled four-cylinder units are used in the Subaru Leone, Alfasud and Lancia Gamma.

No Engine Size Limit

Europeans used to think that there was a limit to engine size and power that could successfully be applied to an f-w-d car. Fiat thought it was about 1,600 cc and 80 hp. Citroen throught it was about 2.3 liters and 125 hp. But General Motors proved with its 7-liter and 8-liter f-w-d V-8s that no such limit does in fact exist. The fact that the biggest f-w-d cars built in Europe today are the 2.2-liter Princess, 2.2-liter Audi 5-cylinder, and 2.4-liter Citroen CX is not a reflection of the state of the art. It reflects the market conditions and a lack of demand for big powerful cars of any type.

There are technical reasons as well as commercial ones for each manufacturer's choice of drive train configuration. A company considering the adoption of f-w-d for a new model must consider very carefully what f-w-d will do to the car concept, how it will affect production costs, and how it can be turned into a competitive advantage in the market place. We will examine all the technical factors in the next chapter and later go into an examination of modern engineering practice on a make-by-make basis. Finally, the complete background on f-w-d will be presented, going back to the start of motorized transport.

More Expensive to Produce?

The matter of cost is one I would like to clear up right now. F-w-d has acquired a reputation for being more expensive to produce. Many auto manufacturers admit production costs are higher for their f-w-d cars than for models with other types of drive train. No doubt they are telling the truth. But read the words carefully. It means what it says and no more. It applies to the f-w-d cars they make and not necessarily to other f-w-d cars.

Back in 1962, a leading Audi engineer, Wilhelm Haupt, stated that his company's f-w-d cars had higher production cost than cars with rear-mounted engines and listed three main reasons:

1. Stronger front suspension required to handle the tractive force and the extra weight of the transmission and final drive without giving up springing qualities.
2. Stronger steering linkage required due to the extra loads imposed by the tractive force.
3. Constant-velocity universal joints needed at front wheel hubs to avoid cyclical drive speed variations.

Volkswagen's technical director for the Made-In-USA models, Dr. Friedrich Goes, confirms that his company's costs (at the Wolfsburg plant) went up with the switch from the Beetle to the Golf (Rabbit). Ford's chief car research engineer, Stuart M. Frey, has no hesitation in saying there is an additional cost involved with front wheel drive. How much? Other Ford engineers put a figure of $50 on it in the case of switching from the rear-axle-drive Pinto to the f-w-d project code-named Erica. How is this calculated? There may be other factors not directly related to f-w-d playing into their calculations.

If you include scrappage of a lot of equipment and machinery for making rear axles, differential gears, pinions and ring gears, then front wheel drive is going to look bad. But if you start from scratch, costing part by part, as if made in factories already tooled for the purpose, the picture will look a lot different. It's making changes in mass-production plants that costs money.

Howard Kehrl, GM vice president in charge of design, engineering, environmental activities, manufacturing and research, told me that he did not think there was necessarily any cost penalty associated with front wheel drive for compact U.S. cars. His reasoning is that you make up for the extra cost of the constant-velocity universal joints at the front wheel hubs by eliminating the propeller shaft and simplifying the rear suspension system.

Savings from Everything at One End

F-w-d cars and cars with rear-mounted engines share the advantage of combining the whole works at one end of the chassis. Money is saved by eliminating the propeller shaft which has at least two universal joints and often comes as a two-piece design with a splined junction and a central support bearing.

If the car is designed with the engine in front (and it is logical to put the engine in front, because the front wheels need space to turn, leaving a narrow section that is just right for an engine but not very good as a luggage compartment), then the rear axle presents the lowest-cost way to get the power from the flywheel to the road wheels.

A live axle also permits the use of a very simple and inexpensive rear suspension system (Hotchkiss drive) with longitudinal semi-elliptic leaf springs that not only carry the load but take up the driving thrust and serve to locate the axle.

With f-w-d, the rear suspension system can be simplified even further since its only duties are the basic load-carrying, wheel-locating, and brake-thrust absorbing functions. Many f-w-d cars with transverse engines use spur gears for the final drive, avoiding the extra cost of the high-precision machined and carefully matched set of pinion and ring gear.

Yet the chassis with the rear-mounted engine has even further opportunities for cutting costs. Here the front suspension can be kept simple and the need for power steering is eliminated, while f-w-d cars of quite modest size and weight can suffer hard steering. The rear suspension system needed with a rear engine is less complex and therefore cheaper than the front suspension system of an f-w-d car. The drive shafts for the rear-engined car can use ordinary universal joints while very expensive constant-velocity joints are required for the f-w-d car.

On the subject of power steering, I hasten to lay the blame on incompetent engineering and not the principle of f-w-d. It's not the

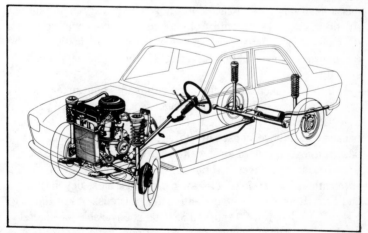

Rear suspension on f-w-d cars can be made extremely simple, lightweight, and needing little space. Only mechanical parts connecting front and rear are the rear wheel brake lines. Exhaust pipe could be shortened but is usually drawn to rear end outlet. This example is the Peugeot 204.

drive system that makes power steering necessary on some f-w-d cars, it's the combination of weight, steering layout, and suspension geometry. For instance, Chrysler equips its Plymouth-Horizon (made in USA) with power steering while the Simca Horizon (made in France) has no need for it. When properly engineered, f-w-d cars big and heavy enough to need power steering tend to belong in a price class where it's usually standard anyway.

Many Fit Automatic Transmissions

Finally, there's the matter of automatic transmissions. Some critics say it's difficult to make f-w-d cars with automatic transmission. Why they should have said is that it may be difficult to fit automatic transmissions designed for cars with front-mounted engines and rear wheel drive into certain f-w-d vehicles, particularly those designed with transverse engines. But there is no technical difficulty about designing an automatic transmission for f-w-d cars.

In the very smallest cars, there may be space problems. The Audi 50/VW Polo design came a year after the Golf/Rabbit which is available with automatic transmission, while the newer and smaller car is not. This decision was made at the outset of the design work. In order to make the car as small and light as possible, the designers did not provide the extra space required for installation of an automatic transmission.

Another example: When the Mini-Minor was designed, there was no thought that a demand would ever exist for automatic transmissions in this type of car. It has never been very important but Austin in collaboration with Automotive Products came up with a unique type of automatic transmission that could be installed in the existing vehicle without making changes in the chassis layout or body structure.

If Citroen and Honda offer semi-automatics only instead of fully automatic transmissions, it is not because of some inherent problem associated with f-w-d or due to installation difficulties. It is simply because they have chosen to do it that way (a decision largely based on cost considerations, with an eye on customer preference).

Renault has never had the slightest difficulty over producing automatic-drive versions of its f-w-d cars regardless of vehicle type and size. Renault offers fully automatic transmissions in the R-5, R-12, R-15, R-18, R-20 and 30 TS. If it's not available for the R-14, it's because Renault does not make an automatic for transverse installation. And if it's not available on the R-4 and R-6, it's because these cars are aimed at the low-priced end of the market where the addition of an automatic transmission would constitute a dispropor-

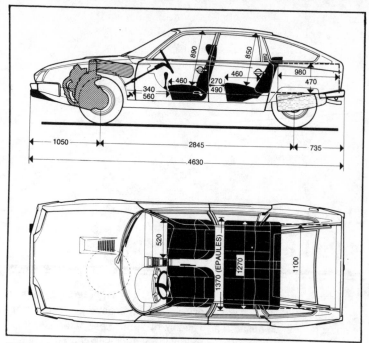

Full-size family car design can be kept within reasonable length and weight by transverse engine mounting and clever streamlining. Front installation of spare wheel frees up trunk space without hurting accessibility to the engine.

tionate amount of the total cost and move the car up into a higher price bracket (where, presumably, it would no longer be competitive).

In the next chapter we'll take a closer look at the question of whether pulling the car by its front wheels actually has any advantages over pushing it by its rear wheels.

Chapter 2
Is Pull Better Than Push?

Advocates of f-w-d have an impressive list of advantages to support their emphatic "yes." Detractors of f-w-d also have powerful arguments at their disposal. The validity of some observations varies according to car size and architecture, engine displacement, configuration and location, and several other design parameters. The relative advantages of front wheel drive also depend greatly on what kind of vehicle is used for comparison (front engine/rear drive or rear-mounted engine).

Simplistic ads for f-w-d cars once likened other cars to wagons being pushed by horses from behind. Silly drawings made the idea of driving the rear wheels fundamentally wrong, with the principle of f-w-d as the only correct way. Of course the corollary won't stand up. Making a vehicle go by applying torque to its wheels, front or rear, is not the same as moving it by a tractive effort applied directly to the chassis or body. The automobile is self-propelled, not a trailer. Driving a car by its front wheels is not the same as towing a trailer and rear wheel drive does not correspond to pushing one.

Is Pull More Logical?

Still, the comparison may have left you with the feeling that there's greater logic in driving the front wheels. But what are the facts? These are the points claimed as advantages for front wheel drive over both rival configurations:

1. Superior traction
2. Higher directional stability

3. Superior cornering characteristics
4. Better ride comfort
5. Better space utilization
6. Greater body style versatility
7. Lighter weight
8. Reduced risk of rollover

The anti-front wheel drive arguments are centered on these points:

1. Uphill traction problems
2. Power on/off steering phenomena
3. Larger turning circle
4. Brake-balance problems
5. Need for power steering
6. Excessive tire wear
7. Higher production cost
8. More costly maintenance and repairs

If the only criterion is traction, then it's logical to drive the wheels that carry the greatest share of the load. Consequently, heavy trucks, with their payload concentrated above the rear axles,

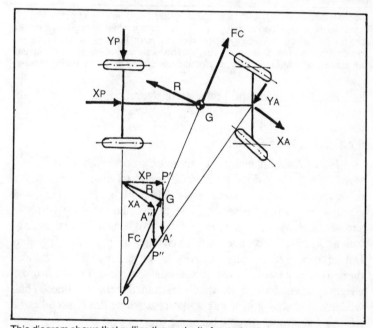

This diagram shows that pulling the car by its front wheels puts lower side forces into the tires than when the car is pushed by its rear wheels (X_A is smaller than X_P) and therefore f-w-d cars can theoretically go faster on curves.

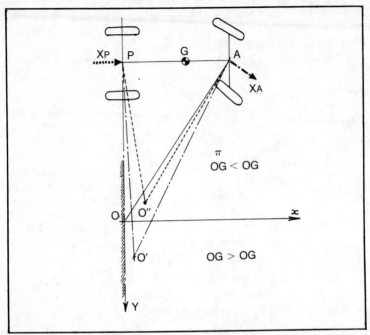

Coordinates show why f-w-d cars tend to understeer: Applying a tractive force at A moves the turning center from its theoretical location to a point giving a longer turn radius 0′. In contrast, applying the tractive force at P brings the turning center to a point that shortens the turn radius, 0″. The example gives both f-w-d and rear drive cars the same center of gravity location, which is rarely the case in practice.

for which traction is the primary consideration, have rear wheel drive.

If All Things Were Even....

Now take a car with perfectly even static weight distribution. Would front wheel drive give equally good traction as rear wheel drive? No—because as soon as you add a driver, passengers, and luggage, you have altered the weight distribution. The result in almost every case, is a rearward bias. When you start driving, weight distribution changes with all changes in speed and direction. During acceleration, when traction is of paramount importance, there is a rearward weight transfer in the car—in other words, weight is taken off the front wheels and added to the rear ones. Thus we have two strong indications that rear wheel drive gives better traction for normal, evenly balanced cars.

Of course, cars usually do not have equal load on front and rear wheels. Rear wheel drive cars with 55/45-percent front/rear weight distribution are quite common. That places less than half the weight on the driving wheels. The same car, converted to f-w-d, would have 55 percent of the weight on the driving wheels. For such weight distribution, the f-w-d cars would have the edge under most conditions.

When a company starts building f-w-d cars, it is never a question of converting an existing model to front wheel drive, however. It would be just as unthinkable to convert a Chevrolet Corvette to front wheel drive as for instance, to disconnect the f-w-d train of the Citroen DS-19 from its engine, add a conventional transmission, propeller shaft, and live rear axle. It could be done, but in both cases, the results would be ridiculous. The further the engineers go to specialize a car for front or rear drive, the more impractical it becomes to alter the drive train layout.

High Front Wheel Loading Common

All current production-model f-w-d cars are designed from scratch as f-w-d cars, static load percentage on the front wheels can go to 60, 65 and even 70 percent. Too great a forward weight bias threatens to introduce other problems, however, particularly in the handling and braking areas. Therefore the weight distribution must be a compromise.

One of the priorities in this compromise is to maximize the benefits of driving the front wheels. Nobody designs the car first, and then decides which wheels should do the driving.

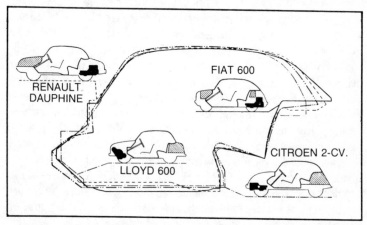

Four economy sedans of almost identical interior dimensions are compared to show advantages of rear-engine layout over f-w-d. The Fiat 600 is the shortest, lightest, and uses the least amount of materials, it also has the lowest production cost.

Cars can be designed to go either way, such as Rover's P6, which was the basis for an f-w-d turbine car, but went into production as the rear-wheel-drive Rover 2000. Such flexibility entails failure to fully exploit potential space utilization of f-w-d.

There is a trend, especially in small cars, towards driving the wheels at the end which holds the engine. You won't find anyone today who will dispute the advantages of driving the rear wheels of a rear-engined car. Some leading auto engineers in Europe say that any front-engined car should also have front wheel drive. Others will say that it depends on size and weight. Fiat, for instance, uses rear engines for its smallest cars, front engine and rear drive for its larger cars, and front wheel drive for its mid-range cars.

"For cars up to a certain engine size," Harry Mundy wrote in *The Autocar* in 1959, "the engine must surely be combined with the transmission at one end of the chassis, if costs are to be reduced and sacrifices in accommodation avoided." On a cost basis, nothing can beat the all-in-the-rear combination for a small car. That's the major reason why Ferdinand Porsche put the engine in the tail of the original Volkswagen and the overriding reason why Fiat builds the 126 with its engine next to the rear wheels.

Nevertheless General Motors has demonstrated that there is no absolute maximum engine size beyond which front wheel drive becomes impossible. The Olds V-8-powered GMC motor home and the 8-liter Cadillac Eldorado have proved that point. Opinions are divided on the question of how well GM succeeded. Mercedes-Benz acquired a Toronado in 1966 for testing and evaluation. The report concluded it was unsuitable for European roads not just because of its massive size but rather due to its excessive understeer, inadequate brakes, and high fuel consumption. The tires wore out in ridiculously short distances. I learned of this experience when talking with Wolf-Dieter Bensinger who was then head of an experimen-

Toronado drive train had center drive shaft running through tunnel in crankcase. Power flowed from torque converter via chain drive to planetary gear sets.

tal engineering section at the Stuttgart works. He said that he personally considered the Toronado a worse mistake than the Corvair.

Working Traction From Stability

But back to the matter of traction. Former chief engineer of Saab, Gunnar Ljungstrom, compared his creation, the Saab-93, with the Volkswagen Beetle and Volvo PV-444 to show the superiority of

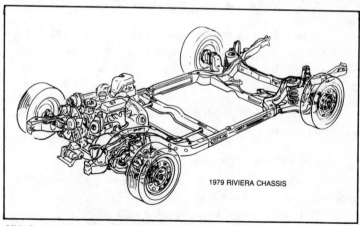

1979 RIVIERA CHASSIS

All-independent suspension was adopted for the f-w-d Riviera chassis, using torsion bars in front and coil springs in rear.

f-w-d over conventional layouts (he was less concerned over the inferiority of f-w-d to the rear-mounted engine in terms of traction, for rear-engine cars had by that time been widely discredited for their lack of dynamic stability and other drawbacks). He made up a chart showing the percentage of weight on the driving wheels:

	Saab	Volkswagen	Volvo
Level, driver only	60	57	45
Level, 4 occupants	56	60	50
20° downhill, driver only	66	52	38
20° downhill, 4 occupants	62	54	43
20° uphill, driver only	54	63	51
20° uphill, 4 occupants	50	68	57

If we can use the sum of the figures for weight percentage on the driving wheels under all conditions as an index number for all-around traction, we get:

1. Volkswagen   354 points
2. Saab   347 points
3. Volvo   284 points

The above figures apply whether the tire-to-roadway coefficient of friction is 15 or 85, if it's rainwet and slick or dry, abrasive tarmac. But something happens that changes the actual quality of traction as the coefficient of friction is lowered. On a slippery hill, it's the front wheel drive car that gets to the top first. The rear-engine car may have better traction but it's the front wheel drive car that has the stability to let the traction work in the right direction and in the right direction only.

With partial wheelspin the f-w-d car still runs straight. It does that because its rear wheels are free of side forces and torque loads. On rear-drive cars, the moment wheelspin sets in, they begin to pull sideways. The f-w-d proponents' claim to superior traction may be false or mythical but the f-w-d car's ability to run straight under low-friction conditions, and thereby give the impression of superior traction, is legitimate and factual.

Directional Stability = Superior Safety

The directional stability of f-w-d cars plays a vital role under a variety of conditions. First of all, as a matter of safety at speed. "Pull is safer than push," said Wilhelm Haupt, a leading Audi engineer. His thesis is that cars are not stable when the tractive force can be deflected by side forces. Therefore, cars with rear wheel drive are

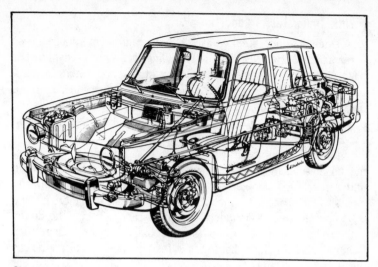

Simplicity of rear-engine layout is demonstrated by the Renault 8. It was very cheap to build, but had stability and handling problems. Also, the need to turn the front wheels stole trunk space that would become available in the tail end if the engine had been moved up front.

not stable. The driving thrust acts through an instantaneous center whose exact location depends on the specific rear suspension design but which generally lies a short distance ahead of the rear wheel axis.

Where do the side forces act? There are two kinds, driver-induced and wind-induced. Driver-induced side forces (centrifugal forces) act through the front tires initially, and subsequently through all four tires. Wind-induced side forces act through the car's center of aerodynamic pressure which on modern cars with average streamlining is located in the cowl area. In rear-wheel-drive cars, the pressure center is therefore located far ahead of the instantaneous center of drive thrust. That makes for a basically unstable condition. On front wheel drive cars the drive thrust is applied through the front suspension linkage and therefore *ahead* of the center of aerodynamic pressure. That makes for a basically stable condition.

The distribution of centrifugal force between front and rear wheels depends on the center of gravity location—not its height but its distance from the front wheels. The shorter the distance, the higher the inherent stability. Front wheel drive cars tend to have a greater concentration of weight at the front end with a center of gravity located closer to the front wheels than is usually the case with rear wheel drive cars. This forward bias in weight distribution is an underlying cause of the understeer characteristic displayed by most f-w-d cars.

A Little Understeer a Good Thing

Does this understeer conflict with the customers' requirements in terms of steering response and handling precision? Is that good or bad? Slight understeer is desirable but strong understeer is unacceptable. What is understeer? It's when the car turns less than the driver directed it to by his steering wheel input (over-steer is the opposite). When a car understeers, it runs with larger slip angles on the front tires than on the rear tires.

No one wants a car with completely neutral steering for that means ceaselessly alternating between a little oversteer and a little understeer, forcing the driver to continuously readjust his command inputs to the changes in vehicle behavior. Chassis designers usually try to put enough basic understeer into a car to provide the driver with predictable response and a restful control situation. Oversteer is an unstable condition that tends to feed on itself and force the car out of control (spin out).

Slight understeer provides the driver with a restful control situation and an ability to go through curves at high speed with no change in vehicle response or attitude. If he enters a turn too fast, he can save the situation by merely backing off on the accelerator—an instinctive action, to which the understeering car responds in the desired fashion. An understeering f-w-d car is invariably in a stable condition and its understeer has a self-diminishing tendency.

Reducing Torque Variations

This probably requires a little more explanation. Let's start with the wheel and its duties. Front wheels steer. They must provide the necessary lateral grip to do this with minimum loss of energy, minimum wear on the equipment, and a maximum of safety, at a variety of speeds.

Steered wheels require greater lateral stability than non-steered wheels because they are subject to higher side forces (all other factors being equal). Because a driving torque applied to steered wheels adds to the side forces acting on them, it seems that front wheel drive is at a disadvantage in terms of directional control.

But the fact is that driven front wheels work with lower side force levels as a result of the driving torque being applied in the direction the wheels are pointing. Since the front wheels of an f-w-d car can tolerate higher side forces than a rear-drive machine of similar weight and weight distribution, it is easy to conclude that the f-w-d car can go through curves at higher speed. But that's only in theory.

As we have seen before, f-w-d cars do not have the same weight distribution. The extra weight carried by their front wheels imposes a limit on their safe cornering speeds. But make no mistake—those speeds can be remarkably high! F-w-d cars have won many races in the past and are prominent in European rallies with many victories to their credit.

The basic understeer of the f-w-d car stems from the greater self-centering force in the front wheels. Driven front wheels run with higher self-aligning torque which means they have higher resistance to deviations from a straight path. Since the tractive force varies with engine speed and accelerator position, some f-w-d cars have demonstrated a nasty habit of changing from understeer to oversteer in the middle of a curve as a result of the driver lifting his foot off the gas pedal. This phenomenon is known as power-on understeer/power-off oversteer. Its cause is easily understood. Front slip angles tend to increase with power-on because the torque applies an additional load to the wheel. That produces understeer. If this torque is suddenly turned off, the forces acting on the wheel are reduced and as a result the slip angle is diminished.

It might seem as if the car's behavior suddenly changed from understeer to oversteer. Oversteer can indeed be induced in front wheel drive cars by taking the foot off the accelerator when negotiating a curve, but it takes great skill, high speed, and very low tire-to-roadway friction coefficients to actually get the car into an oversteering attitude (tail end out, steering with opposite lock). Under normal conditions, what the driver feels is a marked reduction in understeer, an approach to neutral steering characteristics. He must crank the steering wheel back to a lesser input in order to keep the car on the chosen course (constant turn radius).

Sensitivity to accelerator position is, of course, an undesirable trait in a car's behavior and much work has been done to eliminate it. Tire engineering has made a big contribution. Steel-belted radials mounted on wide-base rims, adequately sized, enable the front wheels to accept the torque load variations with minimal changes in tire slip angle, for instance. The rest was done by fine-tuning the suspension geometry and controlling roll steer effects (especially the changes in camber angles on the front wheels as the body leans over in a curve).

Suspension Engineering Confounds Theory

Suspension systems can now be so designed that no metter where the engine is located the car can be given suitable handling characteristics. It is easy to see the theoretical imperfections of the front engine/rear drive layout. The tractive force is not being applied in the direction the car is going whenever the car deviates from a straight path. The tractive force is applied at a tangent to the car's direction of travel. Thus, the front wheels are fighting the rear ones and vice versa. Since the driving wheels are rigidly parallel to the chassis, there is an appreciable difference in the angle between front and rear wheels every time the car has to negotiate a curve. Consequently, changes in direction on a car with a front engine and rear drive mean severe loads on suspension members, steering linkage, hubs, tires, and chassis. Such cars have structural reinforcements to cope with such loads. That means extra weight.

For the f-w-d car, it means weight reduction. We'll discuss the weight-saving aspect of f-w-d in connection with the cost picture later on. First, we have to look at the influence of f-w-d on ride comfort and the risk of rollover accidents.

Help in Getting the "Good Ride"

Ride is something that Americans are most concerned with and f-w-d can contribute to greater ride comfort. That's because it opens the way for all-independent suspension at little or no extra cost. It eliminates the rear axle, the biggest mass of unsprung weight in a conventional car and the worst enemy of a smooth ride. It can be

Ford Escort with rear-axle drive corners in extreme over-steering attitude. In contrast, f-w-d cars invariably tend to understeer (though rally drivers can provoke rear-end breakaway at will). For normal driving, understeer is preferred.

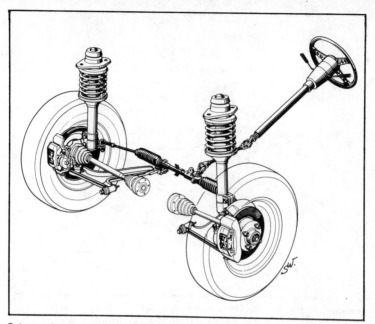

Scirocco front suspension includes lower control arms with an unusually wide base and spring legs mounted aft of the hub center.

replaced by trailing arms, for instance, carrying spindles for freewheeling rear wheels. Alternatively, the wheels can be mounted in a lightweight "dead" axle, needing only a simple attachment since it's free of driving torque and thrust loads. Softer springs with longer deflection travel can be used, further improving the ride.

At the front end, f-w-d is compatible with popular independent suspension systems (MacPherson struts; double wishbones). In fact, lighter parts may be used in some cases. That's just the opposite of what you'd expect, since you've added the driving force to the steering duties of the front wheels. It's actually the rear-drive cars that need front suspension reinforcements and the reason is that, in any curve, the driving thrust is applied at a tangent to the car's direction of travel. The front wheels are fighting the rear ones and vice versa. With f-w-d the conflict is resolved since the rear wheels are simply trailing the front ones.

Yet it's a fact that most f-w-d cars have slightly greater unsprung weight in the front end due to the drive shafts, universal joints, and the use of larger tires. Some engineers have taken advantage of the drive shafts to mount the brakes inboard, adjacent to the final drive unit, which reduces unsprung weight to lower-than-normal levels.

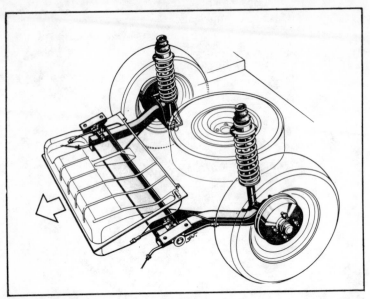

Scirocco rear suspension is independent with trailing arms and coil springlegs, though lateral interconnection exists in the form of a transverse bar near the pivot axis for the trailing arms.

Expensive Vibration Problem Cures

Freedom from vibration plays a big role in ride comfort. Insulation of rear axle and propeller shaft noise and vibration remains a major problem in conventional cars. With f-w-d the problems are different but just as severe. Torque reactions in the drive shafts are about three times stronger than in the drive train of a conventional car. This fact puts extra emphasis on engine mounting systems but does not necessarily increase cost or weight.

Control of vibrations from the drive shafts is mainly dependent on the type of universal joints. With true constant-velocity joints, cyclical feedback from the wheel hubs to the steering gear and transmission controls is eliminated. The angularity of the outer joints varies mainly with steering angles but also with wheel deflection and must be able to change angularity in several planes concurrently. The inner joints have to cope mainly with suspension movements and are almost unaffected by steering movements.

The most elaborate and sophisticated combinations are the most satisfactory but their higher cost restricts their use to high-grade cars, while economy cars demonstrate diminishing acceptability as the combinations become increasingly primitive and less and less expensive.

Even the cheapest combinations, however, benefit from the fact that the drive shafts revolve at wheel speed rather than transmission output speed, i.e., one-quarter to one-third as fast as the propeller shaft in a conventional car. As a result, they do not as easily generate rotational vibration.

Many f-w-d engineers have gone to the extent of placing a torsional vibration damper on the right drive shaft to cushion the effect of torque reversals. Several other f-w-d car makers have added a hydraulic damper on the steering linkage but such devices are common also on conventional cars (GM intermediates, Mercedes-Benz) and even rear-engined models (VW Beetle).

With f-w-d, gear noise is more easily eliminated than in cars using rear axle drive. That's because the entire power train is compact, rigid, and mounted as a unit. Mechanical noise insulation is simpler because all drive elements are contained up front.

Safer and Faster from Lower CG

But now a word about safety. Rollover accidents can happen in many ways. Most cars now in production manage to keep their wheels on the ground even when driven too fast into a curve. They skid and spin before they roll. F-w-d cars tend to have lower center-of-gravity height than other types of cars. The f-w-d layout gives the designers greater freedom to make a low chassis.

The elimination of the propeller shaft and live rear axle make it possible to lower the floor level. Not all f-w-d car designs make full use of this but the opportunity is there and it can be a safety factor of

Adler Trumpf Junior had a four-cylinder engine inside the wheel-base, giving a lengthy hood, but frame design assured low seating and a low center of gravity.

some importance. The wider the track and the lower the center of gravity, the less the risk of rollover from centrifugal force. A low center of gravity also helps cornering stability. There is less weight transfer due to centrifugal force with a lower center of gravity and that means the car can be driven at higher speed on a given curve before the instantaneous tire/road surface friction is exceeded and the tires lose their sidebite.

In the passive safety area, f-w-d does not make much difference. It does not give rise to problems for bumper structures or controlled crumple-rate front ends; nor does it offer much in the way of better opportunities for improved crash-energy absorption. Compared with conventional cars, in some of which the propeller shaft plays a part in energy management, the f-w-d car may have a slight disadvantage.

A rollover can also be the sequel to a spinout and here the same physical laws apply. But there is something that changes the picture in favor of f-w-d cars: They have less risk of spinout due to their inherent understeer (many rear-engine jobs were known for their violent oversteer).

A rollover can also occur when a car veers from the road and heads into a deep ditch. Here we must look for the cause of the veering, not for the result, which can be taken as equal for all cars. But if the car veered because of sidewinds, we know that it was probably not a front wheel drive car with its greater directional stability.

Turning Circle and Braking Capacity

F-w-d cars usually have wider turning circles than rear-drive cars. Some designers resist the possibility of using the full angular range of modern universal joints. Others use joints with a lower range. But there is no technological limit to f-w-d steering angles. Prototypes with f-w-d and 90-degree steering angle capability exist.

F-w-d cars usually have higher front braking capacity than rear-drive cars due to the forward bias in weight distribution. That's an advantage but it also introduces a balance problem for rear braking capacity is correspondingly reduced. The weight transfer that takes place during braking accentuates this problem. It removes load from the rear wheels and adds it on the front. Under braking from high speeds, the rear wheels can easily be unloaded to the point where they can only undertake a very small proportion of the total braking action. If full brake line pressure is applied, the rear wheels will lock, which always leads to instability (side pull and a risk of losing control). Systems to regulate rear brake line pressure are

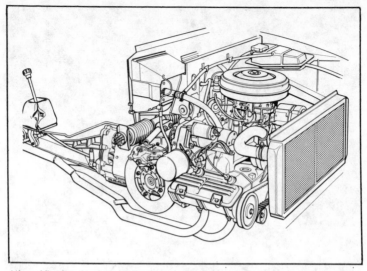

Alfasud flat-four engine shortens front overhang (compared with in-line engines) and gives lower center of gravity, as well as permitting lower and more streamlined hood line.

common on cars of all types but more elaborate devices are needed for f-w-d cars.

Does it reduce overall braking effect? Of course it does. When a car has four tires, the braking duties should ideally be shared equally among them. Since forward weight transfer under deceleration is unavoidable, it becomes apparent that the most effective braking is obtainable with a tail-heavy car (rear-mounted engine). Nose-heavy cars, whether f-w-d or conventional, are doomed to some loss of potential braking capability. How serious is this? Don't lose any sleep over it. Many f-w-d cars have shorter stopping distances than the average for their weight class.

Bad British Experience

One further point claims our attention. F-w-d cars in fleet use have been accused of higher maintenance and repair costs than conventional cars. Is there some innate fragility in f-w-d systems that cannot be eliminated or suitably protected? Not at all. On looking into this question, I find it was an insular problem, non-existent outside the British Isles.

The biggest fleet buyers in Britain are the rent-a-car companies and they suffered some dreadful experiences with certain domestic makes of f-w-d cars. Those cars had shockingly poor quality and most of their defects had nothing to do with the fact that they were

Due to forward weight bias to start with, forward weight transfer during braking, rear wheels on f-w-d cars handle only about 30 percent of the total braking duties. But f-w-d cars can stop in the same (or shorter) distances if their brake systems are properly engineered, as on this Citroen DS-21 with its central hydraulic system.

driven by their front wheels! But the damage was done. The rental firms switched en masse to simple, reliable cars with conventional drive trains (including some from the same source) and their profits improved. The stigma sticks not to a make of car but to the idea of f-w-d.

And that's really meaningless on the strength of what happened in Britain. InterRent in Germany is a VW subsidiary and Europcar in France is a Renault subsidiary. Their fleets consist overwhelmingly of f-w-d cars (not restricted to VW-Audi and Renault only though British cars are not included). The Continental European branches of Hertz, Avis and National use f-w-d cars extensively—but their fleets do not include British-built f-w-d cars!

To sum up, f-w-d may not possess all the qualities that are claimed for it in full measure but the case against f-w-d on technical grounds has been demolished. In fact, the only person I have found who would seriously argue against front wheel drive on technical grounds was Emile Petit who was chief engineer of Salmson in Paris back in the 1920s. I interviewed him in 1967 shortly after Simca and Peugeot had introduced their first front wheel drive cars. Petit maintained that the front wheels were made to steer and that it was a fundamental error to apply driving torque to them. "One must not put all those forces into the same two wheels," Petit insisted. I thought the same argument could be used just as effectively against front wheel brakes and the question remained unresolved when we parted. Not that opponents of f-w-d remain silent!

"Front wheel drive is a fad," said Ferry Porsche, commenting on Volkswagen's turnabout in engineering philosophy in 1973. His company is not likely ever to build a f-w-d car and the reason was explained to me recently by Porsche's chief engineer of car development, Helmuth Bott. He believes Porsche drivers want the driving thrust at the opposite end from the wheels that steer, to balance the car by playing the forces of front and rear against each other. What he means is that the Porsche car offers "oversteer-on-tap", easily provoked and easily controlled.

Despite the common origin of the Porsche and the Volkswagen, the VW management determined that its customers did not share the Porsche drivers' demands. When Porsche lost its contract with Volkswagen for prototype construction and development, the Wolfsburg company went to f-w-d in a big way and it's obviously no fad.

Chapter 3

Constant-Velocity Universal Joints

Universal joints are articulations in rotating shafts that permit the transfer of power at variable angles. Cars with front-mounted engines and rear axle drive have universal joints in the propeller shaft that links the transmission output shaft (attached to the frame) to the final drive input shaft (free to move up and down with the wheels).

F-w-d cars have universal joints in the drive shafts to each wheel. That would be necessary even if the front wheels did not also have to steer the car. The steering duties complicate the demands placed on the universal joints.

To avoid any possible misunderstanding, let's start at the beginning. Shafts are, more or less by definition, straight. They do not like to bend and with one or two notable exceptions are made not to bend. Bending shafts that are not intended to will result in metal fatigue and failure in the shaft. If there is angular displacement between the two ends of a shaft, the shaft must be split to permit each end to operate without having to absorb bending loads.

What Joints Do for Shafts

In a propeller shaft, one split would be enough, theoretically, to give the rear portion of the shaft (and the axle) the required freedom of movement. But if the shaft were split in the middle, the joint would be a long way from either axle or transmission. Special support bearing would have to be installed close to the joint, and that adds cost and complication. Instead, each end of the shaft has its own joint.

This use of two joints has another advantage. Speed fluctuations induced by one joint are cancelled out in the second so that the power flow to the axle comes in as smooth and regular as it went out of the transmission.

The basic form of universal joint provides uniform velocity only when its working at zero angle, in other words, when it's working as part of the shaft and not as a universal joint. A simple universal joint, as used by Cardano and Hooke hundreds of years ago, consists of two yokes on opposite shaft ends, meeting at right angles. The yoke ends are connected by a cross. Each yoke is free to change its angle to the cross but the shaft's rotation is transferred to the cross and therefore to the opposite yoke.

Because the four pins of the cross are positioned at right angles to each other, the joint periodically comes to a point where the entire angular deflection is handled by one side of the joint. There are four such extreme positions during each revolution because as the joint rotates, one pair of cross pins follows the plane of the driven yoke, and therefore the attitude of the intermediate member is continuously changing.

Problems for Velocity Changes

Along the way, the cross is rocking backwards and forwards to accommodate these extreme positions of the yokes. This produces

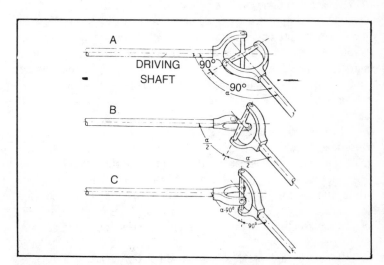

Sketch shows cyclical variations in the rotational speed of the driven shaft with a simple Cardan joint due to one of the two members taking the full angle twice per revolution, slowing down or speeding up the driven shaft four times per revolution.

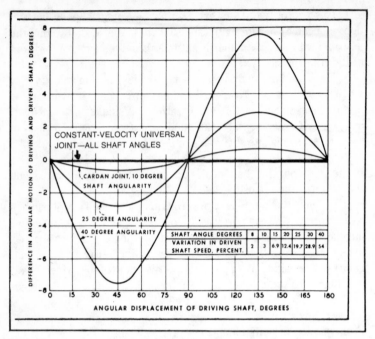

The table within the figure:

SHAFT ANGLE DEGREES	8	10	15	20	25	30	40
VARIATION IN DRIVEN SHAFT SPEED, PERCENT.	2	3	6.9	12.4	19.7	28.9	54

This diagram shows how speed fluctuations increase when joint angularity increases. Zero-line represents constant-velocity joint.

minute accelerations and decelerations in the driven part of the shaft. Assuming that the driving part runs at a steady speed, while the shafts have to operate at a constant angle, the driven part will go faster and slower in a cyclical pattern according to a sine wave of simple harmonic motion. The extent of the speed fluctuations depends on the difference in the effective radii of the crosspins relative to the center-line of the driven shaft. Speed fluctuations increase in severity as the joint angle is sharpened.

In a one-piece propeller shaft with a universal joint at each end the speed fluctuations affect only the middle piece of the shaft. The joint near the rear axle cancels the fluctuations put into the shaft by the joint behind the transmission. This would be adequate for driven front wheels, too, if the wheels did not also have to steer. That introduced angular changes in the horizontal plane and these changes can be far greater than the vertical changes resulting from suspension deflections.

If ordinary universal joints are used on f-w-d cars (especially at the outer end) the result will be vibrations in the steering wheel, increased tire wear, and reduced universal-joint life. If shaft-driven wheels are to be able to steer a vehicle, the shaft must have outer joints that allow the requisite steering angles. Inner joints need angles of 15-18 degrees only, but outer joints (nearest the driving wheels) must accommodate angles up to 45 degrees.

Cardan and Hooke Are Basic

Ordinary universal joints are often called Cardan joints or Hooke joints because of their inventors. Gerolamo Cardano was born in Pavia in 1501, became a mathematician, philosopher and doctor of medicine. He invented a ship's compass about 1550, using a universal joint to keep the compass level regardless of the vessel's rolling and pitching. He was a true scientist of the Renaissance and produced learned papers on a variety of subjects until he died in Rome in 1576.

Robert Hooke (1635-1703) reinvented Cardano's universal joint and applied it to sundials. In Britain, it became known as the Hooke joint. When he built an astronomical telescope tracking device, Hooke also discovered the non-uniform motion characteristics of Cardano's universal joint during a complete revolution of the shaft.

In making further experiments, Hooke discovered he could phase two universal joints to cancel cyclical fluctuations in the rotational speed. To achieve this, identical joint operating angles with exact joint phasing had to be maintained. This is the origin of the back-to-back universal joint used in a number of modern f-w-d cars. The speed fluctuations in the inner member of the outer joint are canceled by the fluctuations in the outer member. The only part that runs at variable velocity is the link yoke that separates the two back-to-back joints. The link yoke contains a center ball and socket to maintain joint phasing—each of the two joints operates through exactly one half of the complete deflection.

The Search for a Constant Velocity Joint

It may seem an unnecessarily complex way of doing what's theoretically a simple job and many inventors searched for a correct theory that would result in a mechanically simple constant-velocity joint. One of the first to throw out the idea of the cross and replace it by a ball was a French engineer, Nemorin Causan. The Causan joint used a central ball between the shaft ends which were carried by segments inside a tilting sleeve. The whole joint was enclosed in a spherical casing. The central ball was connected to forks from both shaft ends and moved on its own center so as to bisect the angle between the shafts. This invention no doubt inspired other pioneers of the constant-velocity joint, such as Fenaille, Weiss and Rzeppa.

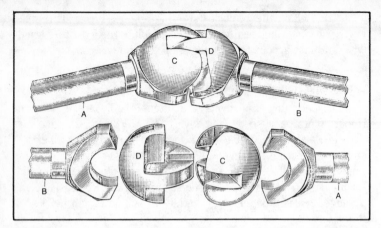

Tracta constant velocity joint used two balls linked by an intricate pattern of keys and slots, with fork-type ball carriers allowing full angular freedom but no speed variations.

The idea of running a plurality of balls in toroidal grooves separating the joint sections that were part of the opposing shafts had also been around for a time. The first multi-ball design was patented by William A. Whitney of Rockford, Illinois, in 1912. It probably was not successful as there was no provision for controlling the ball location. Whitney simplified his invention and received a new patent in 1921 but still the design did not control ball location to assure uniform velocity at all times.

Weiss and Tracta Joint Answers

The first commercially successful constant-velocity joint was patented by Carl W. Weiss of Brooklyn, New York, in 1925. Weiss was head of an engineering company and used to build oil engines. He also invented a continuously variable transmission system about 1924. The Weiss joint was made up of an outer hemi-spherical cage with a number of intersecting toroidal tracks on the inner face, and an inner ball race. The only driving contact was between the balls and their tracks. The ball race was splined to the shaft and the cage attached to the stub-axle. The balls were free to move in one plane only, always aligned so as to bisect the angle of deflection. For instance, with a 30-degree angle, the joint would operate with all contact points in a 15-degree plane.

The Weiss joint was notable for permitting some freedom of movement in the axial plane without upsetting its basic function. The Tracta joint became popular about the same time. It was a novel and ingenious variation on the single central ball theme.

The Tracta joint was enclosed within a spherical casing made up of two overlapping shells (for assembly purposes). What connected the two yokes inside was an intricate assembly of two sectioned hemispheres, pivoting on opposite yokes and connected via keys and

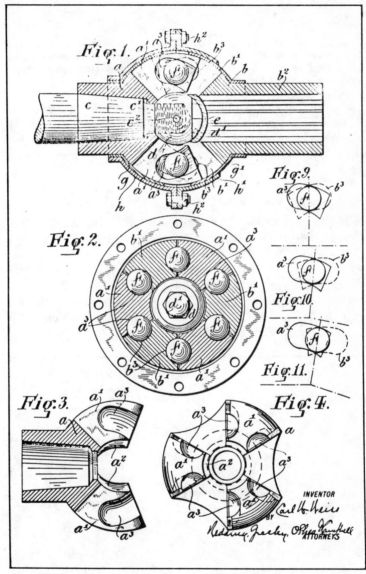

Patent drawings for the Weiss joint shows constant-velocity power transfer via balls running in grooves, automatically aligning themselves to split the joint angle in two equal parts.

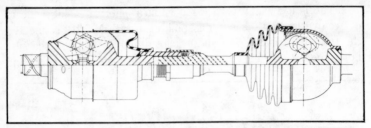

Typical f-w-d shaft with Weiss-Bendix inner (left) and outer constant-velocity joints. Shaft is splined to allow axial play—the shaft has to get longer whenever the wheel is deflected up or down.

slots. The Tracta joint gave constant velocity rotation at angles up to 50 degrees. It is not as compact as the double Cardan joint or joints of the Weiss and Rzeppa types but can handle very high torque. It has been applied more to the steering axle of all-wheel-drive vehicles than to f-w-d cars.

Rzeppa to Birfield, and the Delta

The most sophisticated constant-velocity joint to date is the Rzeppa, patented in 1935 by a Ford engineer, Alfred Hans Rzeppa (1897-1965). In the Rzeppa joint the driving member is an inner spherical race and the driven member a spherical cup, each with six curved ball tracks machined into their surfaces. The drive is transmitted by six steel balls inserted in these tracks, with a spherical cage that locates the member relative to each other. The cage also guides the balls along their tracks.

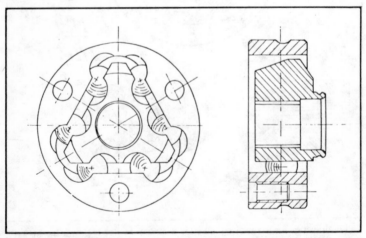

Delta type universal joint is usually preferred for inboard location because of limited angularity. Triple ball tracks assure constant velocity.

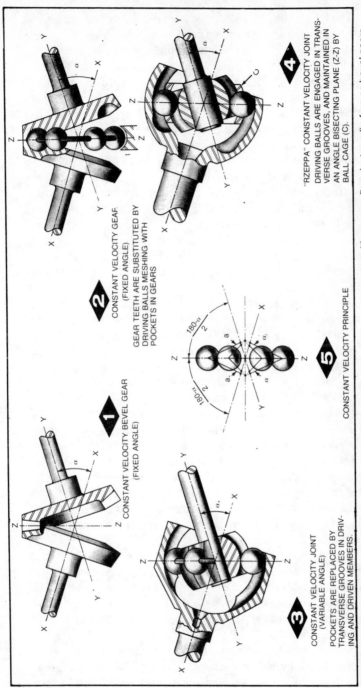

1 CONSTANT VELOCITY BEVEL GEAR
(FIXED ANGLE)

2 CONSTANT VELOCITY GEAR
(FIXED ANGLE)

GEAR TEETH ARE SUBSTITUTED BY DRIVING BALLS MESHING WITH POCKETS IN GEARS

3 CONSTANT VELOCITY JOINT
(VARIABLE ANGLE)

POCKETS ARE REPLACED BY TRANSVERSE GROOVES IN DRIVING AND DRIVEN MEMBERS.

4 "RZEPPA" CONSTANT VELOCITY JOINT

DRIVING BALLS ARE ENGAGED IN TRANSVERSE GROOVES, AND MAINTAINED IN AN ANGLE BISECTING PLANE (Z-Z) BY BALL CAGE (C).

5 CONSTANT VELOCITY PRINCIPLE

$\frac{180-\alpha}{2}$ $\frac{180-\alpha}{2}$

Principle of Rzeppa joint shows driving balls meshing with pockets in the casing to assure positive power flow, while offering full ability to vary transfer angles in motion.

The Rzeppa ball tracks differed from the Weiss design mainly in emanating from a single common point as meridian lines of a sphere while the Weiss tracks formed intersecting channels in the form of a cross with their center lines crossing in two axial, aligned planes. Rzeppa added a spherical three-ball lever to control cage and ball movement to prevent mislocation of the balls during low-angle operation. The locating pin was a feature of all Rzeppa joints until the mid-1950s when the need for it was eliminated by the invention of elliptical tracks to give positive guidance for the balls.

Instead of following exactly the curvature of the balls, the grooves are generated on arcs with a longer radius. The arc centers of the tracks in the inner and outer members are offset in opposite directions so that each pair of matching tracks forms a curved funnel for the balls to run in. The offsets are the smallest possible that assure correct positioning of the balls on the median plane at all times. The refinement was made by Birfield, the British licensee for Spicer universal joints, and was soon adopted by the parent organization.

Under certain conditions, the earliest Rzeppa joints had locking troubles when one groove surface would act as a cam and wedge the balls against the other section. The adoption of the piloting device went a long way to cure that, and the problem does not exist with Birfield-type joints. The Delta joint came along in the mid-Thirties as a lower-cost version of a constant-velocity joint, generally chosen for the inner position on the drive shafts.

Most designers of f-w-d cars use constant-velocity joints at both ends of the drive shafts while others economize and use ordinary universal joints at the inner ends.

This involves a problem that may be somewhat unexpected to the reader and the reason lies in the outer (constant-velocity) joints. These outer joints certainly do what they claim and effectively transmit rotation without speed fluctuation from one shaft to another. But they also faithfully reproduce any fluctations that the driving shaft may deliver to it.

In practice, this means that road surface irregularities which cause vertical suspension deflections will lead to angular changes in the inner universal joint—and if it's not of the constant-velocity type, it will generate speed fluctuations in the shaft which the outer joint will transmit to the wheel and tire and from there will be fed back to the steering wheel.

Delta type joints have restricted angular deflection but tolerate considerable axial variations. A typical Delta joint is made up of an inner and an outer ring with three ball tracks machined in their

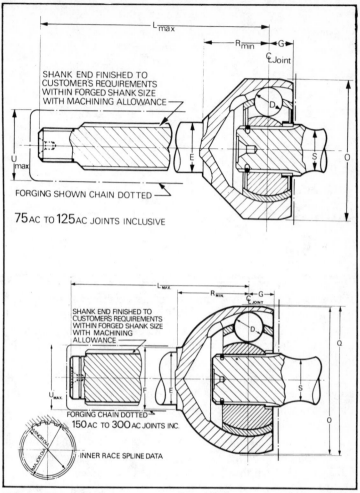

Birfield-Rzeppa joint works without a locating pin by having ball tracks machined with a larger radius than that of the balls, so that the balls automatically gravitate to the center line.

adjacent peripheries. The inner ring is attached to one shaft end and the outer ring to another. The balls are retained by circlips.

Compared with the Weiss joint, where the ball race lines up to bisect the angle of deflection between the shafts, the Delta joint keeps the balls in alignment with the member that carries it. But the rotation of the balls does produce uniform velocity power transmission.

Chapter 4
Citroen

Citroen has been the first name in front wheel drive as long as I have been aware of cars and it's still the first in f-w-d technology today. It would not be logical to start this make-by-make survey with any other car. The rest will follow, more or less in order of descending importance.

Citroen has made nothing but front wheel drive cars in the past 45 years. The current range of Citroen cars comes in two families: the economy cars with air-cooled engines, and the luxury cars with water-cooled engines.

The first of the modern Citroen cars was the DS-19. It went into production in September, 1955, and was discontinued in April, 1975. It was so far ahead of its time that I have selected to make it part of the present scene rather than to treat it as a milestone in history. It also provides a convenient comparison for the vehicle that replaced it, the CX.

Mechanically, the DS-19 was created by an engineering team led by the brilliant Andre Lefebvre (who has been responsible for the original f-w-d Citroen in 1934). The body design came from the studio of a sculptor named Flaminio Bertoni who said he was inspired by an aquatic fowl. Incidentally, DS stands for Desiree Speciale, and the number 19 indicates engine displacement (1900 cc).

A six-cylinder horizontally oopposed engine was designed for this revolutionary new car but in the final analysis, Citroen could not afford to tool for both the vehicle and the engine at the same time so it was decided to use the old four-cylinder engine.

DS-19 cutaway shows front suspension and drive train mechanism with equal-length control arms and air-oil springing. Front disc brakes were mounted inboard on the drive shafts.

Unconventional and All Function

Everything else was new. And not just new but advanced ...futuristic...a revelation. The DS-19 was designed to provide maximum ride comfort and safety without regard to whatever complication might be necessary to obtain it. The result was a totally unconventional kind of car. A central hydraulic system, for instance, took care of springing, power steering, gear-shifting and braking. The body was styled not for fashion but for aerodynamic efficiency.

The engine was placed vertically within the 123-inch wheelbase and the front wheels carried 70 percent of the car's static weight of 2,569 pounds. This 70/30 weight distribution assured a near-total absence of traction problems. Normally it would have aggravated the brake-balance problems of f-w-d cars but Citroen's central hydraulic system also sensed weight transfer and automatically adjusted brake force distribution accordingly (while also providing automatic level control). Normally such weight distribution would have led to slow steering response and excessive understeer but the Citroen engineers got around that by a combination of center-point steering (vertical steering axis with no offset—zero scrub radius), larger tire size on the front wheels than on the rear ones, and much wider track in front than in the rear.

The transmission was mounted ahead of the final drive unit. It was a four-speed gearbox with all-indirect ratios and column shift, with synchromesh on second, third and top gears. All driving gears except the reverse pinion had helical-cut teeth. It was a design of exemplary simplicity in that the mainshaft (input shaft) was splined to the clutch, and the secondary shaft doubled as pinion shaft for the spiral bevel final drive. Both transmission and final drive casings were aluminum die casting.

The drive shafts were long, and had Delta-type inner joints, and the outer joints were made up of two Cardan-type joints placed back to back. Manufactured by Glaenzer-Spicer, they were claimed to run with constant velocity up to angularities of more than 40 degrees. Wheel bearings were enough in diameter to surround the entire universal joint, whose outboard member formed part of the hub.

Steering was by power-assisted rack and pinion geared at 12:1 overall to give a 38-foot turning diameter. Front brakes were discs mounted inboard (the DS-19 represents the world's first production-model use of disc brakes).

Instead of the double A-arm and torsion bar independent front suspension of earlier models, the DS-19 had a new design with two parallel L-arms, positioned one above the other, with the chassis ends forming a pivot shaft and the wheel ends carrying ball joints. These arms were high-grade spring steel forgings, their elasticity being the only concession towards horizontal compliance in the system. The upper L-arm pivot had a splined extension connected to a rocker arm, whose upper end worked against the oleo-pneumatic spring unit, while its lower end was linked to a stabilizer bar.

At the rear end, the wheels were mounted on single, parallel trailing arms, carrying similar spring units, with a stabilizer bar. Both front and rear roll centers were at ground level, which meant that (apart from the slight effect of the spring units on roll) the car had no roll stiffness other than what the stabilizers provided.

The four-cylinder long-stroke engine had a cast iron block with steel cylinder liners and an aluminum cylinder head and weighed 312 pounds. It delivered 75 hp at 4,500 rpm and had a peak torque of 14 m-kg at 3,000 rpm, giving the car a top speed of 95 mph.

Transmission could be called semi-automatic for there was no clutch pedal. The clutch was automatic, being operated by the central hydraulic system (with a vacuum-type governor). In moving off from standstill, the clutch was set to start engaging at 750 rpm and being fully engaged at 850 rpm. With the car in motion, the clutch was automatically disengaged by movement of the shift lever, while a check valve connected to the accelerator linkage controlled the rate of engagement. But there was nothing automatic about the speed selection. The lever worked in a quadrant marked Start-Reverse-Neutral-1-2-3-4. Pushing the lever beyond Reverse position engaged the starter motor and the clutch remined disengaged until the lever had been moved back to Neutral so as to avoid accidental reversing.

ID-19 and Evolution of the Theme

A simplified companion model called the ID-19 appeared in 1956. It was not equipped with power steering and had a standard clutch with a normal H-pattern four-speed column shift.

On the DS-19, minor interior and body changes were made in 1959 and 1960. For the 1961 models the clutch governor was changed to a centrifugal type and a 12-volt electrical system replaced the 6-volt installation. The engine received new pistons, a new carburetor, a new 5-bearing crankshaft, and power output went up to 83 hp at 4,500 rpm.

The 1962 models had a larger brake pedal and a redesigned instrument panel with provision for a radio. For 1963 the front end was redesigned with smaller and relocated air intakes. Headlamps were enclosed. Two years later the range was extended upwards with the addition of the DS-21 powered by a 2.1 liter version of the same engine, rated at 100 hp. The DS-21 had a 110-mph top speed.

The D series was regrouped for 1970. The ID-19, ID-20 and DS-19 were discontinued. Instead, the new lineup read D Special, D Super, DS-20 and DS-21. The D Special had a 2-liter engine rated at 91 horsepower and a conventional clutch. The D Special replaced the ID-19 and the D Super was a continuation of the ID-20. The D Super got a more powerful (103 hp) version of the same engine and a

The DS-21 was built on a 123-inch wheelbase and had the engine mounted longitudinally behind the front wheel axis, protruding into the cowl structure.

1966 CITROEN DS-21

Unified power pack for the DS-21 shows left side of engine with radiator and ducted fan in front. It was a four-cylinder hemi-head unit with strong low-end torque and high rpm limit.

conventional clutch. The 103-hp engine was also found in the DS-20, but in combination with an automatic clutch. The DS-21 had a 2,175-cc engine with electronic fuel injection rated at 124 hp, giving the car a top speed of 116 mph. For 1973 the DS-21 was renamed DS-23 and a five-speed gearbox became available. The top speed went to 124 mph. At the same time the D-Special was given more power and a D-Super 5 was added outfitted with the former DS-21 engine.

Current Family of Economy FWDs: the 2 CV

Before we examine the current luxury cars from Citroen, it is proper to look at the evolution of the economy cars, for, inevitably, there has been a certain amount of cross-breeding, with luxury-car features being applied to the economy cars and developments from the smaller cars being adopted for the larger ones.

The current family of economy cars begins with the 2 CV (CV stands for Cheval Vapeur, meaning hp, and the engine was so small it was rated at only 2 taxable hp in France). It is still in production today, instantly recognizable as the same car that made its debut as a 1949 model. During its 30-year career, it has undergone more than 1,000 modifications and 5.5 million have been built (not counting derivatives sold under other names).

The 2 CV is a four-door sedan built on a 95-inch wheelbase with a curb weight of only 1,160 pounds. To combine roominess and comfort with that kind of lightness and fuel economy calls for extraordinary solutions. In fact, both the engineering and design of the 2 CV are exceptional.

Lightness of construction took precedence over low manufacturing cost. The frame, for instance, was Duralinox light alloy casting. Instead of a metal roof there was a canvas top with a plexiglas rear window, stretching from windshield frame to tail end panel (about 5 inches above the bumper). Door glass could not be lowered into the door panels. Rear doors had fixed windows. Front door windows were horizontally split, the lower half swinging up to give an opening for arm-waving, etc. Seats were simple steel-tube frames with canvas to form a back and bottom. The hood was a corrugated-steel clamshell.

The engine was an air-cooled flat-twin located in the nose of the chassis with the four-speed gearbox aft of the final drive unit. The drive shafts carried inboard drum brakes and both inner and outer universal joints were Cardan-type. Citroen felt it could save the

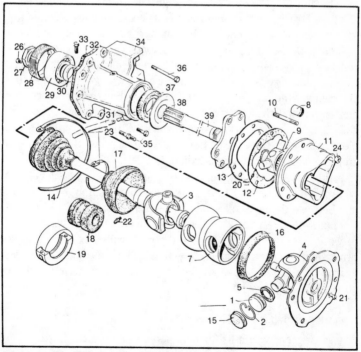

DS-21 drive shafts combined Delta-type inner joints with double Cardan-type outer joints. Axial variations were absorbed by the inner joints.

Citroens 2 CV in its original form shows overall layout and extremely lightweight construction.

extra cost of constant-velocity joints because of the low power involved. The engine had only 375 cc displacement and delivered 9 hp at 3,500 rpm.

Each wheel was carried on a single control arm, leading arms in front, and trailing arms in the rear. Each control arm was linked to a spring unit—one on each side that served both front and rear suspension. The spring unit was a horizontal cylinder containing two coil springs, each being compressed from the middle towards its end by the action of rods from the control arms reaching through the coils and capping them deep inside the cylinder. Each wheel carried an inertia coil and the control arm pivots carried friction-type shock absorbers. The system was simple and light. It gave a soft ride with plenty of wheel travel. Roll centers were at ground level and roll stiffness was practically non-existent.

Steel tubes running across the frame carried the suspension control arms. The front tube determined the position of the power unit because the gearbox needed a certain clearance to avoid interference with the tube. As a result, the final drive unit was pushed forward from its ideal position on the front wheel axis, forcing the drive shafts to run permanently with a backwards angle. This was accepted, again, because of the low power transmitted and the correspondingly low power losses.

Remarkable Debut and Success

Nearly one and a half million people saw the car at the Paris Auto Show in October, 1948. Their reaction: astonishment, perplexity, incredulity. The press found it laughable—with one exception, a

Swiss weekly (*Automobil Revue*) whose editor Robert Braunschweig predicted a brilliant future for the car. He was right.

In 1950 the order book was filled for the next six years' production. The first major modification was the introduction of an optional 425-cc engine rated at 12 hp, in 1954. Top speed was 45 mph (compared with 40 mph for the base model). The following year models equipped with the larger engine also received a clutch with centrifugal control (to ease driving in city traffic with frequent starts and stops).

For 1957 the canvas top was shortened, ending at the backlight base, to make room for a metal trunk lid. On the 1960 model the corrugated hood gave way to a smoother steel stamping with five

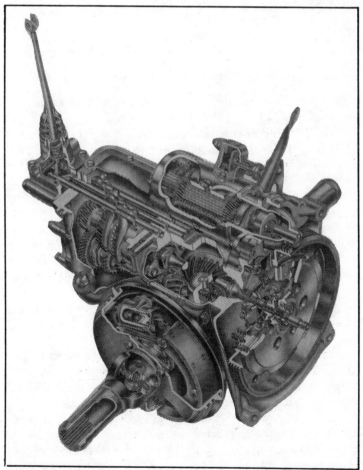

Transaxle for the 2 CV included spiral bevel final drive. Drums were carried inboard and plain Cardan joints were used at both ends.

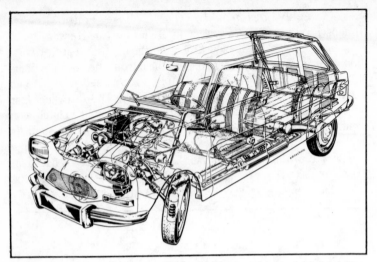
Ami-8 cutaway shows interconnected front and rear springs and details of drive train and steering linkage. It has inboard front disc brakes.

stiffening ribs and the cowl louvres were replaced by a triangular air-evacuation duct.

For 1962 power output from the 425-cc engine increased to 13.5 hp at 4,000 rpm and top speed to 53 mph. A year later peak-power speed was raised to 5,000 rpm and output was boosted to 16.5 hp. This allowed the final drive ratio to be lowered from 3.875:1 to 3.625:1, improving highway fuel economy and reducing engine noise at speed. Top speed went up to 60 mph.

Various suspension refinements were incorporated in the 1963 models which also boasted a new instrument panel that contained a fuel gauge for the first time. Electric wipers replaced the vacuum type. The brake pedal mechanism was modified in 1964 and hydraulic brake lines enlarged. For 1965 the gearbox ratios were changed to make better use of the engine's higher-rpm capacity and improve road performance without detracting from the fuel economy.

The 1966 models were the first to use constant-velocity outer universal joints. Hydraulic shock absorbers were fitted at the rear end but the front ones remained friction-type. During the model year a 12-volt electrical system was adopted.

A further power increase to 21 hp at 5,450 rpm was made for the 1968 models but the gearing was revised again and the final drive ratio reverted to 3.825:1 so that top speed remained unchanged. The engine was enlarged to 435 cc for 1970 with an output of 24 hp at 6,750 rpm. Final drive gearing was shortened to 4.125:1, giving a

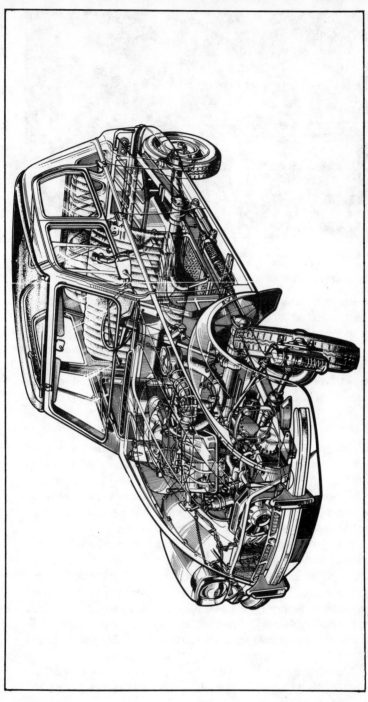

Two-cylinder 2 CV/Dyane engine is almost invisible behind the fan. Underhood area allows plenty of extra space for storing spare wheel, etc.

65

Mehari recreational/utility vehicle is built on 2 CV chassis. Body is all plastic. Windshield folds down and doors can be removed. Ragtop and poles can be packed away in a simple operation.

top speed of 63.5 mph with 45-mpg fuel economy. And a larger engine of 602 cc became optional. It delivered 28.5 hp and boosted top speed to 68.5 mph, with 38.5-mph fuel economy.

The 1972 models became available with a new variation in the drive train. A double-Cardan type outer joint was combined with a Rzeppa-type constant-velocity inner joint. This more than satisfies all demands of the technical purist.

Offspring of the 2 CV

Until now, we have concentrated on the 2 CV to the exclusion of its derivatives, the Dyane, Ami-6, Ami-8, and Mehari. All were built on the 2 CV chassis which kept the manufacturing costs low. The Ami-6 came first, going into production in 1961. The idea behind its creation was to start filling the huge gap in the Citroen model range that existed between the 2 CV and the D-series.

It was a four-door sedan with a stylish front end including a low air intake and oval headlamps. At the rear, the reverse-slant rear window allowed a normal trunk lid to be combined with a high roofline giving adequate headroom for rear seat occupants The 602-cc version of the flat-twin engine was designed for the Ami-6. For its first two years, it delivered 22 hp at 4,500 rpm. Without changing displacement, its output was raised to 25 hp in 1963, 28 hp in 1965, and 35 hp in 1968.

The Dyane was released in 1967. It was essentially a deluxe version of the 2 CV with its own sheet metal and interior fittings and trim. It began its life with the 425 cc engine but for 1968 it received the new 435-cc unit. At the same time the 602-cc engine (from the Ami-6) became optional in the Dyane.

A further variation was the Mehari, a sports-cum-utility vehicle with a boxy all-plastic open body and canvas top. It went into production in 1969 and is being built today practically without modification.

The Ami-6 was replaced by the Ami-8 in 1969. It had a redesigned body with much cleaner lines, and was built in station wagon form as well as the usual sedan. The 602-cc engine was retained with the same drive train except that disc brakes replaced the drum brakes on the drive shafts.

A special coupe version of the Ami-8 was built in 1969/70 for a fleet test of the single-rotor Wankel engine Citroen was developing. The rotary engine took the place of the flat-twin, using the standard Ami-8 clutch and transmission. But it never became a production model. For 1974 a new model known as the Ami Super became available. It was an Ami-8 chassis and body, with the flat-four engine from the GS.

All-New GS with a Flat Four

The GS was a totally new car when it appeared in August, 1970, combining an improved oleo-pneumatic suspension system from the

LN-Ami-8 engine is air-cooled but cooling fins are enclosed by ducting. Inboard disc brakes are patented and made by Citroen.

Latest addition to the Citroen small-car range is the Visa, replacing the Ami-8 and filling the gap between the Dyane and the GS. It has a new flat-twin, optionally with the Peugeot 104 engine.

D-series with the general chassis layout of the 2 CV in a streamlined body shell.

The GS sedan was built on a 100.4-inch wheelbase and had an overall length of 162.2 inches. The car had a front track of 54.25 inches and a 33.5-foot turning diameter with rack and pinion steering geared at 3.75 turns lock to lock. It had a curb weight of 1,975 pounds with 63.5 percent resting on the front wheels, 36.5 percent on the rear wheels.

The engine was an air-cooled flat-four mounted ahead of the front wheel axis, a lightweight unit with aluminum block and cylinder heads delivering 55.5 hp at 6,500 rpm from 1015 cc displacement. Standard transmission was a four-speed gearbox while a new semi-automatic drive was optional. The drive shafts carried inboard disc brakes and the inner universal joints were of the Tri-Axe (Delta) type while the outer joints were Rzeppa-type ball couplings.

The four-speed gearbox had all-indirect ratios with top gear giving a 1.12:1 reduction. The final drive ratio was 4.375:1, which meant that the car ran 14.2 mph per 1,000 rpm. It had a top speed of 92.5 mph and 24.5 mpg fuel economy.

The C-Matic system consisted of a three-speed gear-box of the countershaft type with a Ferodo Verto hydraulic torque converter that could be put out of action by an automatic lockup clutch. It eliminated the clutch pedal and reduced the driver's shifting duties but gave him full freedom to select gears. Both worked with a floorshift—a Citroen first since its adoption of f-w-d. In another cute switch, the handbrake was dash-mounted, right where others usually put the radio.

In front suspension design Citroen reverted to upper and lower A-arms for the GS. The upper arm carried a rod which worked against the oleo-pneumatic spring unit. At the rear end a straight trailing-arm design based on that of the D-series was used. Stabilizer bars were used both front and rear to provide the necessary roll stiffness.

In 1971 an enlarged engine (1,220 cc) was made optional. In September 1973 a special vesion known as the GS Birotor went into limited production powered by a Comotor twin-rotor Wankel engine. It was combined with the C-Matic drive and gave the car a performance far above the standard models. I drove the GS Birotor extensively in France and found it had a top speed of 112 mph with sparkling acceleration but a disastrously low gas mileage of about 15 mph. The Birotor was discontinued in April, 1976.

The four-cylinder GS has gone on without any substantial engineering changes and has been tremendously successful in the market place. A model designated GS-X3 was an enlarged (1,299 cc) version of the same engine raising power output to 65 hp at 5,500 rpm. This has enabled the final drive ratio to be brought down to 3.825:1 with revised reduction steps in the gearbox, bringing top gear reduction to 1.09:1 and raising road speed per 1,000 rpm to 15.4 mph. The standard engine displacement has been increased to 1,129 cc, boosting power output to 56 hp at 5,750 rpm.

Peugeot Input: LN and Visa

To complete our survey of Citroen's economy cars, the LN was added in 1976 and the Visa as a 1979 model. These two are related to

Citroen created the GS by making a flat-four based on the Dyane flat-twin and developing a new aerodynamic body style that was to mark all Citroen cars in the 1970s and '80s.

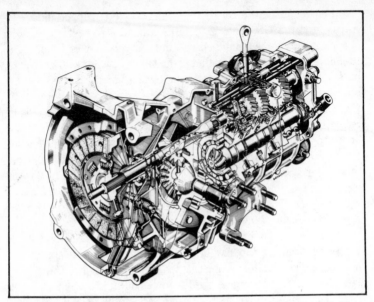

GS transaxle is composed of a four-speed gearbox and spiral bevel final drive. Gearbox input shaft runs on crankshaft axis on top of differential.

the 2 CV family only in the engine department but the vehicles are of totally different type, having originated at Peugeot (Citroen was taken over by Peugeot at the start of 1975).

The LN is basically the Peugeot 104 coupe powered by Citroen's 602-cc flat-twin engine. It is short and light with an 88-inch wheelbase and an overall length of 133.25 inches and a curb weight of 1,557 pounds (distributed 60.5 percent front and 39.5 percent rear). It has a top speed of 75 mph and gives fuel mileage from 32.5 to 40 mpg.

The Visa stems from the four-door Peugeot 104 and Citroen has retained the underbody structure and front and rear suspension, steering and brake system but has changed all the body skin, the outer sheet metal, so that the car has a genuine Citroen appearance. The body nose is made of plastic and integrated with the bumper. It is better streamlined than the Peugeot, and the rear fender treatment follows along the lines of the GS. For the Visa, Citroen developed a new 650-cc version of the flat-twin engine. It will also be available with the Peugeot 104 four-cylinder water-cooled engine.

SM: The Finest of Them All

One more ingredient remains before we can jump to the CX. And that ingredient is the most fantastic f-w-d car of all time, a

Low height of GS flat-four is obvious from the size of the disc brake rotors whose hubs carry the inner Delta-type universal joints.

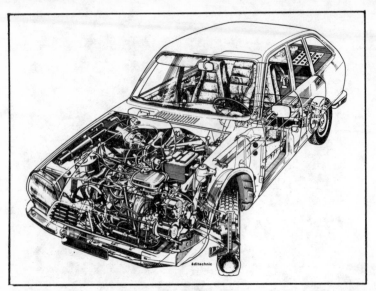

Transverse engine installations at Citroen began with the GS Birotor. The same unitized power pack was intended for the CX which was then under development.

vehicle of mixed parentage, produced from 1970 to 1974 as the Citroen SM.

The Citroen SM was the fastest f-w-d production car ever made, a streamlined sports coupe built on a 116.125-inch wheelbase with an overall length of 192.625 inches. Front track was 60.1 inches, and rear track 52.25 inches. The engine was built by Maserati of Modena (Citroen held a stake in Maserati from 1968 to 1974) and is basically the same power unit that's still used in the Maserati Merak. The 2.7-liter engine weighed 308 pounds and was 12.25 inches long but delivered 180 hp at 6,250 rpm. It was a V-six with the banks disposed at 90 degrees and four chain-driven overhead camshafts.

Despite the engine's compact size and low weight, Citroen resisted the temptation to gain interior space by pushing it forward in the chassis. The entire power unit was carried behind the front wheel axis with a five-speed transmission located ahead of the final drive unit. Both fourth and fifth gears were over-drives and the final drive ratio was 4.375:1.

The drive shafts carried inboard disc brakes and the inner joints were of the Tri-Axe type with double Cardan joints at the wheel ends. From the D-series came the center-point steering geometry with a vertical steering axis and no scrub radius. Curb weight was a mere 3,197 pounds, and the front wheels carried 62.1 percent of

Citroen SM was a high-performance "grand tourisme" that introduced several innovations in f-w-d engineering. SM stands for Super-Maserati since it was powered by a Maserati V-six engine.

that, the rear wheels 37.9 percent. Naturally, the SM had oleo-pneumatic spring units.

The front suspension system worked on the same principles as that of the D-series but the equal-length control arms were hinged in a trailing position on the SM while the DS used leading arms. This gave the SM higher anti-dive effect under braking. The rear suspension was basically the same as used on the D series. Where the SM really broke new ground was in the steering department. It was no less than a truly new concept in directional control. The steering gear was so quick that it gave only two turns lock to lock. That would make it an impossible car to drive without power assist and it would be unsafe with ordinary power assist. Citroen's engineers made the fast steering ratio acceptable by inventing a system of variable power assist. The amount of power assist available varied with vehicle speed and steering wheel position so that you got full power at low speeds, for parking and maneuvering, and very little at high speed when maximum stability was desired. The power steering pump was part of the central hydraulic system. But the power steering circuit was regulated by a speed-sensing device driven by the transmission. It was a centrifugal mechanism with flyweights that operated levers which in turn actuated hydraulic slide valves to adjust the pressure within the power steering circuit.

After initially testing the SM in France, I used one for several trips in America and included one in a 3-way comparison test at Bridgehampton race circuit with the Mercedes-Benz 450 SLC and the Jaguar XK-E with the V-12 engine where the Citroen came out on top. The SM had a top speed of 135-140 mph and would do the standing quarter-mile in 17 seconds flat. Fuel consumption varied. I got nearly 20 mpg on a high-speed run from Providence to New York and averaged about 16.5 mpg in all-around use. Naturally, the SM was to have considerable influence on the CX luxury car which was then on the drawing board.

CX: The Most Advanced Family Car

This was 1970, and Citroen was giving a lot of prominence to the rotary engine in its planning. Therefore the CX was designed for both the twin-rotor Comotor unit and the four-cylinder D-series engines. In both cases a transverse installation was chosen—a new departure for Citroen. It was the creation of a reorganized design office, working in groups rather than as individuals. It is difficult to say who did what but some of the key names behind the CX are Ravenel and Estaque (overall concept), Debladis (engine), Grosseau (drive train), Allera (suspension and steering), Clavel (safety) and Opron (body).

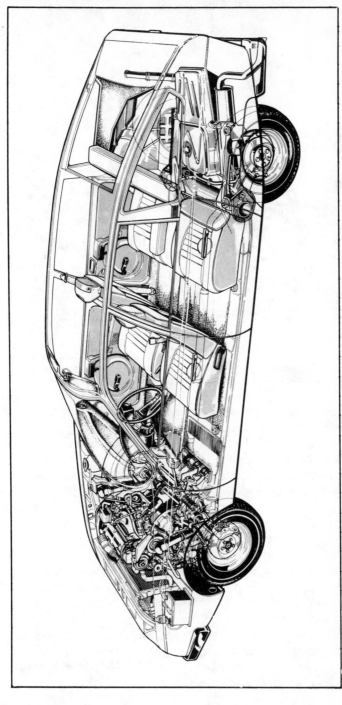

CX cutaway shows total concentration of drive train elements at the front end. Transverse engine installation necessitated move to outboard front discs.

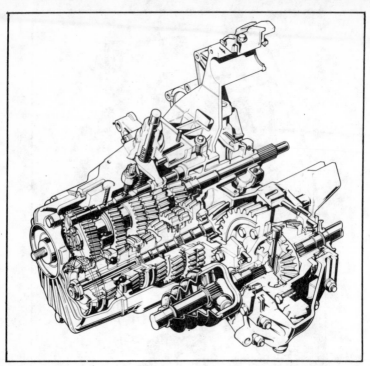

Five-speed transaxle used on CX GTi and 2500 Diesel. Final drive by helical spur gears is driven straight off gearbox output shaft.

Throughout it had to be kept in mind that this car project would eventually have to replace the entire D-series. It had to be a four-door sedan. It should be lower and lighter with smaller frontal area and a lower drag coefficient.

As it took form, it was seen that the piston engine had to be installed transversely (as was the rotary). Production plans for the rotary version of the CX were shelved while the tooling was being completed. Only the four-cylinder job was to come into being. The engine was offset to the right side of the chassis with the gearbox on the left. The countershaft carried an output pinion which turned a large spur gear that replaced the usual ring gear (bevel gears were avoided here because all rotation was taking place in the same plane). Both series were available with the three-speed semi-automatic C-Matic.

The final drive was offset to the left and drive-shafts of unequal length were avoided by splitting the right-hand shaft and providing a center bearing for non-oscillating center section. At each wheel were Rzeppa-joints and at equal distance from these couplings were

Tri-Axe joints. Because of the power train layout, there was no space for inboard disc brakes and the discs and calipers were consequently moved out to the wheels, riding right on the tire center line.

The central hydraulic system for the CX evolved from the D-series with influences from the GS and SM. The brakes were basically GS-type while the variable-assist power steering was adopted from the SM. The front suspension design owes much to the GS, with parallel control arms and a hefty stabilizer bar and oleo-pneumatic spring units connected to the upper control arms. The control arms were not A-arms but had a simple 1-profile, sharing the horizontal compliance between their torsional elasticity and the flexibility of their mountings. For the first time, Citroen built anti-dive into its front suspension. The rear suspension system had simple trailing arms as on the DS, GS, and SM. Front and rear roll centers were at ground level.

The CX went into production in August, 1974, with two basic versions, CX-2000 and CX-2200. The CX-2000 was powered by the 1985-cc engine and had a 4.77:1 final drive ratio. Manual steering was standard, power steering optional. Variable-assist power steering was standard on the CX-2200 which used the 2.175-cc engine and a 4.583:1 final drive ratio. Both had 20-percent overdrive on fourth gears.

CX 2400 GTi has electronic fuel injection and five-speed transmission as standard. Variable-assist power steering was developed from the SM.

Both were built on a 112-inch wheelbase and were 182.3 inches long overall. Front track was 58 inches and the turning diameter 35.5 feet. The non-assisted steering had a 24.5:1 overall ratio giving 4½ turns lock to lock but the power steering was much faster —almost as quick as in the SM—with a 13.5:1 ratio and 2½ turns lock to lock.

The CX-2200 had a 2,822-pound curb weight and a top speed of 111 mph. It could go from standstill to 60 mph in 11.5 seconds and its fuel consumption averaged 23 mpg. After a year it was replaced by the CX-2400 using the 2,347-cc engine (with carburetor) which had the same performance but better fuel economy despite no change in the gearing.

In September, 1975, a CX-2200 Diesel became available and it evolved into the CX-2500 Diesel in April, 1978. In May, 1977, Citroen launched its CX-2400 GTi with electronic fuel injection, raising power from 115 hp at 5,500 rpm to 128 hp at 4,800 rpm. The GTi received a five-speed transmission as standard. Fourth and fifth are overdrives (28 percent in top gear) and though the final drive ratio remains at 4.77:1, the GTi goes 21 mph per 1,000 rpm in top gear compared with 19.3 mph for the carburetor version. C-Matic was made available as an option for the GTi and the five-speed for the CX-2500 D.

A long-wheelbase (121.85-inch) Prestige model joined the range for 1976. The names Confort, Super and Pallas also denote specific models in the CX series but are trim-level distinctions rather than having to do with technical specifications.

What next from Citroen? The CX remains the most advanced family-type sedan in production and no doubt has a long career in front of it. But there will be a lot of action to renew the rest of the economy-car range in the coming years. The LN was just a stopgap and the Visa is just the beginning of things to come.

Chapter 5
Renault

Nobody builds more f-w-d cars in a year than Renault. In the space of less than 15 years, this French company changed from cars with "everything at the rear" to front-mounted engines and f-w-d. Oddly, Renault's first f-w-d vehicle was not a car but a van. It appeared in 1958 and was called Estafette. It was the creation of Yves Georges who was later to replace Fernand Picard as Renault's technical director. The Estafette is still in production today, practically without change from its 1958 specifications.

The engine was mounted ahead of the front wheel axis between the front seats with the transaxle behind it. All-independent suspension with coil springs was used with upper and lower A-frame control arms in front and lateral swing arms in the rear. Drive shafts used double Cardan-type outer joints and Delta-type inner joints and the right-side shaft was fitted with a torsional damper.

When Estafette production began, Yves Georges and his staff were deep into engineering a new small car to replace the 4 CV with its rear-mounted engine, a model that had been developed during the war and been in continuous production since 1947. The new car project was code-named "112," but it was to be marketed as the R-4 (a reference to the engine size of four taxable hp, as for the 4 CV "quatre-chevaux"). As it turned out, it became a station wagon rather than a sedan. Later, it was also built as a light van and a pickup truck version was added in 1978.

Competition Forced F-W-D

F-w-d was chosen for the R-4 because it was intended to compete against Citroen's 2 CV and its derivatives. That meant it had to

Estafette van and minibus were first Renaults with f-w-d. The four-cylinder Dauphine engine was mounted in-line ahead of the front wheel axis and rear suspension was independent with transverse arms and coil springs.

be a lightweight, relatively compact car of great versatility, which excluded the possibility of continuing the rear-mounted engine configuration. The engine had to be front-mounted, and to Yves Georges's way of thinking, it was then necessary, in a car of its price class, to drive the front wheels. This offered remarkably little technical difficulty, for the entire 4 CV power train could be lifted for use in the R-4!

In the 4 CV the engine was mounted in the tail, the transaxle riding ahead of the rear wheel axis, with pendulum-type swing axles taking the drive to the wheels. It was simply a matter of moving the whole assembly forwards. The pinion and ring gear already turned in the right direction so the only drive line change was the addition of constant-velocity universal joints and the only control modification needed was to re-route the gearshift linkage.

This was very expedient for manufacturing reasons but it also dictated the engine location in the chassis—vertically aft of the front wheel center line with the transaxle in front. The transmission was a three-speed unit with synchromesh on the two upper gears. Delta-type inner joints were matched with double Cardan-type outer joints, as on the Estafette. With a final drive ratio of 4.721 the R-4L ran 14.5 mph per 1,000 rpm in top gear. It had a top speed of 62.5 mph and gave a gasoline mileage of 39-42.5 mpg.

R-4 Range up to Super

The R-4 range was composed of the R-3 (with a 600 cc engine), the R-4 (747 cc engine) and R-4L (747 cc engine). Production started

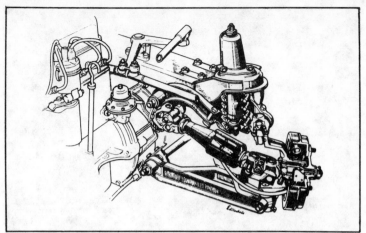

Drive shafts on the Estafette had rubber-bushing vibration dampers, double-Cardan outer joints and offset inner Cardan joints.

in August, 1961, and soon reached 1,000 cars a day. The R-3 version was discontinued in 1962 due to lack of demand.

As on the Estafette, all-independent suspension was used, but for the R-4 torsion bars were chosen. At front, they ran from the pivot shaft of the lower control arm to an anchorage point on the platform frame cross-member below the front seats. At the rear, the torsion bars were mounted across the frame, one ahead of the other, each linked to the trailing arm that carried its wheel. Because the trailing arms had equal length, the wheelbase was longer on the right side (96.2 inches vs. 94.3 on the left). The R-4L was 144 inches long overall and weighed 1,323 pounds with full tanks but no payload. In common with the 4 CV and Dauphine, the R-4 series used rack and pinion steering and drum brakes for all wheels. Tires were 135-330 with 145-330 as an option.

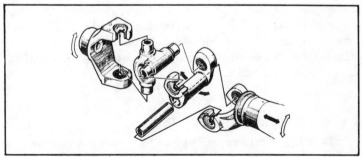

Inner universal joints on Estafette drive shafts were a special design with triple links and axial offset.

R-4 GTL is top model in the 4-series. Over 5 million of these economy cars have been built since 1961.

For 1963, an R-4 Super was added powered by an 845-cc engine delivering 26.5 hp. The 1964 models were given a wider rear track of 49 inches (instead of 47.4). Bigger front brake drums were fitted for 1965 and they got bigger still for 1966. A fully synchronized four-speed transmission was adopted in September, 1967 and springs were strengthened to give greater payload capacity.

More power came on tap in 1970 along with various refinements in equipment and safety design. The basic engine was enlarged from 747 to 782 cc for the 1972 model whose steering gear was slowed down from 17:1 to 20:1 to lower the muscle effort. A new transmission was adopted in 1973 (same as used in the R-5 and R-6). It had a new shift pattern. At the same time the brake system was improved by the addition of a load-sensitive brake force regulator in the hydraulic lines to the rear wheels. Over five million R-4s have been built and Renault is still producing them in sizeable numbers though it will admittedly have to give way to a more modern design in the near future.

Project 114 Abandoned for the R-16

In 1961 Renault started its Project 114—a far more ambitious project—a compact family car with a 1½-liter engine and 90-mph top speed competing in the most hotly contested market segment and a new field for Renault. Project 114 was a four-door sedan of classic profile with a conventional trunk and an engine bay able to accommodate either a four-cylinder or a six-cylinder engine. It was not an f-w-d design but followed the Fregate layout with front-mounted engine and rear wheel drive with all-independent suspension. Studies of the investments necessary to build this vehicle, coupled with market research reports that indicated extremely low sales volume at the projected price, led to the death of Project 114.

Instead, Yves Georges revived a highly original concept that existed only as a styling mockup made in 1958. It was a car of comparable dimensions, but without a separate trunk, and despite a long hood, it offered a roomier interior. This design was developed into a car that went into production in February, 1965, as the R-16.

For its time, the R-16 was a uniquely functional design with all sorts of wagon-type features combined with a four-door family sedan of fastback appearance (with a rear hatch). It had a curb weight of 2,160 pounds and was 166.5 inches long overall. Its front/rear weight distribution was 56/44 percent which assured a level ride

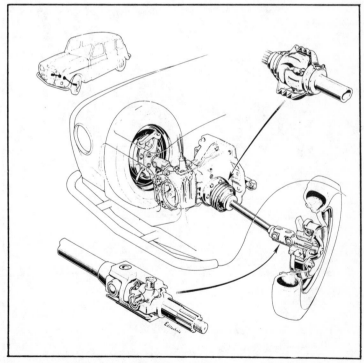

R-4 universal joints were of the Delta type nearest the differential and double Cardan-type nearest the wheel hubs.

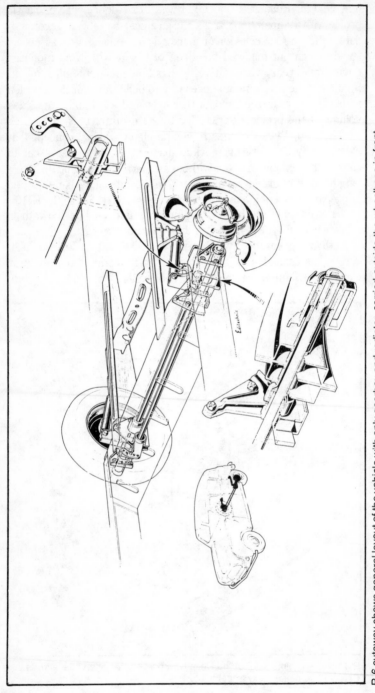

R-6 cutaway shows general layout of the vehicle with only gearbox and radiator carried outside the wheelbase in front.

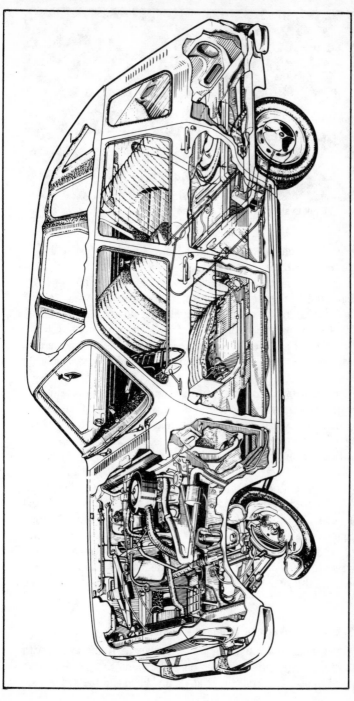

Renault 6 came into being as an enlarged and modernized version of the R-4. It's a four-door wagon-type sedan. R-6 cutaway shows general layout of the vehicle with only gearbox and radiator carried outside the wheelbase in front.

R-16 was meant to steal sales from Citroen by offering a f-w-d four-door sedan priced below the ID-19.

with relatively quick steering response and basic understeer with adequate down-the-road stability.

The R-16 engine was a light alloy overhead-valve four of 1,470 cc delivering 58.5 hp at 5,000 rpm. The whole unit weighed 203 pounds without the clutch. It was mounted inboard of the wheelbase, DS-19 fashion, with the transaxle in front. The transmission was a synchromesh four-speed unit with column shift. An automatic transmission of Renault's own manufacture became available in March, 1969.

The Renault automatic transmission consisted of a Ferodo three-element hydraulic torque converter, a three-speed Ravigneaux-type planetary gear unit, and a spiral bevel final drive Perhaps its most remarkable advance was the use of an electronic control unit rather than the usual hydraulic "brain."

The R-16 used double Cardan-type outer joints and Weiss constant-velocity inner joints for its tubular drive shafts. The Weiss joints had a maximum working angle of 20 degrees and allowed axial play up to 1.57 inches. With a turning diameter of 32.9 feet, the rack and pinion steering needed 4 turns lock to lock and no power assist was offered. Floating-caliper solid disc brakes with rotors of 9.8-inch diameter were used on the R-16 front wheels with drums of 9-inch diameter in the rear wheels.

Big Positive Camber and Unequal Wheelbases

Front suspension used upper and lower A-frame arms, with torsion bars linked to the lower ones. Suspension geometry was arranged to place the roll center at ground level and the swivel axis was inclined at 13 degrees. The full range of wheel deflection was 8.27 inches (3.15 in jounce and 5.12 in rebound) and camber angles are practically constant, varying from less than 1 degree positive in full jounce to less than one degree negative in full rebound. Keep in mind that these angles refer to the car as being level which means that with 9-degree body roll on a sharp turn, the outside front wheel runs with nearly 10 degrees of positive camber in a situation where zero or a slight negative camber would be desirable for maximum traction and side bite.

Rear suspension on the R-16 was similar in principle to the R-4 design with trailing arms and transverse torsion bars. The torsion bars are coaxial with the trailing arm pivot axis which means that they would meet in the middle unless steps were taken to offset them relative to each other. This was done by shifting the whole left rear suspension assembly backwards, so that the car has unequal wheelbases on the two sides, 106.75 inches on the left and 104.5 on the right.

The rear roll center was also at ground level, giving a horizontal roll axis. Like Citroen's DS-19, the R-16 depended on front and rear stabilizer bars for its roll stiffness. The effective radius of the rear trailing arms was 15.75 inches and their pivot points, at design height, were fractionally under 10 inches above ground level. Rear wheel travel was unusually generous at 11.81 inches (7.28 in jounce and 4.53 in rebound).

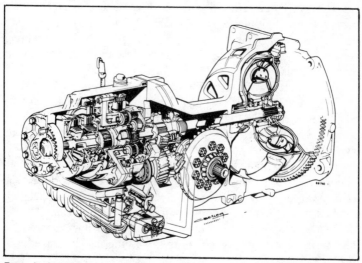

Renault pioneered the automatic transmission with an electronic control. The R-16 unit consists of a hydraulic torque converter and three-speed planetary transmission.

Some body and interior modifications were made in 1966. For 1967 a brake-system warning light was added, reverse gear position was changed, and the automatic choke was discontinued. A 16 TS model was added in 1968 with larger-size front disc brakes. Power brakes became standard on the 1970 models and at the same time engine displacement was increased to 1,565 cc, raising power output to 65 hp. The 16 TX was added for 1973 with a 1.7-liter engine delivering 93 hp at 6,000 rpm and five-speed transmission. For 1974 the TX became available also with automatic drive.

The R-16 range was redefined for 1975, starting with the 16 L (55 hp), including the 16 TL (55 or 65 hp), 16 TS (83 hp), 16 TX (93 hp for the five-speed and 90 hp with automatic drive). A year later, the 16 TL and 16 TS disappeared from the lineup. The R-16 is still in production but its days are numbered. Its niche in the market is being invaded from below by the R-14 and from above by the R-20. These two are quite recent creations and will be described later.

In-Between R-6: Comfort and Economy

The next f-w-d Renault, chronologically speaking, is the R-6, it grew out of Project 118, which started in 1965 as a result of Renault's realization that a number of its customers wanted something more comfortable and better equipped than an R-4 but could not afford an R-16.

The problem of styling such a vehicle was submitted to Carrozzeria Ghia in Torino. Renault's own body designers also made their own proposal. As it turned out, the Ghia design was a rustic-looking utility vehicle that did not at all correspond with the marketing concept. Fortunately, Renault's own proposal was further removed from the bleak austerity of the R-4 and it was adopted for the R-6 which went into production in September, 1968.

It was a boxy four-door sedan/wagon with a sloping tailgate combining R-16 space and comfort with R-4 economy. Overall length was 157.3 inches and the R-6 had a curb weight of 1,885 pounds. The layout followed closely along R-4 lines. It was powered by an 845-cc engine with an output of 34 hp at 5,000 rpm, installed aft of the front wheel axis. A final drive ratio of 4.125:1 gave the car a road speed of 14.5 mph per 1,000 rpm in top gear. A four-speed all-indirect gearbox was standard. Steering was by rack and pinion. It gave much faster response than on the R-4 for on the R-6 it was geared for 3.33 turns lock to lock whereas the R-4 steering demanded 4.5 turns.

The R-6 brake system had 9-inch drums on the front wheels and 6.3-inch drums on the rear ones. Front suspension was based on the

R-4 design with unequal-length A-frame control arms and longitudinal torsion bars. Rear suspension was simply scaled up from the R-4 using the same sort of geometry with parallel trailing arms and transverse torsion bars.

As is the case with its smaller brother, the R-6 is still in production. Both are likely to be replaced by new designs with transverse four-cylinder engines mounted outside the wheelbase, thereby freeing up much of the space occupied by the R-4 and R-6 engines for useful purposes and at the same time saving weight by shortening the overall length. For bigger cars with more powerful engines, Renault seems to favor the longitudinal-outboard installation as first used on the R-12.

R-12 Changed the Pattern

The R-12 went into production in September, 1969. It had started in 1963 in collaboration with Ford do Brasil as Project 117 and the design was to break with earlier Renault practice in more ways than one. The engine was carried outside the wheelbase in the nose of the vehicle and coil springs were used all around. And it did *not* have all-independent suspension. Breaking with the functional design approach of the R-6 and R-16 bodies, the R-12 was a four-door notchback sedan with a conventional trunk. A station wagon with its own roofline and tailgate was added in 1971.

Built on a 96.2-inch wheelbase with a front track of 51.6 inches, the R-12 had a curb weight of 1,938 pounds, each of the front wheels carrying a load of 566 pounds and giving a 58.4/41.6 percent front/rear weight distribution. With an 8-degree swivel-axis inclination, it had a positive scrub radius of 0.47 inches. Front roll center was located 1.08 inches above ground level and the rear roll center 12.6 inches above ground level, adding to the basic under-steering tendency due to the weight concentration up front.

Two transverse A-frame control arms were used in the front suspension with coil spring struts standing on the upper arms. The lower control arm was a wide-based steel pressing and the upper control arm consisted of a lateral arm and a diagonal drag strut. The lower control arms were connected via a stabilizer bar.

Unusual Compensation for Oversteer

Since the weight distribution of the R-12 made for strong understeer during power-on cornering, the car demanded special measures to guard against power-off oversteer. This was solved by adding roll oversteer in the rear suspension on the theory that this

Four trim and power levels are offered in the R-12 four-door sedan. The R-12 is also built as a station wagon.

would reduce the likelihood of drivers lifting off the accelerator in the middle of a curve.

At design height, the trailing arms are closer to the ground at the axle end than at their pivots. In a cornering situation, lateral weight transfer adds load on the outside wheel, compressing the spring and levelling the trailing arm so that the wheel is pushed back relative to the body. The opposite happens on the inside so that wheel is pulled forward. This turns the axle away from the turn center to counteract the understeer at the front end.

With a full load of passengers and baggage, the weight distribution is so altered that no roll steer effect is needed. In fact, it could be detrimental to the vehicle's stability in cornering. And it's automatically cancelled, for the load moves the trailing arms into a horizontal plane and body roll on a curve will pull both wheels forward by the same amount so that any roll steer effect is eliminated.

The gearbox and final drive unit were bolted to the clutch bell-housing to form a rigid assembly suspended in the monocoque body shell at four points. Renault's automatic transmission was optional on the R-12 from the outset. The 1,289-cc engine was a development of the 1,108 cc design used in the R-8 delivering 54 hp at 5,250 rpm. It was geared to run 16.5 mph per 1,000 rpm in top gear with a 3.77:1 final drive ratio.

Outer joints were double Cardan type, and inner joints were of the Rzeppa type. Rack and pinion steering gave four turns lock to lock and a turning diameter of 35.2 feet. Brakes were 9-inch discs in front mounted in the wheels with drums of 7-inch diameter in the back. A pressure-limiting valve was inserted in the hydraulic lines to the drums. It is weight-sensitive, being controlled by the angle of the

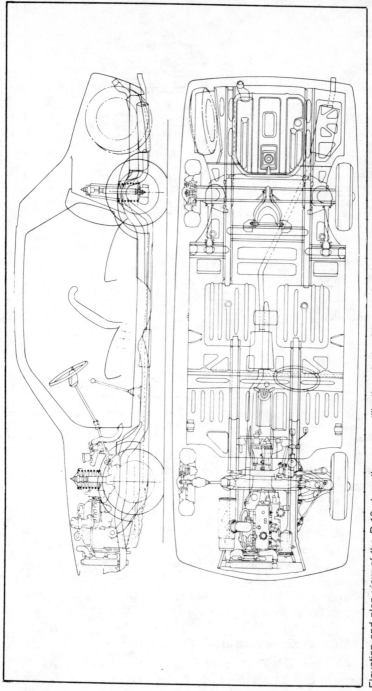

Elevation and plan view of the R-12 show the space utilization obtained by moving the power unit into the front overhang.

91

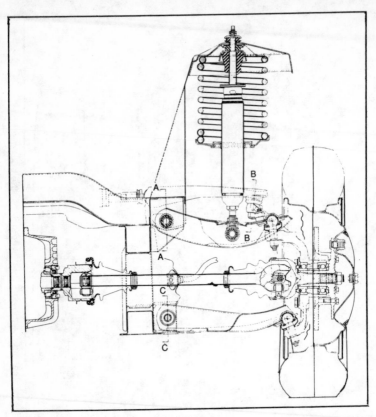

R-12 switched to coil springs instead of torsion bars and went to Delta-type universal joints at both ends of the drive shafts.

A-bracket in the rear suspension. There was no provision for power assist for either brakes or steering though both could have used it to great advantage.

The R-12 Gordini was introduced in the summer of 1970 as a high-performance version suitable for rally work. It was equipped with the 1,565 cc light-alloy engine from the R-16 coupled to a five-speed transmission and power disc brakes on all four wheels. The gearbox came from the R-8 Gordini and had synchromesh on all forward gears. Final drive ratio was 3.77:1 giving a road speed of 18.1 mph per 1,000 rpm in top gear. The steering was speeded up to give only 2.6 turns lock to lock but no servo was available.

Sports Car Versions: R-15 and R-17

As early as 1963 Renault had been planning for a sports car version of the R-16. Project 115 looked very promising but the

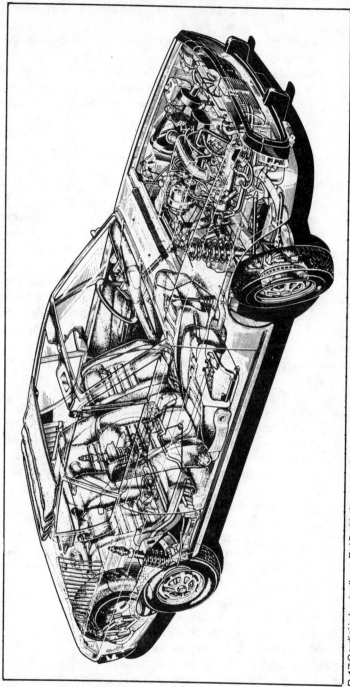

R-17 Gordini is basically an R-15 with the rear side glass filled in and powered by a fuel-injected R-16 engine.

notchback coupe looked clumsy when a maximum of body panels from the sedan was used.

To make its success as a sports car an almost totally different body would be required and that caused Project 115 to be put back on the shelf. In the design of the R-12 Renault faced the facts from the outset, and planned for a sports coupe having its own body entirely but using the same floor plan and wheelbase, and the same power train, suspension, steering and brakes. The R-15 and R-17 sports coupe went into production in July, 1971. The R-17 TS was equipped with the fuel-injected engine from the R-12 Gordini.

Le Car: The Notable R-5

In the late 1960s Renault made some market studies that led it to begin questioning the age-old superstition that French customers won't buy large numbers of two-door cars. At the same time, the designers happened to propose a pretty little car that, due to its short length and neat roofline, could only be built as a two-door model. It was a concept that had evolved from a city-car feasibility study. It was a simple but fascinating design, suitable for a basic economy car, a family car for young couples, a baby "personal" car, a utility car, a second car in a two-car family, and a four-passenger sports coupe. Renault decided to produce it, engineered from off-the-shelf components mostly borrowed from the R-6. The new car, called R-5, went into production in January, 1972.

It is built on a 96-inch wheelbase and weights 1,730 pounds. Front track is 50.6 inches and rear track 49 inches. Overall, the car is only 138 inches long and has a turn diameter of 32.3 feet. R-5 power train components were inherited from the R-6, which dictated the engine location. At first, three sizes of four-cylinder units were offered, 782 cc, 845 cc, and 956 cc. Later, engines of 1,108 and 1,285 cc were to be added.

The R-5 drive shafts use Delta-type inner joints and double Cardan-type outer joints. Overall gearing depends on which engine is used, ranging from 14.6 to 19.6 mph per 1,000 rpm in top gear. Early models inherited the umbrella-handle gearshift on the dash from the R-4 and R-6 but this was modified to a remote-control floorshift in 1973.

Though the front suspension system was derived from the R-6, it was not identical, having no interchangeable parts. Instead of the R-6's lower control arm made up of a transverse link and a drag strut, the R-5 had a one-piece A-frame control arm. The lower control arm was linked to a torsion bar whose rear end was anchored in a frame crossmember under the front seat. A stabilizer bar connected the lower control arms on the hind side while the rack and pinion steering linkage crossed in front of the engine.

Rear suspension in the R-5 was independent with trailing arms and transverse torsion bars. The main difference from R-6 practice was the use of vertically mounted shock absorbers rather than horizontal ones. Its brake system relied on 9-inch front discs mounted in the wheels with rear drums of 7-inch diameter.

The latest model in this series is the Alpine introduced in 1977. It's powered by a 93-hp version of the 1,397-cc engine matched to a five-speed gearbox, giving the car a top speed of 110 mph. It also has a rear stabilizer bar and a special front bumper with an aerodynamic deflector. The R-5 Alpine has turned into a successful competition car and has placed well in several international rallies. The R-5 has become one of Renault's best-selling models and it appears destined for a long production life.

Unusual Features on the Big R-30

I mentioned earlier that the R-14 and R-20 combined to take the place of the R-16. The 20 is a big, heavy car sharing the body of the 30 TS, which was introduced in February, 1975. It was designed and developed in parallel with Renault's BRV (Basic Research Vehicle) which was first shown at the London Engineering Conference on Automotive Safety in 1974. Yves Georges was connected with both

From every angle, the R-5 looks right. It was intended as a replacement for the R-4 but has established a completely different market.

in his new office as director of applied research while Hubert Seznec, who had left Citroen after 14 years at Quai de Javel to join Renault in 1967, was responsible for production-car engineering.

The R-30 concept was a large, luxury-market four-door hatchback sedan with a powerful V-six engine carried in the front overhang. It was built on a 105.12-inch wheelbase and had front and rear track of 56.9 and 56.7 inches. With its overall length of 178 inches, it's impressive that its curb weight is no more than 2,911 pounds. In comparison, the R-16 TX Automatic, which is nearly a foot shorter, and is powered by a four-cylinder engine, has a curb weight of 2,405 pounds. Front/rear weight distribution on the 30TS was 62.3/37.7 percent.

The overhanging engine installation was made possible by the fact that the power unit has light alloy block and cylinder heads keeping its complete weight down to 331 pounds. It sits in the longitudinal plane with a transaxle using a spiral bevel ring gear and pinion. The standard transmission is a four-speed synchromesh gearbox with Renault's electronic-control three-speed automatic as an option. When the automatic is used, the torque converter takes the place of the clutch next to the flywheel with the output shaft running past the final drive to the planetary gearing at the rear. Drive shafts have Rzeppa-type inner joints and double-Cardan outer joints. With synchromesh transmission, the car was geared for a speed of 20 mph per 1,000 rpm. It has a top speed of 115 mph, can reach 50 mph from standstill in 7 seconds and cover the standing quarter-mile in 17 seconds.

The 30 TS has all-coil suspension with quite ingenious linkages. At the front end is a one-piece A-frame lower control arm and a short and straight upper control arm linked to a drag strut. A coil-spring and shock absorber unit is mounted on the upper control arm about halfway between the pivot axis and the ball joint. The spring base also provides an attachment for the stabilizer bar.

Rear suspension layout is a variation on Renault's typical trailing-arm designs. What's new here is that the trailing arms do not support the hub carriers. Instead, the hubs are secured to transverse arms (having a slight trailing angle) that locate the wheels laterally. These arms provide bases for the vertical coil springs and separately mounted shock absorbers and carry vertical rods linked to the stabilizer bar. The trailing arms are bolted to the transverse arms and serve to locate the wheels in the fore-and-aft plane.

Ample wheel travel was assured at both ends with a range of 8.72 inches in front and 11.8 inches in the rear. Power-assisted rack and pinion steering with a 17.8:1 ratio was standardized with hyd-

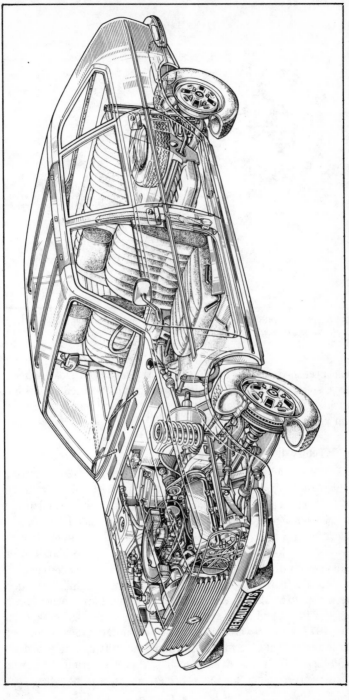

Top-of-the-line model R-30 TS carried V-six engine in the front overhang and uses relatively short wheelbase. Power steering is standard.

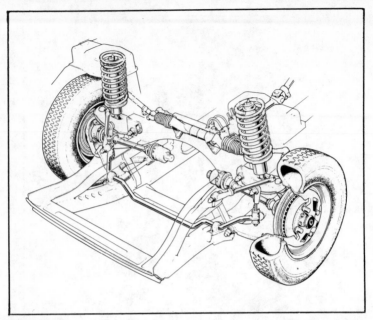

Front suspension on the R-30 TS relies on the same principles as the R-12 design but is considerably heftier and drive shafts have more sophisticated universal joints.

raulic pressure varied according to steering angle and a load-sensing valve, so as to reduce the assist for making high-speed curves but provide full assist for parking. Four-wheel disc brakes were used with ventilated rotors in front and solid ones in the rear.

R-20: Four-cylinder in the Big Body

At the end of 1975 Renault introduced the R-20. It was a combination of the four-cylinder engine from the R-16 TX with the R-30 vehicle. To make the change of engine position, the pinion and ring gear engagement had to be shifted from one side to the other, otherwise the car would have had one forward speed and four in reverse. For the rest, it was just a matter of turning the whole power train back to front and arranging the motor mounts accordingly.

Curb weight was cut to 2,590 pounds and weight distribution evened out to 61/39 percent. Speed capacity and performance levels were far lower and drums replaced the rear wheel disc brakes. In June, 1977, a 20-TS was added with a brand-new overhead-camshaft 2-liter engine that gave the car a top speed of 100 mph and standstill to 50-mph acceleration in 8.2 seconds. Power steering and power brakes were retained for the entire 20-series.

R-14 and the Transverse Engine

In the meantime, the R-14 had arrived to fill out the middle of the range. It went into production in May, 1976. Code-named Project 121, its design was started in 1970. It's a four-door sedan with a hatchback, and the body consequently belongs in the R-4/R-6/R-16 family. But the engineering design introduced yet another departure for Renault in introducing the transverse engine. It came not by a change of design policy or any technical discovery. It was simply a practical decision resulting from Renault's joint production of engines with Peugeot at Douvrin. Peugeot has an engine design suitable for any size from 900 cc to 1,300 cc with a complete drive line for transverse installation. Renault wanted to make use of it and the R-14 was designed around the engine and drive train rather than the other way around.

The R-14 engine is inclined backwards at 72 degrees with the transmission located centrally beneath the engine and ahead of the front wheel axis. The R-14 drive train is related to that used for the Peugeot 104. From the clutch, the power flows through a 1.26:1 reduction gear to the transmission mainshaft. The car is geared with a 3.866:1 final drive ratio to run 15.9 mph per 1,00 rpm in top gear.

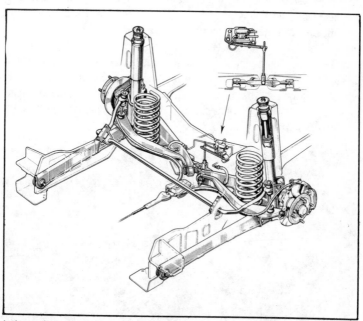

Independent rear suspension on the R-30 TS is a totally new design with semi-trailing arm geometry. Shock absorbers are mounted separately from the coil springs.

Most modern car in the Renault lineup may be this R-14 four-door hatchback sedan. Unlike the R-12 and R-20, it is not available with automatic transmission.

The R-14 has a top speed of 90 mph and returns a fuel economy of 27 mpg in normal use. All-independent suspension is used with a MacPherson system in front and by trailing arms and transverse torsion bars in the rear. A front stabilizer is included. The steering is by rack and pinion. The geometry is set to give low steering effort for small steering angles and progressively high steering effort is demanded with increasing steering angles. The car handles with more finesse than the R-12, its understeer not nearly so strong, and consequently with less need for roll oversteer which is practically absent due to a negative camber setting of 1.5 degrees.

The R-14 weighs 1,907.5 pounds and 60.7 percent of it is carried by the front wheels. Wheelbase is 99.6 inches and rear track is slightly wider than at front (54 inches vs. 53.2) Since the overall width is 64 inches, that provides the car with a wide stance. With an overall length of 158.5 inches, it has modest overhang at both ends: 28.6 inches in front and 30.3 inches in the rear.

R-18 is a modernized and upgraded R-12 for world markets. It will be produced in the U.S. by American Motors.

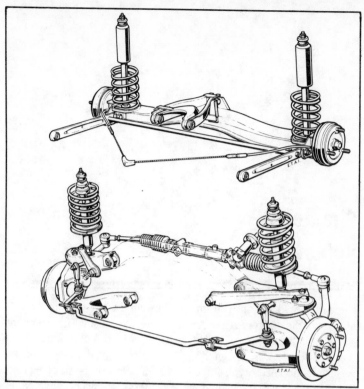

Front and rear suspension system of the R-18 are inherited from the R-12 but contain several refinements such as drag struts on the upper control arms.

R-18: The Future's in Wisconsin

The latest newcomer in the Renault stable is the R-18, which went into production in February, 1978. Developed since 1974 as Project 134, it is basically an updated and upgraded R-12, sharing the R-12 power train and chassis assemblies. Like the R-12 it is a four-door notchback sedan with a conventional trunk. There can be no question of its replacing the R-16. Renault sees it as a conquest car—something that will bring Fiats, Opels, and Fords as trade-ins. A separate station wagon body does not yet exist but is a future possibility.

According to Renault, the R-18 is not just one car but a range of cars because it is offered with such variety of power trains. Two engine sizes are available (1,397 and 1,647 cc) with four-speed and five-speed synchromesh transmissions as well as Renault's electronic-control automatic. This is the first car that will be assembled by American Motors in Wisconsin, according to Renault's plans.

Chapter 6
Volkswagen

The first f-w-d car to bear the Volkswagen label was an outside design and did not come from Audi. It came from a small independent car manufacturer, NSU of Neckarsulm, which Volkswagen took over in 1969. It was designed by Ewald Praxl and developed to the pre-production prototype stage by NSU in 1968. Volkswagen inherited the design and tooled up for the K-70, as it was code-named, in its Salzgitter works, where it went into production in September, 1970. It remained in production until 1974. In all, Volkswagen built 210,082 cars of the K-70 type.

The K-70 was a four-door sedan built on a 105.9-inch wheelbase with an overall length of 174 inches. It had a narrow front track of 54.7 inches and a wide rear track of 56.1 inches. The engine was a slant-four carried above the final drive unit, the front wheel axis running in a plane between cylinders 3 and 4. The transmission was located directly behind the flywheel and clutch in the normal manner but its output shaft took the drive forward at countershaft level. Both inner and outer joints were of the constant-velocity type. Curb weight was 2,315 pounds of which the front wheels carried 59.5 percent. With a full load (1,015 pounds of passengers and baggage), the front wheels still carried 49 percent of the total weight.

Two versions of the water-cooled, in-line, four-clinder 1,595 cc power unit with overhead camshaft and aluminum cylinder head were made. The low-compression unit was rated at 75 hp and the high-compression unit at 90 hp. With the 75 hp engine, the K-70 had a top speed of 92 mph and could accelerate from standstill to 60 mph

First f-w-d car to carry the VW label was the NSU-designed K-70. It was a roomy and practical car of good quality but too costly to produce.

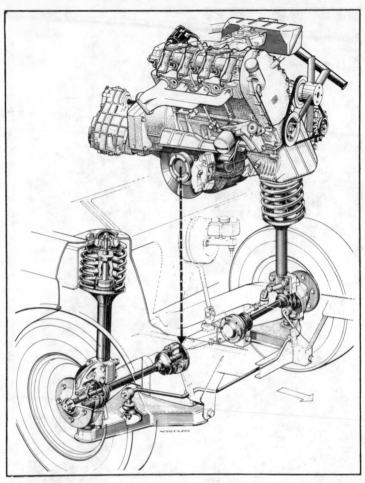

Slant-four engine in the K-70 drove the front wheels via Delta-type inner joints and Rzeppa-type outer joints.

in under 16 seconds. The more powerful engine gave the car a top speed of 98 mph and 0-60 acceleration in 13.5 seconds. Both versions had the same four-speed transmission with all-indirect gears and the same final drive ratio of 4.375:1.

Front wheels were suspended by means of lower A-frame control arms and MacPherson struts with coil springs and concentric shock absorbers. A stabilizer bar crossed the chassis in front of the suspension with the steering linkage behind. The rack and pinion steering gear had an 18.5:1 ratio giving four turns lock to lock with a 32.5-foot turning diameter. Front disc brakes were mounted inboard and carried as spring weight.

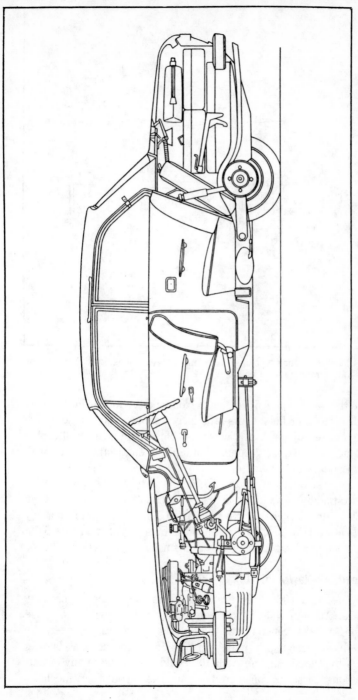

With an overhanging slant-four, the Audi 60 had excellent space utilization and the power unit was light enough to avoid hurting the car's road manners.

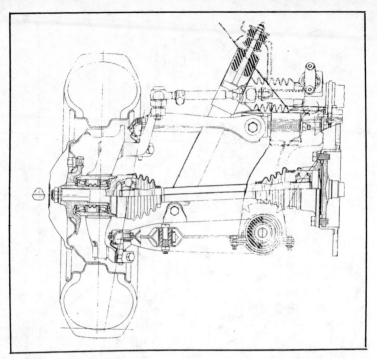

The Audi used Rzeppa-type outer joints and Delta-type inner joints with a sliding pot to accommodate axial travel.

more than ample at 7.56 inches in front and 8.4 inches in the rear. Front roll center height was 1.89 inches above ground level which gave a nose-down roll axis when combined with a rear roll center 10.3 inches above the ground. That tends to endow the vehicle with a firm understeer characteristic.

Several variations of this basic vehicle were built up to 1972. The first addition was the Super-90 from 1967 powered by a 90-hp 1,760-cc engine. Then came the 75L in 1968. It was mechanically identical with the base model but had higher-grade trim. In 1969 the Audi 60 was added, equipped with a smaller (1,496 cc) engine.

Refined, All-New Audi 100

The Audi 100 appeared in 1969 and was a completely new vehicle. At the outset it was not certain that it would in fact use f-w-d, however. Since it was to be designed on a clean sheet, the most basic design principles were taken up for debate. Ludwig Kraus explained that the Audi 100 could have gone in any of four directions: First, he considered the American type of car, mechani-

The rear suspension consisted of semi-trailing arms with vertical coil-spring legs and a small-diameter stabilizer bar. The semi-trailing arms were of tubular construction and had a very wide base. Their pivot axes ran at an angle of about 20 degrees relative to the rear wheel center line and the arms were arranged to provide some toe-in at design height with increasing toe-in as load was added. As a result, body roll on curves would increase the toe-in of the outer rear wheel, producing a degree of roll oversteer to counter-act the progressive understeer of the front end.

The K-70 was a good car but it was an expensive vehicle to produce and Volkswagen had to sell it at an unjustifiably high price to avoid taking a loss on it. Consequently, it never became a popular model. Eventually it was pushed out of the market, most of all by Volkswagen's own Passat. The Passat became known in America as the Dasher. It was not a true Volkswagen design but a VW edition of an Audi design known in America as the Fox and in Europe as the 80.

Audi 75, Audi 80, Audi Fox to Dasher

The Audi 80 belongs in a family of cars that starts with the 1965-model Audi 75. The Audi 75 came into being as a four-cylinder four-stroke version of the three-cylinder two-stroke DKW F-102 which it superseded. The chassis and body design came from Auto Union and were mainly the work of Wilhelm Haupt while the new four-cylinder engine had been designed at Mercedes-Benz by Ludwig Kraus. It was a slant-four of 1,696 cc tilted about 30 degrees to the right and carried entirely ahead of the front wheel center line with the transaxle behind it. The four-speed transmission had all-indirect gears and the hypoid level final drive gave a reduction of 3.888:1. It came as a column shift. There was no automatic option at first.

Front suspension comprised upper and lower A-frame control arms with longitudinal torsion bars and a stabilizer. Front disc brakes were mounted inboard, and the drive shafts had constant-velocity universal joints at both ends. The outer joints were of the Rzeppa type and the inner joints of the Delta type. The rack and pinion steering gear gave a turning diameter of 35.75 feet with 3¼ turns lock to lock. The rear wheels were carried on a tubular "dead" beam axle located by a single trailing arm on each side linked to transverse torsion bars, with a track bar for lateral location of the axle.

The Audi 75 was a compact four-door sedan built on a 98-inch wheelbase with a 52.4-inch track in front and 52.2 inch track in the rear. Curb weight was 2,161 pounds with a front/rear weight distribution of 60/40. The springing was fairly soft and wheel travel

cally simple, with low production cost and low maintenance demands, with a fashionable body shape. This was rejected as being harmful to Audi's image as a marque. Kraus considered a high-powered car of compact size with great performance and sporty styling to attract the youth market. This was rejected on the grounds that it meant entering an overcrowded market of uncertain potential. He considered creating a revolutionary car, an avant-garde design that could run for many years' production without needing updating, introducing new engineering features and original styling concepts at the same time. This was rejected as being too risky for a relatively small organization like Audi.

The fourth alternative was the one that got the nod. It was the typical European solution, a roomy family car with a high degree of technical refinement combined with robust construction and body lines that were right for the taste of the time, neither old-fashioned nor innovative, but a common-sense design.

Detailed design objectives included good fuel economy with above-average performance levels which necessitated lightweight construction and good aerodynamics. High priority was also placed

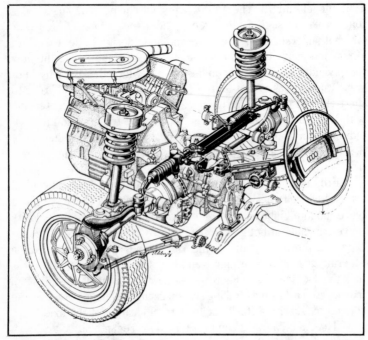

Audi 100 front suspension had upper and lower control arms with coil spring legs mounted on the upper control arm. Rack and pinion steering gear was outfitted with a hydraulic damper.

The Audi 100 was built to match the Mercedes-Benz 220 for interior dimensions while offering f-w-d at a lower price. It had a dry weight of 2,315 pounds.

on roadholding, stability in cornering as well as down the road, and consistent handling characteristics in all climates and all road conditions. Out of these considerations came the decision to go with f-w-d.

· The design formula followed closely along the lines of existing Audi models with a slant-four engine carried as front overhang, inboard front disc brakes, rack and pinion steering, and a "dead" beam rear axle attached by trailing arms.

The Audi 100 became a four-door sedan with a 105.5-inch wheelbase and a curb weight of 2,315 pounds. The 1760-cc engine was offered in three stages of tune, 80, 90 and 100 hp. The four-speed all-indirect transmission was available with either column- or floor-shift and an automatic transmission was in preparation, becoming optional in 1970. Final drive ratio was 3.88:1 giving the most powerful version a top speed of 107.5 mph and 0-60 mph acceleration in 11.5 seconds.

The front suspension introduced a new principle in Audi engineering, MacPherson-type struts in combination with two control arms. The strut had its base on the upper control arm. The lower control arm was a wide-based A-frame linked to a stabilizer bar. The reason for using two control arms (when one would be enough) was to provide a strong anti-dive effect. At the rear end transverse torsion bars were used with telescopic shock absorbers mounted vertically on the beam axle. The rear wheels carried brake drums.

The car had a 34.4-feet turning diameter and the steering was geared for 3.9 turns, lock to lock. Front roll center was located 3.6 inches above ground level and the rear roll center 8.45 inches above

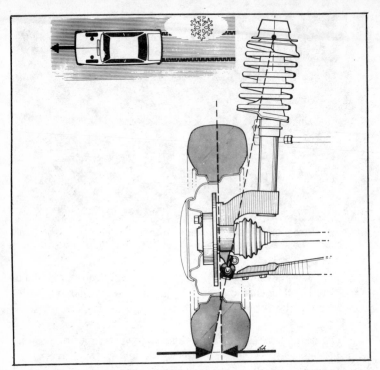

Because of the Audi 80's diagonal pattern of dual-circuit braking, the front wheels were given a negative scrub radius to maintain directional stability on surfaces of irregular friction coefficient.

ground level. Front springs were softer than the rear ones and the rear stabilizer bar had slightly more than half the strength of the front one. As a result, the car's roll-steer characteristic was understeer in front and oversteer in the rear suspension.

A 1.9-liter engine went into the 100-S two-door fast-back coupe that came out in 1970. It delivered 112 hp and had shorter wheelbase (100.8 inches) ventilated front discs and wider tires (185/70 HR-14 instead of 165 SR-14). The 1.9-liter engine was adopted for the Audi 100-GL which was added to the line in 1972.

Audi 80 Into VW Dasher

Volkswagen's f-w-d involvement began in May, 1968, with a car project known as EA838 (EA stands for Entwick-lungs-Auftrag, which is German for Development Order). EA 838 was entrusted to the chief engineer of Audi, Ludwig Kraus, in 1970 (Volkswagen had acquired control of the Audi company in 1965). This became the Audi 80 and went into production in 1972. The following year Volkswagen was given its own version of the same car to be marketed as the Passat in Europe (Dasher in the U.S.). When the 80 appeared it replaced all the former models in the junior series (75, 60, Super 90).

The Audi 80 was built as a two-door and four-door sedan with a wheelbase of 97.25 inches and an overall length of 164.4 inches. It had closely similar front and rear tracks (52.8 and 52.6 inches). The body structure was a monocoque shell designed by computer so that the weight was concentrated where the stress levels indicated a need for strength and removed from wherever it was not needed. This enabled the engineers to bring the car's curb weight down to 1,841 pounds.

A new slant-four engine family was created for the 80 with displacements of 1,297 and 1,471 cc, giving 60 and 75 hp. Engine

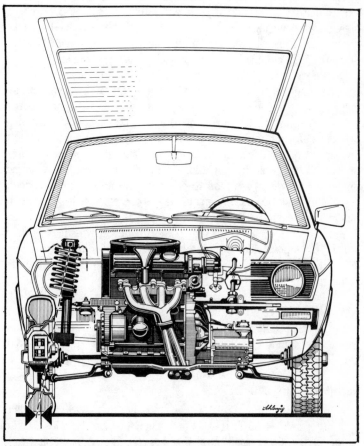

Unitized power package installation on the Audi 50 was extremely tight-fitting, leaving no space for an optional automatic transmission.

location followed earlier Audi practice but the suspension design showed considerable advance over the 100-series. At the front end, a true MacPherson system was adopted with lower A-frame control arms and coil-spring struts abutting against an extension of the cowl structure. At the rear end, torsion bars were discarded in favor of coil springs surrounding the shock absorbers.

Questionable Diagonal Braking Circuit

The brake system had outboard front discs and rear drums with a new diagonal hydraulic brake circuit (which meant that in case of failure in the primary circuit, the secondary circuit provides braking in a diagonal pattern (both front and one rear wheel). This led to the development of a new front suspension geometry with offset swivel axis (negative scrub radius). This was intended to keep the car on a straight path during braking after failure of the primary hydraulic circuit. This principle has since spread to all VW and Audi cars. Despite these companies' great publicity efforts to sell the idea as a great safety device, it's not necessarily a good thing.

Its opponents (notably Fiat) point out that hydraulic brake failure is an extremely rare occurrence and it's rarer still that when it occurs, the car must be brought to a stop under conditions which present different coefficients of tire-to-roadway friction for the left and right wheels (dry and abrasive on one side and wet and slippery on the other). But the negative scrub radius cannot be obtained unless the universal joint and steering arm are accommodated deep inside the wheel so as to practically become part of the hub. Such designs necessitate oversize wheel bearings and certain other reinforcements—and that adds to the unsprung weight. In other words, for a possible advantage in a one-in-a-million situation, you are putting up with a drawback that's in effect every moment the car is in motion.

The VW Passat (Dasher) went into production in April, 1973. In contrast with the Audi 80, which was a notchback sedan, the Passat came in three different body styles: hatchback coupe, hatchback sedan, and four-door station wagon. Mechanically the Passat was identical to the Audi 80.

Rabbit Start in 1970

In the meantime, Volkswagen had another f-w-d car project under way at Wolfsburg. It was known as EA-337 and had its start in April, 1970, when the director of research and development, Prof. Werner Holste, laid down the design objectives and overall layout for a Beetle-replacement and made Hans Georg Wenderoth, a top NSU

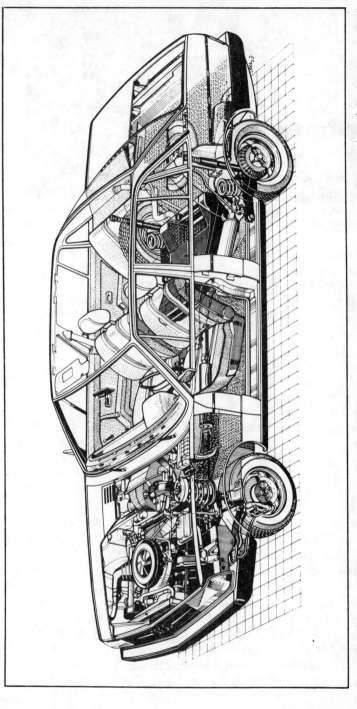

Non-independent rear suspension was retained for the 1977 Audi 100, and a MacPherson type front suspension was adopted. Fuel tank was moved inside the wheelbase.

113

Audi Avant four-door hatchback is powered by a 136-hp five-cylinder gasoline engine with fuel injection.

man who had been transferred to Wolfsburg, executive engineer for the car that was to become the Golf (Rabbit in the U.S.).

As chief development engineer, Friedrich Goes played a key part in making this car a fine example of f-w-d engineering. In the autumn of 1974 I sat in his office as he explained how the Golf came into being. The task was to develop a very light and compact vehicle to be built in two versions, four-to-five passenger sedan, and a two-plus-two sport coupe (Scirocco).

Because of its compact layout, the transverse engine cum front wheel drive was chosen. Two engines, overhead-cam designs derived from the Audi 80, of 1,100 and 1,500 cc were developed. Their installation shows a strange variation, for the small unit slants forward, while the larger one slants backwards. Striving for short overall length with the greatest possible interior length led to the design of a hatchback type of body with minimal body overhang front and rear. The car literally has a wheel in each corner.

Optimum space utilization and weight distribution transversely as well as from front to rear brought with it an unusually wide track. The combination of long wheelbase in relation to the overall length and optimum track width for the car's overall width with the advantageous center-of-gravity location obtained by the f-w-d and transverse engine layout presented a useful starting point for meeting the goals with respect to handling characteristics. MacPherson suspension with lower control arms and inclined spring legs was chosen for the front end. The use of a front stabilizer was avoided by working out the geometry for a very high roll center.

The A-frame lower control arms are asymmetrical in design and pivot on shafts anchored in the body shell. The spring struts are

Volkswagen Passat (Dasher) was based on the Audi 80 with slant-four engine installed longitudinally. It comes with four-speed manual or three-speed automatic transmission.

secured by bolts to the wheel hubs. Maintenance-free ball joints are fitted between the hubs and lower control arms. The upper end of the spring leg is supported by a rubber mounting with an integral ball bearing. The shock absorber inside the strut is of the twin-tube type with a replaceable cartridge and a piston rod guided by low-friction Teflon bearings.

The front spring rate is slightly progressive in jounce because of the diminishing length of the effective leverage of the lower control arm. The spring rate rises by 30.5 percent from design height to full load during which stage the front axle load is not greatly increased—only about 15 percent. As a result, the steering effort is remarkably unaffected by changes in load.

Particular attention was paid to obtaining a relatively inelastic connection between the front wheels and the steering gear. For this

With Golf's arrival in 1974, Vokswagen adopted the transverse engine layout. It is built as two-door and four-door hatchback sedans with manual or automatic transmission.

reason VW chose rack and pinion steering. It works with low friction and brings significant feedback sensitivity so that a steering damper was found not to be needed. The steering geometry was designed for progressive action and the ratio is gradually varied from 18.5 in the central position to 17:1 at extreme left or right. The steering lock range is 3½ turns.

Innovation in Rear Suspension

Without a newly developed rear suspension the Golf would not have become as compact as it is nor would it have attained its excellent road-holding ability. The design is called a connected trailing arm rear axle and is remarkable for combining the best properties of a live rear axle and certain advantages of independent suspension with minimum need for layout redesign and extra space. The rear suspension plays a vital role in assuring the Golf of its light understeer throughout its load range.

The problem stems from the fact that the rear wheels carry three-quarters of the weight of the passengers (one in front, two in the back). Because of space considerations the trailing arm rear axle was the only design that could be used. This design combines the advantages of the live axle (constant track width and parallel wheels at all times) with those of independent wheel suspension (low unsprung masses). In addition, the trailing arm rear axle requires considerably less space under the vehicle floor pan compared to the independent semi-trailing arm rear suspension. The constant camber configuration permits the smallest possible wheel housing. The small space occupied by moving parts permits simple exhaust pipe ducting and the best possible utilization of the space between the wheels.

The disadvantage of the trailing arm axle so far has been the narrow supporting basis with either ensuing high elasticity in the transverse direction or unsatisfactory ride-noise damping. The supporting base dimension in the VW connected trailing arm rear axle is 44.5 inches or nearly the complete car width. Very low elasticities in the transverse direction despite large-volume silentblocs result in excellent ride-noise damping.

The two trailing arms are connected by a so-called open profile. Open profiles are torsionally soft and consequently the travel of one wheel, especially when the travel is slight, only insignificantly affects the other wheel. Torsional stiffness can be changed by modification of profile thickness. This effect is used for roll stabilization. The connected trailing arm rear axle, therefore, does not need a separate stabilizer.

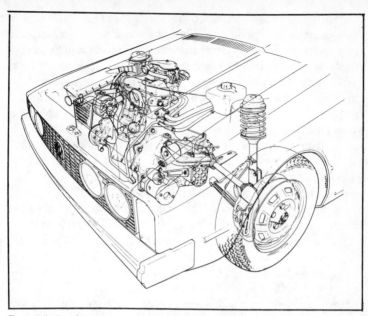

Four-cylinder Scirocco engine slants backwards and is offset to the right. MacPherson-type front suspension is shared with the Golf.

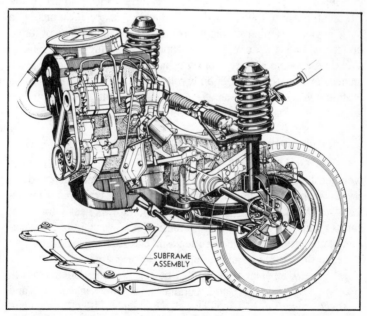

SUBFRAME ASSEMBLY

Audi 80 and VW Passat carry their engines in a cradle and rear gearbox mount acts to control torque reactions in the fore-and-aft plane.

Springing is accomplished by spring-damper units with a super-progressive spring rate. They are wound with variable pitch using a wire with an inconstant diameter. This combination gives a progressive spring rate and therefore makes it possible to employ a shorter spring with shorter wheel travel. This in turn requires less space for the wheel housing. Changes in vehicle load cause lesser variations of car attitude. The ride comfort for widely changing wheel loads is significantly better when compared to linear springs and the natural frequencies of the body can be maintained constant.

Severe bottoming caused by extreme bumps is prevented by a rubber spring that becomes effective above full-load position. The total wheel travel is approximately 7.5 inches and 2.36 inches of wheel travel is available above the full-load point which provides for excellent ride comfort even at full load. The effective spring rate at full load is double the rate at design height. This permits the natural frequency of the rear axle to remain constant regardless of the load.

The basic adjustment of the axle has a negative camber of one degree without any toe-in or toe-out. Trailing arm torsion slightly increases camber when both wheels of the axle are in "bump" position, such as in straight ahead driving, and at increasing load.

Negative camber was selected to have a certain allowance for camber changes caused by roll or side forces and to improve the lateral stiffness of the rear axle at higher lateral accelerations. The basic negative camber of one degree results in an increase of toe-in of approximately 15 minutes per 4 inches of spring travel. This is slightly over-compensated for by reducing toe-in 20 minutes per 4 inches of wheel travel under body roll. Camber change at body roll is in the negative direction as well and runs to slightly more than one degree per 4 inches of wheel travel.

Golf/Rabbit Changes Since Introduction

The Golf went into production in the summer of 1974. It weighed 1,720 pounds and was 146 inches long overall. It shared the Beetle's wheelbase of 94.5 inches and had wider track: 54.7 inches front and 53.5 inches rear. Its turn diameter was nearly four feet shorter than the Beetle's at 32.2 feet. The first round of modifications came after 11 months' production. The steering gear ratio was increased to 20.8:1 in an attempt to reduce the wheel effort.

For 1976 an enlarged engine (1,600 cc) became optional for the Golf S and LS while the Golf L continued with the original 1,100 and 1,500 cc power units. The GTI with a fuel-injected 1,600 cc engine made its debut in September, 1976, and shortly afterwards the Golf-diesel went into production.

Audi 50: Short, Light Family Car

While the Golf and Scirocco were being developed at Wolfsburg, Ludwig Kraus at Audi in Ingolstadt was busy on a stlll smaller vehicle which went into production in October, 1974, as the Audi 50. The goal was not to build a minicar but to design a four-seater family car two feet shorter than the Audi 80 with a weight target of no more than 1,325 pounds.

These objectives fixed certain architectural elements, such as the hatchback body and the transverse engine with f-w-d. While the Golf was designed for automatic transmission, the Audi 50 was to be made only with a four-speed gearbox. That saved some critical space at the front end. Also in contrast with the Golf which exists in both two-door and four-door versions, it was decided to make the Audi 50 exclusively as a two-door model.

There are many points of resemblance between the Audi 50 and the Golf but also many points of dissimilarity. The Audi engine is the same 1,100 cc unit that's used in the Golf, installed transversely and tilted forward at 15 degrees. The transmission is the same. Front suspension on the Audi 50 is a MacPherson type and steering by rack and pinion. In contrast with the Golf, there is a front stabilizer bar (which serves double duty as part of the lower control arm exactly as shown in Earle S. MacPherson's original patent). And on the Audi the spring strut base is offset towards the rear end of the front wheel hub carrier, which has the effect of assuring the same lightness of steering on entering difficult curves at speed as when changing lanes on the expressway.

Because of the differences in front suspension design, Kraus found it advisable to install a vibration damper on the right-hand drive shaft. The rear suspension system is similar in basic principle but differs in execution. The transverse link of the Golf's trailing arms have been moved back from the pivot points and forms a U-shaped beam axle linking the trailing arms at midpoint. The layout is not unlike that of the Saab 96, as a matter of fact. It is intended to provide some measure of negative camber when cornering (roll understeer).

The Audi 50 did not miss its weight target by much, ending up with a curb weight of 1,510 pounds. Built on a 91.7-inch wheelbase, its overall length is no more than 137.4 inches. "You can't make a four-seater much shorter than that," Friedrich Goes told me, "unless you go to a rear-mounted engine."

Front track is 51.2 inches and rear track 51.6 inches. The steering is geared to give 3.5 turns lock to lock with a turning diameter of 31.5 feet. The final dive ratio is 4.267:1 which gives a

119

Volkswagen Derby is a notchback version of the hatchback Polo (which is practically identical with the Audi 50). All three share the same engine and drive train.

road speed of 15.1 mph per 1,000 rpm in fourth gear. It can reach 50 mph from standstill in 9.6 seconds and has a top speed of 88 mph. Average fuel economy works out to 32.2 mpg.

Audi 50 Becomes VW Polo/Derby

In March, 1975, Volkswagen began production of its own version of the Audi 50 under the model name of Polo. It differed from the Audi mainly in having a smaller engine of 895 cc and drum brakes all around instead of front discs as on the Audi. In February, 1977, Volkswagen produced yet a different version of the same car wearing the Derby label. It differs from the Polo in having a hatchback body with a conventional trunk.

Evolution of the Audi 100

It remains to look at the evolution of the Audi 100 to complete the picture of the Volkswagen group's use of f-w-d. No major changes occurred until 1975. Then the front discs were moved outboard and the front suspension modified to provide a negative scrub radius. The rear drums were redesigned with fins for better cooling and longer lining life. Rear wheel brake lines were equipped with a load-sensitive pressure regulator to prevent premature locking. The column shift quietly disappeared as all models used a console shift for both four-speed synchromesh and automatic transmission.

In September, 1976, a new 100-series went into production developed under the direction of Ferdinand Piech who replaced

Ludwig Kraus on the latter's retirement. The four-cylinder engine went to 2 liters displacement and a new in-line five-cylinder engine was added. Both front and rear suspension systems were totally new. At the front end, Piech used a pure McPherson setup even to the extent of using the stabilizer bar as a component of the load control arm (as on the Audi 50).

The rear wheels were connected by a "dead" beam axle as before, but the suspension geometry and means of springing was entirely different. The axle was located by short trailing arms with vertical coil springs mounted ahead of the axle. Telescopic shock absorbers were mounted behind the springs and closer to the wheel hubs. A track rod located the axle laterally and a stabilizer bar was connected to the two trailing arms. This system was free of roll steer effects, giving a well-balanced car with consistent cornering behavior.

The car weighed 2,448 pounds in its basic form with the 1.6-liter engine, 2,536 pounds with the 4-cylinder two-liter, and 2,580 pounds with the 2.2-liter five-cylinder unit. Wheelbase was 105.7 inches and front and rear track 62 and 56.9 inches. Top speed ranged from 100 mph (1.6 liter) via 111 mph (2-liter) to 118 mph (2.2-liter). Acceleration figures for the three cars, from zero to 60 mph, are 16, 12.25 and 9.5 seconds. All the above figures refer to the standard four-speed transmission. The automatic takes about 3 mph off the top speed and adds two to three seconds to the acceleration times.

Audi is testing a new 170-hp twin-rotor Wankel engine in the current 100-series vehicle and this is expected to become the replacement for the NSU Ro-80 at some future date, probably in 1980.

As for the Audi 80, it has had one body change: new front and rear sections, introduced in August, 1976. Mechanically, it has benefited from a multitude of detail improvements but no basic engineering alterations. A new 80-series will be announced for 1979 but specifications are not available as we go to press.

Chapter 7

Fiat and Lancia

Fiat is one of the few companies in the world that simultaneously produces conventional cars (front-mounted engine and rear wheel drive), cars with rear-mounted engines, and f-w-d cars. Fiat has only four f-w-d models and they are very closely related. But one of them has been Europe's best-selling car for five years, regardless of drive system and price. That's the 127, sold with both Fiat and Seat name plates (Seat is Fiat's subsidiary in Spain).

Autobianchi's Primula Led the Way

It was not Fiat's first f-w-d production model but the second, the 128 having preceded it by two years. And the first Fiat-designed f-w-d production car was sold under another label: Autobianchi. The Autobianchi Primula went into production in March, 1965, after four years of design and development work. The man who was primarily responsible for its creation was Ettore Cordiano who is now engineering director for Fiat's car division.

His instructions for the Primula were to create a medium-class family car as dissimilar to the Fiat 1100 as possible but having comparable power, dimensions, and seating capacity. The design must permit production in relatively low volume at a low enough cost enabling the car to be marketed at a reasonable and competitive price. Consequently, Cordiano designed the Primula for a long production life to spread out the amortization of the tooling costs over a number of years so as to have an adequate number of cars to share these costs. It was also decided to use Fiat engines already in

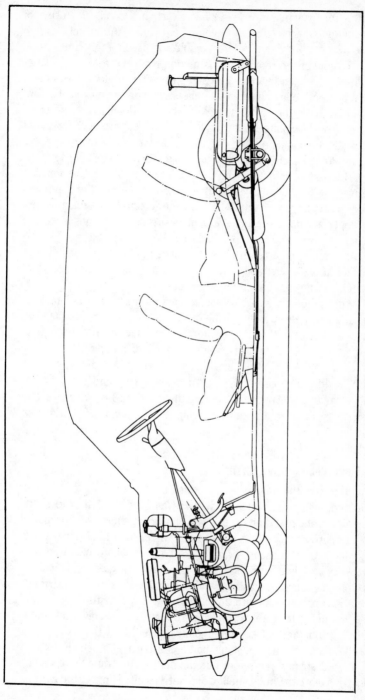

Autobianchi Primula was the forerunner of all f-w-d Fiats built to date. Four-cylinder Fiat engine was mounted transversely.

production which was a first-class shortcut not only in terms of production cost but also in development time. Autobianchi was to build its own body shell and assemble the car in its own plants.

To obtain the maximum distinction from the Fiat 1100, Cordiano decided on a hatchback design in two forms, two-door coupe and four-door sedan. That would take care of providing visual difference. To make the car technically different, Cordiano chose front wheel drive. Looking back into Fiat's f-w-d experience, Cordiano had at his fingertips a large bank of information and even patents. Fiat was not exactly starting from zero in f-w-d technology.

Because of this, Cordiano had the freedom to opt for technically "brave" solutions such as a transversely mounted engine and unequal-length drive shafts. That meant designing and manufacturing a special transaxle and developing a special mounting system for the power unit. The transaxle had to be kept as short as possible so as to fit in between the front wheel housings. Due to tooling cost considerations, Cordiano was locked into a conventional gearbox location, facing the clutch and flywheel.

Other modifications made necessary by the transverse installation and a 15-degree forwards tilt included a different oil sump and oil pump intake, a relocated water pump and cylinder head water outlet, new intake and exhaust manifolds, carburetor and air cleaner.

The 1,221-cc Fiat engine delivered 54 hp at 5,400 rpm. The four-speed transmission had all-indirect gears and used helical spur-gear transfer to the final drive unit with its 3.846:1 ratio. The gearshift was mounted on the steering column, giving a full-width flat floor.

Unequal Length Drive Shafts

Because the final drive unit was offset to the left, the shaft to the right wheel was nearly twice as long as the left side shaft. Cordiano anticipated problems with this arrangement and prepared an alternative design with a split right-wheel shaft to obtain oscillating shafts of equal length and a short center shaft anchored to a bracket extending from the crankcase. But the expected difficulties (handling, steering, tracking) did not materialize and the Primula went into production with unequal-length drive shafts.

Cordiano tried for a low-cost combination of universal joints, avoiding constant-velocity inner joints on the theory that axial sliding freedom was more important than uniform drive speed. Early test cars used splined pot-joints but this led to the transfer of engine vibrations into the body shell. Constant-velocity joints of the Rzeppa

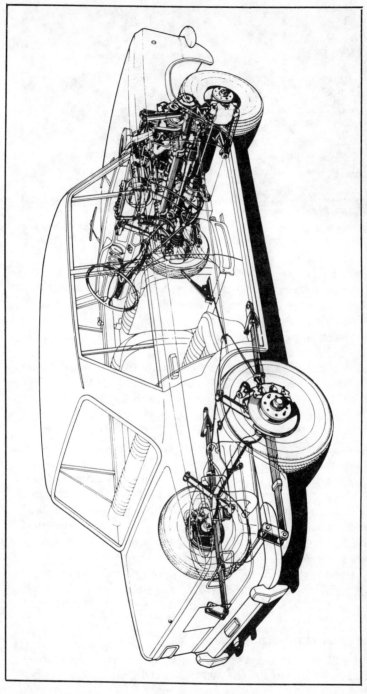

Autobianchi A-111 cutaway shows front and rear suspension systems inherited from the Primula with a brand-new and wider body shell.

Fiat 128 was built in three versions, two-door sedan, four-door sedan, and two-door station wagon. It was a new design, not a scaled-down Primula.

type were then tried at both ends but with no improvement (thought to be due to their lack of axial compliance). Finally, a pot-joint with rollers instead of splines was developed and this gave satisfactory results.

Front suspension on the Primula had A-frame lower control arms and a transverse leaf spring serving as upper control arm. Telescopic shock absorbers were mounted on top of the outer spring attachments. Rear suspension consisted of longitudinal leaf springs shackled at the rear end and clamped to a tubular 'dead' beam axle kinked at both ends to cross the chassis below hub level (to get a lower cargo platform behind the rear seat). The rear suspension also included a weight-sensing device that was connected to a pressure-control valve in the brake lines to the rear wheels. Four-wheel disc brakes with vacuum power assist were standard on the Primula.

Steering was by rack and pinion geared for 3½ turns lock to lock with a turning diameter of 38.7 feet. With its 90.5-inch wheelbase and front track of 52.4 inches, the Primula had an overall length of 149 inches and a curb weight of 1,885 pounds, divided 60/40-percent between front and rear wheels.

It was geared to run 16.2 mph at 1,000 rpm and had a top speed of 87 mph. It could go from standstill to 50 mph in 15 seconds and was able to climb a 35-percent grade in first gear.

Fiat 128 and Autobianchi Mini

With the Primula in production, Cordiano immediately tackled two new f-w-d projects, one car, smaller and lighter than the Primula, to be built and sold as a Fiat, and a minicar for Autobianchi. The Fiat project was to be the 128, going into production in March, 1969, and the minicar became the Autobianchi A-112, introduced in November, 1969. At the same time the Primula was updated with newly styled bodies, a more powerful engine (the 1,438-cc Fiat 124 unit), an improved steering linkage, and renamed A-111. It was produced up to 1973.

The A-112 was a little box on wheels, no more than 126 inches long with its 80.25-inch wheelbase and weighing only 1,445 pounds in 60/40-percent front/rear distribution. The Fiat 128 was a small family car available as two- and four-door sedan and two-door station wagon. It has an overall length of 152 inches with a wheelbase of 96.4 inches and a front track of 51.5 inches. It weighed 1800 pounds as a two-door sedan carrying 60 percent on its front wheels. I am treating the two together for their chassis layout and engineering follow identical principles and show how Cordiano's thinking had evolved since the Primula was on the drawing board.

Engines were positioned the same way, transversely and ahead of the front wheel axis with the transaxles offset to the left, driving the wheels via unequal-length shafts. The Fiat 128 had a completely new and technically advanced 1,116-cc engine while the A-112 inherited the 903-cc engine from the Fiat 850. MacPherson suspension was adopted at front with the spring legs mounted above the hub carriers and slightly splayed. The lower control arms were made up of steel rods, one member being a drag strut and at the same time forming the ends of a stabilizer bar and the other a lateral link attached at a slight leading angle.

Chassis components of the Fiat 128 are gem-like in all their simplicity. Rear suspension may be the ultimate in low cost.

127

Fiat 128 transaxle is built integrally with the engine. The same mechanical unit is used in the Ritmo.

Independent rear suspension was adopted with A-frame control arms linked to a low-mounted transverse leaf spring doing double duty as a stabilizer bar. Telescopic shock absorbers provided an upper anchorage point and dictated the suspension geometry.

Both cars had a slightly positive scrub radius and a roll axis aiding towards slight understeer, with a front roll center at ground level and the rear roll center three inches above. Brake systems were also similar with discs in front and drums in the rear and the usual weight'sensitive proportioning valve. Both had rack and pinion steeering and both used four-speed floorshifts.

The A-112 had a final drive ratio of 4.692:1, giving a road speed of 14 mph per 1,000 rpm in top gear and a maximum speed of 85 mph, with 0-60 mph acceleration in 18.5 seconds. With its 4.077:1 final drive ratio, the Fiat 128 ran 15.1 mph per 1,000 rpm and had a top speed of 91 mph. Going from standstill to 60 mph was a matter of 16.5 seconds.

Abarth, Brazil and the Ritmo

Autobianchi added an Abarth version of the A-112 in 1971 and in 1973 Pininfarina proposed a roadster version called Giovani which was exhibited at Geneva but never got into production. The Abarth version got a larger (1,050 cc) engine rated at 70 hp for 1978. Fiat's 128 has evolved steadily over the years, adding a sports coupe and a 1.3-liter engine in 1973. The 128 SL 1300 in turn became the 3P for 1975 with new sheet metal but mechanically the same.

The Fiat 147 made in Brazil is based on the 128 and the new Ritmo, unveiled in April, 1978, is essentially a new and more modern body built around the 128's mechanical components. It had its start as Project X-1/38 in November, 1973, just as the fuel crisis hit the Western World and the concept was aimed from the start at improved fuel economy. That has resulted in a range of three engine sizes with progressively lower final drive ratios: the 4.077:1 gearing is retained for the 1,100-cc version. The 1.3-liter is geared at 3.765:1 and the 1.5-liter at 3.588:1.

Five-speed transmissions are available on all models and an automatic transmission (purchased from Volkswagen—the Golf design) is offered for the 1.5-liter. All are made to run economically at high speed (with a streamlined body having a drag coefficient of 0.38). The 1.1-liter has a top speed of 90 mph and gives 28.3 mpg when cruising at 70 mph. That drops to 28.0 for the 1.3-liter, with its

Fiat Ritmo takes over where the 128 stops. It's more refined, quieter, more economical, and offers five-speed transmission plus an automatic option.

Ritmo front end shows extra-long right-side drive shaft, articulated steering shaft, and sharp tilt of the MacPherson spring legs.

93-mph top speed, and to 27.3 mpg for the 1.5-liter with its 100-mph top speed.

What about the Fiat 127? It was a new body for the A-112 components, built as a two-door fastback introduced in 1971. It was built on a longer wheelbase (87.6-inches) than the A-112 to serve as a real family car and provide a useful back seat and a roomy trunk. It grew to 141.5 inches in overall length and a curb weight of 1,517 pounds. Two years later a hatchback became available and Seat

Ritmo rear suspension is basically as on the 128. Fuel tank is still outside the wheelbase but does not extend far behind the wheels or main rear body shell cross-member.

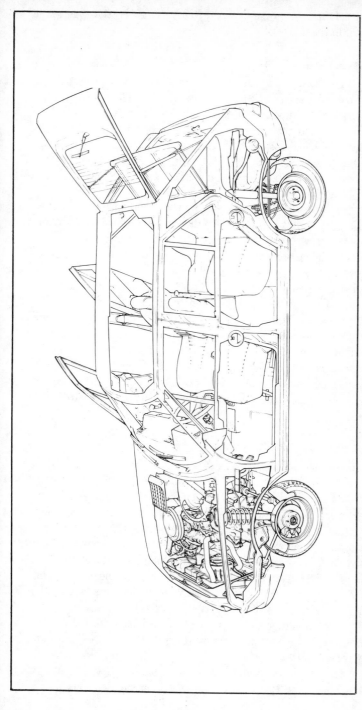

Overall cutaway of the Fiat Ritmo shows excellent space utilization and a body structure that combines the aerodynamic with the practical in a happy union.

added a four-door version. For 1978 the 147 engine was made optional in the 127.

Lancia Flavia and Fulvia

Fiat took control of Lancia in 1969 and thereby acquired a stable of f-w-d cars. Lancia switched to f-w-d in 1960 when the Flavia went into production and added the smaller Fulvia in 1963. Both were creations of Antonio Fessia, a former Fiat engineer and f-w-d enthusiast who had lectured at the University of Bologna from 1940 to 1945 and came to Lancia in 1956 from the Politecnico di Milano. His main assistants were Giorgio Romanini, Giuseppe Gillio, and Francesco de Virgilio.

"It is the product of a logical mind which has analyzed the needs of a category of motorists to which thought is rarely given," Robert Branschweig wrote after a preview of the Flavia. These are motorists who desire a high-class car but without a large engine or a body that takes up a great deal of room.

Harry Mundy was in agreement: "I have been an admirer of Lancia's purposeful design approach to the automobile for many years. Their engineers are never afraid to break away from the orthodox path to achieve a desired purpose. The Flavia carries on this tradition, for the use of a flat-four engine, combined with the transmission, and driving the front wheels, is an ideal solution to obtain a compact layout and yet provide sufficient internal space and comfort for six people—not forgetting plenty of room for their luggage."

Fessia's Remarkable Conception

Fessia had been preoccupied with auto safety for a long time and his design priorities were thus established: First, front wheel drive, arranged to ensure absolute regularity of power transmission and a turning diameter no greater than for conventional cars. Second, the structure of the body skeleton, chassis and mechanical organs had to be extremely robust even if that meant a weight penalty. Third, the engine had to be extremely lightweight and must present an installation package of short length and low height. Fourth, power disc brakes with dual hydraulic circuits were to be used. Fifth, large-size tires were chosen, to give secure road grip under all load conditions, at high speed and with high side forces, and offering the greatest security in case of sudden loss of pressure. And sixth, the car must have low running costs and be simple to maintain.

When the Flavia design was cleared for production, it was a remarkably roomy four-door sedan of compact dimensions with a

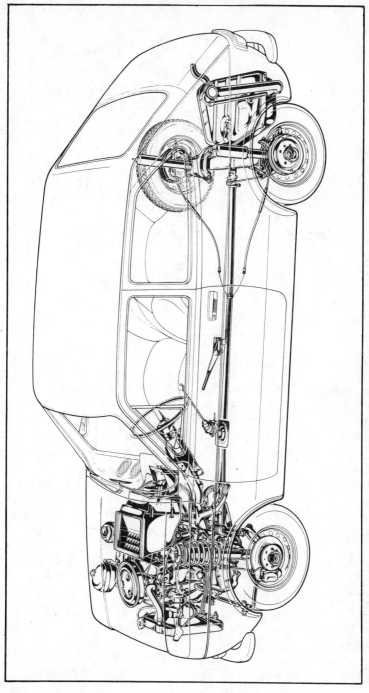

Fiat 127 provides a model example of packaging with all mechanical elements concentrated around the front wheel axis.

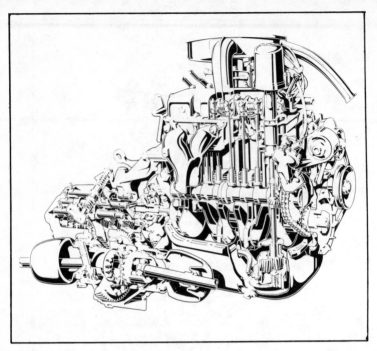

Unified power package of the Fiat 127 combines pushrod OHV 903 cc engine with ultra-compact four-speed transaxle.

curb weight of 2,700 pounds and an overall length a fraction over 180 inches. It had a top speed of 92 mph and gave an average fuel economy of 23 mpg. It was an outstanding combination of qualities that are difficult to unite in one single car. How was it done?

First, the engine was a flat-four all-aluminum job of 1,500 cc displacement, positioned ahead of the front wheel axis. It delivered 78 hp at 5,400 rpm and was matched with a four-speed transaxle having a final drive ratio of 4.10:1, giving 18.1 mph per 1,000 rpm in top gear. Birfield-Rzeppa joints were used near the wheels and Delta-type joints near the differential. Radial tires were standard (Michelin X steel-belted or Pirelli Cinturato fabric-belted).

Fessia wanted leaf springs in both front and rear suspension systems and designed a front end with A-frame control arms and a transverse leaf spring crossing the chassis above the transaxle, plus a stabilizer bar. Rear suspension was non-independent with a tubular "dead" beam axle carrying the wheel hubs and longitudinal leaf springs on each side.

Placing the seating between front and rear suspensions—with no waste of space—effectively fixed the wheelbase at 104.33 inches.

Prototype sports model with detachable roof section, using A-112 chassis, was made by Pininfarina in 1973.

Front track was 51.2 and rear track 50.4 inches. Steering was by worm and roller geared at an 18.2:1 ratio, giving 4½ turns lock to lock with a 36.3-foot turning diameter. Disc brakes, mounted outboard at all wheels, were combined with a vacuum-booster. All four discs were 11 inches in diameter making for an important effective radius and pratically fade-free brakes. A coupe and a convertible were added to the Flavia line for 1962.

In September, 1963, Lancia offered a more powerful 1.8-liter engine. Coupes and convertibles equipped with this 88-hp engine were given a 3.90:1 final drive ratio which raised top speed to 108 mph. The Flavia 1.8 sedan could reach 100 mph. Fuel injection was offered for the 1966 models raising power to 108 hp. In April, 1967, all Flavia models received new bodies with crisper styling. A two-liter 131-hp version of the Flavia engine was introduced in July, 1969. In April, 1971, Fiat decided to kill the Flavia name and redesigned the sedan body while the sports models were dropped. The

Lancia Flavia was a roomy and comfortable sedan of very compact dimensions. The whole car was designed with great attention to safety.

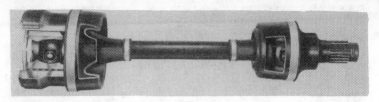

Lancia Flavia drive shafts had Birfield-Rzeppa joints at both ends. The outer joint is seen at left.

1.5 and 1.8-liter engines were discontinued and the new model was called Lancia 2000. It lasted only about 20 months in production.

10-Year Run for the Fulvia

After about 1965 it was no longer the Flavia that spearheaded Lancia's march of progress. It was the Fulvia which began its career as a boxy little sedan in March, 1963. It looked like a scaled-down Flavia but differed technically in more matters than dimensions. First, the engine was a V-4. Not so strange, for V-4 engines had been used in the first Flavia prototypes but gave way to the flat-four. In the smaller car, Fessia felt that the narrow-angle V-4 offered advantages over the flat-four (fewer parts, lighter weight, lower cost). As in the Flavia, the engine was carried outside the wheelbase with a transaxle behind. It delivered 58 hp at 6,000 rpm from 1,091 cc and pulled a 4.777:1 final drive ratio via a four-speed gearbox with direct drive on top. In contrast with the Flavia, it used a floorshift.

The Fulvia weighed 2,270 pounds and was 162 inches long. With a front track of 51.2 inches and a 97.6-inch wheelbase, it had a turning diameter of 31.4 feet. Steering was by worm and roller, geared slow at 4.25 turns lock to lock. Front and rear suspension systems were scaled-down editions of the Flavia designs and the Flavia brake system with four very large discs was copied, reducing disc size no more than required by the 14-inch wheel rim design.

For 1965 Lancia added a Fulvia coupe and increased engine size to 1,216 cc. The coupe was built on a shortened wheelbase of 91.75 inches and weight was reduced to 1,975 pounds. Two years later came the optional 1,298-cc engine rated at 90 hp, and for 1968, a Fulvia Sport with an aluminum body by Zagato. For 1970 the Fulvia 1600 HF was added to the line, sharing the coupe body and powered by a 1,584 cc version of the same engine delivering 114 hp coupled with a five-speed gearbox. At the end of that year the sedan was discontinued. Then the Zagato-bodied model was chopped and in 1974 the only Fulvia still in production was the 1.3-liter coupe. No Fulvias were listed in the 1973 lineup.

Lancia Fulvia was launched in 1963 as a high-priced alternative to the Fiat 1100 with a narrow-angle V-four engine.

Transverse-Engined Beta

Fessia died in 1968 and Sergio Camuffo became technical director of Lancia. He had concentrated on developing the Fulvia as an all-Lancia car but after the takeover by Fiat he was assigned to create a new car series using Fiat power units. The result was the Beta which first appeared in 1972 with the 1,600-cc twin-cam engine from the Fiat 125.

Its overall layout and engineering principles were inherited from the Autobianchi A-111. But it was a more developed design

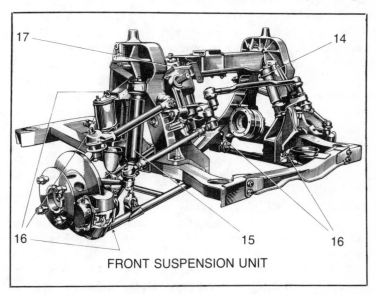

FRONT SUSPENSION UNIT

Front suspension of the Fulvia had elaborate control arm design with steering arms and linkage behind the front wheel center axis.

| BETA BERLINA | BETA HPE | BETA COUPE | BETA SPIDER | BETA MONTECARLO |

Lancia Beta range is all f-w-d except one model, the Montecarlo (alias Scorpion) which has the same unified power package moved back to a midships position.

with greater technical refinement. The engine was installed transversely ahead of the front wheel axis and tilted backwards at about 20 degrees. The helical spur gear final drive unit was offset to the left but drive shafts were now equal in length and Delta-type inner joints were used in conjunction with Rzeppa-type outer joints.

Front suspension is a MacPherson system with lower A-frame control arms and inclined spring legs extending from the wheel hub carriers, and a stabilizer bar. At the rear end is a setup with the same type of spring leg and mounting and a lower control arm consisting of two parallel transverse rods. Drag struts to each hub carrier are integral parts of the stabilizer bar.

Rack and pinion steering is used, with a 20.5:1 ratio giving a 33-feet turning diameter with an even 4 turns lock to lock. The four-wheel disc brakes have power assist and discs are nearly 10 inches in diameter. A proportioning valve linked to a mechanical load-sensing device limits brake line pressure to the rear wheels to prevent locking. Fiat's five-speed transmission was adapted to the Lancia transaxle, with fifth overdrive and a 4.21:1 final drive ratio. When the 1,800-cc engine became available for the Beta, the ratio was changed to 4.07:1, which had the double job of raising top speed and reducing fuel consumption.

A smaller version of the same engine, 1,438 cc, as originally used in the 1967 Fiat 124 Spider, was added to the Beta options in 1973 with a 4.46:1 final drive ratio. The Beta sedan is a four-door fastback built on a 100-inch wheelbase with an overall length of 169 inches. It weighs 2,400 pounds of which the front wheels carry 60 percent.

A coupe on a shortened wheelbase (92.5 inches) was added in June, 1973, and the HPE sportswagon followed in March, 1975. All share the same power trains and chassis units and constitute a fine example of modular construction. In addition, the Beta power train is

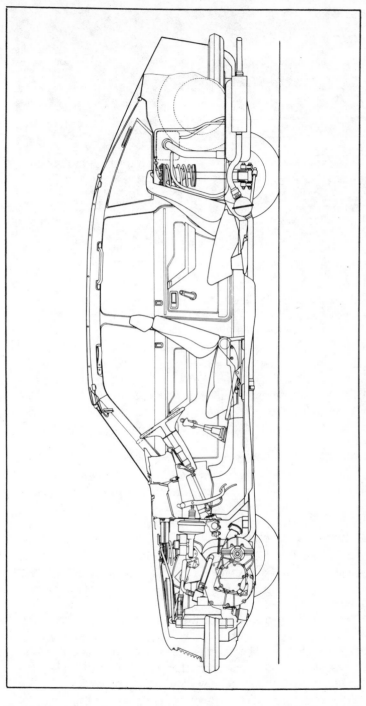

Sectioned view of the Beta shows compact power train, tall rear spring legs, and vertical storage of spare wheel.

Lancia Gamma is a luxury and prestige car intended to replace the Fiat 130. It reverts to the Flavia concept of a flat-four engine.

used to drive the rear wheels of the Scorpion—a sports model with a midships-mounted engine having the same relationship to the Beta as Fiat's X-1/9 has to the 128.

In the wake of the fuel crisis, Fiat prepared a 1,297-cc version of the twin-cam 124 engine and used it for the Beta 1300 launched in November, 1974. A year later the 2-liter replaced the 1.8-liter and the final drive ratio was lengthened to 3,785:1, bringing top speed up to 112 mph. The Beta 2000 sedan accelerated from standstill to 60 mph in 10 seconds flat and covers the standing quarter-mile in 17 seconds.

In the spring of 1978, Lancia began building automatic transmissions for the Beta. The design comes from Automotive Products in England and consists of a hydraulic torque converter and a train of bevel gears giving three forward speeds.

Flat Four Lancia Gamma

With the Beta safely launched and its further development becoming a matter of routine, Camuffo and his engineering staff concentrated on their next project, a luxury car to replace the Fiat 130.

Regardless of the fact that the Fiat 130 was a conventional notchback sedan powered by a front-mounted V-six engine driving the rear wheels, Lancia felt that their car should have f-w-d. Fiat was taking its V-six out of production so Lancia was allowed to plan and make its own engine for the new luxury car, the Gamma.

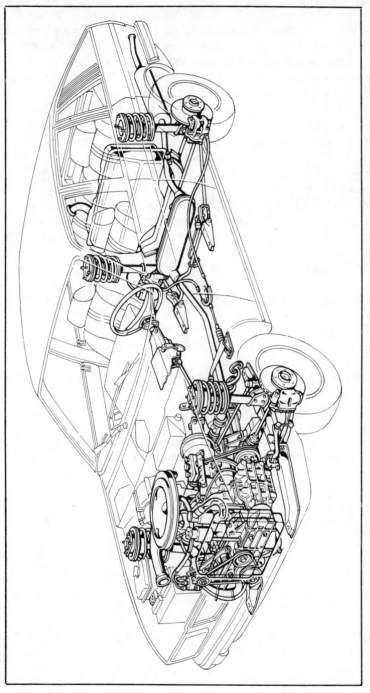

Gamma front and rear suspension systems are upscaled from the Beta with various differences in the control arms and linkages.

141

Camuffo reverted to the Flavia concept and made it a flat-four, in the same location, and with the same drive train configuration. Displacement was 2,484 cc and power output 140 hp. A five-speed gearbox was made standard with the prospect of an automatic transmission at some future date. It pulls a 3.70:1 final drive ratio which gives the car a road speed of 20.2 mph per 1,000 rpm.

Front and rear suspension systems were scaled up from Beta designs and adapted to the Gamma. A new power brake system with four-wheel discs was developed with ventilated rotors in the front wheels. Power-assisted rack and pinion steering was chosen, giving three turns lock to lock with a turning diameter of 34.4 feet. Wheelbase is short for a car in this class and overall length has been kept to 180.3 inches. Because the engine is all aluminum, it does not cause weight distribution problems, nor do its 298 pounds add greatly to the vehicle weight which comes out at an even 3,000 pounds. Front/rear weight distribution is 63/37 percent.

The Gamma was first shown in March, 1976. A 2-liter version of the same engine became optional in November of that year. The Gamma competes against the Audi 100, BMW 525, Citroen CX 2400, Mercedes-Benz 250, Opel Senator, Peugeot 604, Renault 30 TS and Volvo 264 DL. A Gamma coupe was added in 1977 with a Pininfarina body on a shorter (100.6 inches) wheelbase.

The Gamma 2500 has a top speed of 121 mph and goes from standstill to 60 mph in under 10 seconds. With its low-drag body it has reasonable fuel consumption at speed: 27.5 mpg at a steady speed of 60 mph and, cruising at 100 mph, it still gives 16.2 mpg.

At the low end of the range, Lancia is preparing a new series known as Epsilon. It will share its mechanical elements with the Fiat Ritmo and feature its own body with a Lancia look.

Chapter 8
Svenska Aeroplan/Saab

The cars of the Swedish Aeroplane Works have always had f-w-d. Saab is a relatively recent make, production having begun in 1950, and no great soul-searching was undertaken before making the decision to use f-w-d. It came about sort of casually.

At the end of World War II the executives of the Swedish Aeroplane Works realized that the company would have to diversify into a line of peacetime consumer goods to keep its factories busy and meet its payroll. After brief consideration of going into household appliances and prefabricated houses, the company determined that it should stay in the transport sector and manufacture equipment that could get maximum benefits from its knowhow and experience in aeronautical engineering. Only one product met the requirements: automobiles.

The task of developing a car was entrusted to Gunnar Ljungstrom whose previous engineering experience included stepless automatic transmissions, aircraft engine accessories, gas turbines, and aircraft wing structure—a background highly unlikely to lead its owner to create an ordinary car. He took no notice of what was being produced in the U.S., Britain, and France in 1945 but was guided exclusively by common sense.

The Logical First Saab

He correctly assumed that the demand for small cars in Sweden, which had grown fast in the 1937-39 period, would continue to grow. His design should be a light family car intended to compete

Streamlined prototype from 1947 gives no hint of engine location or drive system in the car that Svenska Aeroplan was to produce.

with the smallest Fords and Opels in price. For his technical inspiration he went to a German car that had sold well in pre-war Sweden, the DKW (whose origin and technical makeup are described in Chapter 17.

The DKW appealed to Ljungstrom because of its mechanical simplicity—a two-cylinder two-stroke engine mounted in front and driving the front wheels, leaving great freedom to design the passenger compartment and the overall "envelope." That's why, in a nutshell, the Saab became an f-w-d car.

It would not be logical for an aircraft manufacturer about to go into the auto business to disregard aerodynamics. It had to be a streamliner and give visual proof of the company's basis in flying. Industrial designer Sixten Sason was invited to submit some proposals. He came in with one design that was immediately liked by all and instantly approved.

Relying heavily on local junkyards for parts, Ljungstrom had his first prototype running in 1946. It was the company's 92nd design project so it was designated Saab-92. In parallel with the slow and painstaking development work, tooling orders went out and arrangements were made to purchase components Svenska Aeroplan could not produce itself. That included the engine, at first. It was an updated DKW copy designed and built by Hans Muller in North Germany.

The Saab-92 prototype was presented at a press preview in June, 1947. It was a four-to-five passenger car with a 97.2-inch wheelbase and an overall length of 154 inches. The shorter the body, the more difficult it is to streamline, and here Sixten Sason has succeeded brilliantly. The fastback roofline was made possible by using a very low back seat, and the "soft nose" with its sloping hood was many years ahead of its time. It was built as a two-door sedan only and did not have a trunk lid. It weighted 1,687 pounds.

With an output of 25 hp from the 764-cc parallel-twin, the Saab-92 had a top speed of 65 mph with acceleration to match but gave excellent fuel economy. Owners had to mix oil into the gasoline in proportions of 1/25, as was common for other cars and motorcycles with two-stroke engines.

The engine was installed transversely ahead of the front wheel axis with a three-speed transmission battling the Dynastarter for space on the left side of the flywheel, and spur gear drive to the centrally located final drive unit. A column shift mechanism was used. Drive shafts had Delta-type inner universal joints and double Cardan-type outer joints.

Front suspension was independent with leading arms and transverse torsion bars in an arrangement where each torsion bar can perhaps best be described as two-thirds of a stabilizer bar. The torsion bars crossed each other in a narrow X pattern with eccentric anchorage points in the inner body structure. Telescopic shock absorbers were mounted on top of the hub carriers.

Rack and pinion steering was used with a parallelogram linkage to steering arms pointing forward from the hub carriers. Brakes were Lockheed hydraulic with 8-inch drums on all wheels. The wheels were disproportionately large, shod with 5.00-15 tires.

Rear suspension was also independent with trailing arms and transverse torsion bars. This gave a ground-level roll axis, which in

First production-model Saab was powered by a two-cylinder two-stroke engine mounted in the nose of the car.

Saab-92 engine was mounted transversely, with transverse gearbox connected to final drive unit, horizontally to the rear.

combination with a narrow track of 46.5 inches front and rear gave the car a tendency to oversteer once the side force exceeded a certain value, a characteristic that demanded great driving skill and quick reflexes for fast driving on winding roads.

Changes For 92B and 93 Models

No chassis changes were made for the Saab-92B that went into production in 1953. The engine had its output raised to 28 hp and the body was partially redesigned with a larger rear window and, yes, a trunk lid.

Far more important changes were made for the Saab-93, appearing as a 1956 model. Hans Muller had designed a three-cylinder engine (also based on pre-war DKW practice). Some time earlier, Svenska Aeroplan had completed its own engine plant in Gothenburg and taken over production of the parallel-twin. This plant had also been tooled up to make the three-cylinder two-stroke.

It delivered 33 hp from 748 cc displacement and was turned around from its transverse position to an in-line overhanging location

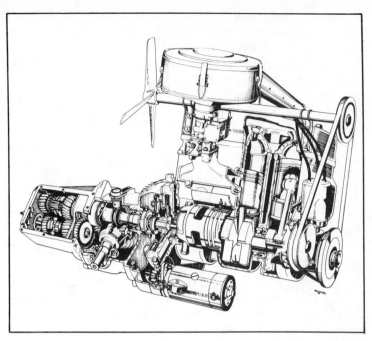

Saab switched to longitudinal engine location when adding a third cylinder on the two-stroke engine. Power unit was mounted ahead of the front wheel axis.

Saab-93 engine was fairly light and hardly took up any room at all. It was mounted ahead of the radiator with most of the accessories on the firewall.

with a transaxle including a spiral bevel pinion and ring gear instead of the earlier arrangement with all rotation taking place in the same plane. Column shift was retained for the new 3-speed gearbox.

Front and rear suspension systems were completely new. At the front end, a coil-spring setup with unequal-length A-frame control arms was adopted. Due to the presence of the drive shafts, the coil springs were mounted on top of the upper control arms.

Independent rear suspension was discarded in favor of a "dead" beam axle of drop-center aspect, located by trailing arms and a track rod. At the same time track was increased to 48 inches front and rear. These modifications made the Saab-93 a much better balanced car, less capricious in its cornering behavior. Wheel-base was increased to 98 inches and weight went up to 1,775 pounds.

The First Sonett

A prototype open two-seater created a sensation at the Stockholm auto show in 1956. It was called the Saab Sonett. It was the spare-time project of the company's top development engineer, Rolf Mellde, who was also a keen rally driver. Mechanically, it was a Saab-93 on a shorter chassis. Mellde had tuned the engine to 57.5 hp and with its lightweight plastic body the whole car weighed 1,103 pounds dry. It had sports-car acceleration and a 103-mph top speed. The Sonett (unofficially Saab-94) was never placed in production, but the public interest in this car had demonstrated to Svenska Aeroplan that there was a market potential for that type of car and the idea was to be revived in the 1960s.

The car evolved into the Saab-93B for 1957, with improved brakes and a host of body modifications including a one-piece windshield. In 1958 a sports model called GT 750 was introduced

Sonett sports prototype from 1956 never became a production model but the company never forgot the sensation it created.

Side section of the Saab 96 shows its space-utilization secrets. Low rear seat makes sloping roofline possible.

(for export only). The engine had been tuned to deliver 45 hp and a four-speed transmission was fitted. A station wagon designated Saab-95 appeared in 1959 and the sedan version was updated to 93F specification.

The 96 and Refined Two-Strokes

In February, 1960, the Saab-96 replaced the 93F. Extensive body changes were matched by an enlarged engine, now of 841 cc displacement delivering 38 hp. Chassis improvements did not involve any change of principle but tuning of the existing system. The Saab-96 had 7 inches of wheel travel available in the front suspension. The roll center was unusually high at 4.6 inches above ground level. Rear springs were 50 percent stiffer than the front ones and wheel travel was restricted to 3.3 inches. Because of its non-independent rear suspension the roll center was quite high at 10.25 inches above ground level.

Meanwhile, Rolf Mellde wanted to see if the Saab engine would be competitive as a Formula-Junior power plant, and built a single-seater in 1960. It was raced in several events but was outclassed by more advanced machinery with four-stroke engines.

It was becoming quite clear to Gunnar Ljungstrom that time was running out for the two-stroke as a production car engine. But the company had invested heavily in manufacturing equipment for two-strokes and did not plan for switching to four-strokes. Development engineers Kjell Knutson and Josef Eklund did wonders to bring the two-stroke up to the requirements of the customers of the day, but it was too late.

New models with more power and better equipment failed to attract new customers. In 1962 came the GT 850 with a triple-

Sonet II went into limited production with a three-cylinder two-stroke engine and plastic bodywork.

carburetor engine delivering 52 hp, four-speed transmission, and front disc brakes. It had automatic engine oiling. It was later renamed Sport for European markets and Montecarlo 850 for sale in America. Not only faster, it was also quieter and more comfortable than the baseline Saab-96. It went from standstill to 50 mph in 12.3 seconds and had a top speed of 85 mph. Overall fuel consumption was 36.2 mpg.

Sonett II And Sonett III

About this time Svenska Aeroplan decided to offer a model with a real sports car body in addition to the high-performance sedan. Sixten Sason and Bjorn Karlstrom submitted designs and although Sason's made greater use of standard parts and could be expected to have lower manufacturing cost, the management picked the Karlstrom proposal, a two-seater coupe of very restricted interior space. It was announced in March, 1966.

Apart from the shorter wheelbase of 84.75 inches, this Saab-97 was mechanically similar to the GT 850 but much lighter with its plastic body shell at 1,565 pounds curb weight. It was marketed as the Sonett II for about three years, selling in very small numbers. It led to the Sonett III, a better-looking car with body designed by Sergio Coggiola of Torino, built on an 85-inch wheelbase and powered by a different engine. It was code-named Saab-98 and was produced from 1970 to 1973.

First Four-Stroke a V-4

In the meantime, Rolf Mellde had found a four-stroke engine that met his standards for performance and reliability, which fit into the Saab-96, and which was available in any quantity Svenska Aeroplan might need. It was the Ford V-4 made for the Taunus 12M, an engine that was also used in a French sports car at the same time, the Matra 530.

The Saab-96 V-4 went into production in September, 1966. Its power train was 112 pounds heavier than the triple-carburetor three-cylinder engine and transaxle, which raised the car's weight to 1,932 pounds. Because of the engine's overhanging position, front/rear weight distribution went from 60/40 to 63/37 percent. It changed the character of the car and sales immediately picked up. For 1969 the Saab-96 acquired power brakes, lower-geared steering, and various body modifications. The two-stroke engine was kept in production up to 1969 and then dropped completely. The 96 V-4 is still in production (by Valmet in Finland) with basically the same specifications.

Project Gudmund for All-New 99

The present company is now Saab-Scania and makes only the 99, which stemmed from a design study code-named Project Gudmund that dates back to 1956. Project Gudmund was a different kind of car aimed at the more affluent market Svenska Aeroplan expected to prevail in the 1970s and 1980s. It was to be a wide and spacious family car with a smooth, quiet, and powerful engine, something that would appeal to the traditional Volvo buyer without losing the old-line Saab customer.

Ricardo & Company was engaged to design and develop a four-cylinder overhead-cam engine for the new car, and through contacts with Ricardo, Svenska Aeroplan found out that Triumph was developing a very similar engine. From that information evolved a plan to use Triumph engines in order to save time and cut production cost. The first batch of 20 test engines were delivered in 1963.

Final version of the Sonett was powered by a V-4 engine produced by Ford of Germany. This is the first production model without bumpers.

Saab 99 GLE four-door sedan with hatchback comes with all-coil suspension and a choice of manual or automatic transmission.

Gudmund prototypes were on the road as early as June, 1965, with disguised bodies wearing fake Daihatsu identification crisscrossing Europe from Spain to Lappland.

Rolf Mellde was in charge of the project while Gunnar Ljungstrom, now past 65, acting as a consultant. Sixten Sason and his talented assistant, Bjorn Envall, developed the body design. Production began in November, 1967. The original Saab-99 two-door sedan was built on a 97-inch wheelbase with a wide front track of 54.7 inches and an even wider rear track of 55.1 inches. It was 171 inches long overall and weighed 2,500 pounds.

The engine was installed longitudinally on the front wheel axis and tilted 45 degrees to the right. Flywheel and clutch were at the front end with an idler gear taking the drive to the four-speed transmission below the front part of the block. The gearbox output shaft carried a pinion meshing with a spiral bevel rung gear. Rzeppa-type joints were adopted for the outboard position, with Delta-type inner joints.

A final drive ratio of 4.22:1 gave the car a road speed of 17.7 mph per 1,000 rpm in top gear, a reasonable number in view of the relatively small 1,709-cc displacement and the car's weight and carrying capacity. That gave a top speed of 93.5 mph and zero-to-sixty mph acceleration in 15 seconds with an average fuel economy of 26 mpg.

Front and rear suspension systems followed the same principles utilized for the 96 with coil springs all around. At the front end, unequal-length A-frame control arms with springs and shock absorbers above the upper arms were used while the rear end continued as a non-independent design with a beam axle located by trailing arms and a track rod. Rack and pinion steering geared at 3.33 turns lock to lock for a 33.5-feet turning diameter led to demands for power steering—something previously unheard-of at Svenska Aeroplan Power brakes, however, were standard, with discs on all four wheels. Wheel size was not one inch but two inches smaller than on the 96, using 165 SR 13 tires.

In 1969, an export version of the Saab-99 was launched with an 1,850 cc version of the same engine using fuel injection and delivering 95 hp at 5,200 rpm. For this model an automatic transmission developed on the basis of the Borg-Warner Type 35 was optional. A four-door 99 sedan was added in 1970.

Turbo Climax to Variations

Then Rolf Mellde left Saab-Scania in order to take over as chief development engineer of Volvo and Henrik Gustavsson took over the duties of improving the Saab cars. First came the EMS at the end of 1973, powered by a 110-hp 2-liter engine. Saab-Scania had completed its own engine plant and transferred manufacturing from Triumph to Saab-Scania in 1972. Then came the Combi-Coupe

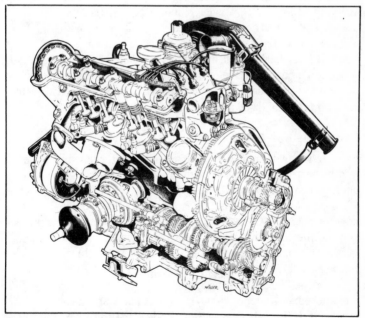

Power flows from the front of the Saab-99 crankshaft via clutch and spur-gear train to countershaft-transmission below crankcase.

The Saab-99 Turbo was, in 1978, the world's fastest f-w-d car in regular production. It's ideal for long-distance travel.

(Wagonback in the U.S.), a hatchback version of the two-door sedan, early in 1974. It was followed by a GLE four-door hatchback in 1976.

The most amazing version of the Saab-99 is the Turbo which made its debut in September, 1977. An AiResearch turbocharger boosts peak power output from the 2-liter engine to 145 hp and top speed to 115 mph. It provides smooth six-cylinder-like torque and does not affect fuel consumption except at high rpm. With the Turbo in its 99 range, Saab now occupies a unique position in the world of f-w-d. But can Saab-Scania live on this high line car series alone? No. It needs a modern replacement for the 96. What will it be? It will be the new Lancia Epsilon made in Italy with Saab-Scania merely acting as importers and distributors.

Remarkable New 900 Series

For its own production, Saab-Scania is determined to compete in a higher price class. For a time the company was considering putting an in-line six-cylinder engine into a long-hood version of the 99. A prototype was built and tested but was rejected in favor of a new project using the power trains from the 99 series. This project became the Saab 900 which went into production in September, 1978. The power ranges from 108 hp (twin-carb) via 118 (K-Jetronic) to 145 (Turbo).

For the 900 is not just a model, it's a series. Two basic bodies are offered: two-door hatchback and four-door hatchback. The baseline GL is available with both bodies and the twin-carburetor version of the 1,985-cc engine with either four-speed manual or three-speed automatic transmission. The GLE is powered by the fuel-injected engine in combination with automatic transmission and comes only as a four-door. The EMS comes only as a two-door with fuel-injection and manual transmission. The Turbo is available with both body types and manual transmission only.

The 900 replaces the Wagonback versions of the 99 but the 99 two- and four-door sedans will continue in production for an indefinite period. Bodies for the two series are produced in different plants and final assembly takes place on separate, side-by-side lines.

The 900 project began several years ago and its timing was determined by U.S. federal safety standards. When Saab found that modifications to the 99 to pass the 30-mph barrier crash test would demand as high costs as tooling for a new body, the decision was made to make a new body for all markets. This permitted the combination of specific deformation-pattern requirements with manufacturing improvements such as the combination of several parts into one single stamping before welding into the body shell. By such techniques Saab-Scania was able to make a longer, roomier car at a minimal increase in overall weight and cost.

Many Results of Longer Wheelbase

Saab's goals in the dynamic-behavior area dictated an improvement in weight distribution. This was solved by moving the front

Turbocharged Saab engine turns the 99 from a docile family car into a fire-breathing highway rocket. Turbo bypass conserves fuel economy when full power is not needed.

wheel about two inches forward. It may have been judged desirable simultaneously to move the rear wheels backwards but that would have involved a major change in the body floor and was consequently ruled out. As a result, the 900 series was able to share the 99 body floor. It has new front fenders, a new hood, larger-area windshield, new roof and side panels, and new front and rear bumper systems. The 900 is 8.27 inches longer than the 99 Wagonback and 12.6 inches longer than the 99 sedan. The 900 body has improved aerodynamics. All models have a new front spoiler and the Turbo has a rear spoiler.

The 900 series also features a completely new engine mounting system, made possible by the increase in body dimensions. New large-base rubber mounts help minimize vibrations and assure low noise transfer to the interior. Yet the mounting system is fixed in critical points so that the shift lever does not rock during throttle reversals.

Handling Inspires Confidence and Speed

Driving the 900 is a revelation. Despite being 45 pounds heavier than the 99 Wagonback, the 900 GL feels like a lighter car. Its dynamic response has been much improved, so that the driver gets true information back from the steering wheel and has his commands obeyed without delay. This has been achieved through persevering development work and involves a new steering system, revised rear suspension, and modified front end geometry. The new rack and pinion steering gear is more precise, the rear suspension practically eliminates roll steer effects, and the front end geometry does not permit toe-in changes during spring deflections.

In combination with the evened-out weight distribution and lower polar moment of inertia, these suspension design changes have helped give the Saab 900 greater steering precision without loss of ride comfort. The 99 has a certain initial understeer and a certain inertia in its response that do not encourage fast driving on winding roads. But the 900 tells you, in its language of steering wheel feedback, body roll, and overall balance, exactly what its capabilities are and sort of eggs you on to use its cornering power to the maximum.

But that doesn't mean you have to be a leadfoot to enjoy driving the 900. Its rewards in terms of driving joy show up even in leisurely motoring, continuously reassuring you of its general competence and instant readiness for the unexpected. Even if the driver is caught off guard, the car won't be—and it will respond to emergency action in a safe, predictable manner, always remaining under full control.

Improved weight distribution has been obtained by moving the front wheels forward about two inches, giving a more favorable disposition of the major masses relative to the wheelbase and therefore a lower polar moment of inertia.

Fifteen-inch wheels have been retained for the 900, giving the Saab a number of advantages over competitors with smaller wheels in the areas of traction under reduced-friction conditions, rough-road ride and handling, and ground clearance.

The news in the front suspension is the elimination of toe-in/toe-out changes during wheel deflection, thereby improving the car's down-the-road stability as well as assuring consistent steering characteristics on curves. The front roll center has been raised to about 7 inches above road level so that the car has plenty of roll stiffness without a stabilizer bar.

A tubular axle forms the basis of the rear suspension, as on the 99. But the 900 has new geometry with the control-arm lengths and pivot points carefully calculated to counteract any tendency for rear wheel steering effects during spring deflection. It's a more expensive suspension system but it pays off in terms of driving pleasure.

Adequate anti-dive has been built into the front suspension and the rear axle itself acts as a stabilizer bar, giving great roll stiffness at the back end. The 900 is totally free of throttle-steering phenomena (as occur in some other front-wheel-drive cars, tending to go wide during power-on cornering but sharply shortening the turn radius if you lift your foot off the accelerator).

Power Steering Radial Tires, & Better Brakes

Turn diameter on the 900 has been kept short (about 32 feet) and the standard steering gear takes 4.2 turns lock to lock. That's fast enough to keep steering wheel movement within reasonable limits on Swedish roads and at the same time gives an agreeably low steering effort.

For the first time, Saab is offering power steering. After exhaustive testing, the choice came down to ZF or Saginaw and in the final analysis the contract went to the American supplier. Two straight-ratio systems are used, one for the 900 GLE giving 3.7 turns lock to lock, and an even quicker one for the fuel-injected 900 EMS and 900 Turbo with 3.5 turns lock to lock. Both work flawlessly, without any trace of pump catch even on quick steering reversals and without the tendency to overshoot that's often associated with a car maker's first attempt to adopt power steering to his products.

Tires are a vital part of the chassis and here Saab has stopped at nothing. All 900 models have steel-belted radials with 165 SR 15 on the GL and GLE and 175/70 HR 15 on the EMS. Pirelli P-6 were chosen for the two-door Turbo (in 195/60 HR 15 size) as the ultimate for high-speed handling, while the four-door Turbo comes with Michelin TRX 180/65 HR 390 tires as the best combination of ride comfort, high-speed capacity, and cornering stability.

The Turbo and EMS are equipped with Saab's own four-speed gearbox and the GLE comes exclusively with automatic transmission. The automatic is the latest version of Borg-Warner's type 35 which can now be described as generally satisfactory. Four-wheel power disc brakes based on the 99 system are used on the 900. But there is something new here: The outer pads in the front wheel calipers have semi-metallic pads (For higher heat resistance).

Despite slightly heavier weight, the Saab 900 offers performance levels similar to the 99 up and down the range. Saab's fuel-economy figures (test cycle established by Sweden's Konsumentverket) show overall figures of 24 mpg for the GL and EMS, 22.4 for the Turbo and 21.4 for the GLE.

Although the company is increasing its production capacity to 130,000 cars a year, Saab will never become a dominant factor in any market and the management wants to compete in a class where each car can sell on its own particular merit and bring a healthy profit (instead of trying to compete with Europe's mass-producers). With the introduction of its 900 series, Saab takes a step into a price class with products that are not only competitive but outstanding for their combination of qualities—safety, fuel-economy, performance, durability, versatility, and driving pleasure.

Chapter 9
Austin Design Office

A whole family of f-w-d cars, marketed with a variety of different labels, all now belonging to the British Leyland organization, have originated in the same place, the Austin Design Office in Birmingham. The first one, which is still in production, was the 15th project since the engineering departments of Austin and Morris were merged and therefore called ADO-15. Its first official names were Austin Seven and Morris Mini-Minor, going into production in October, 1959.

The ADO-15 project got its start in 1955 when Sir Leonard P. Lord, head of British Motor Corporation, got irritated at the success of the "bubble cars" (Isetta, Heinkel, Zundapp Janus, Fuldamobil and others) and decided to produce a vehicle of similar size that was also a true automobile. He gave the order to BMC's overall engineering boss, Turkish-born Alec Issigonis, who had just been lured back to the fold after three years with Alvis, having formerly been with Morris since 1937. His primary assistant on ADO-15 was Charles Griffin, an excellent man who had come up through the ranks of the technical department at the Nuffield Organization after starting his career as a draftsman with Wolseley in 1940.

Remarkable Response to Bubble Cars

They looked at some bubble cars, and of course, L. P. Lord had rejected that line of approach. They looked at everything BMC was already building and knew they had to come up with something quite

The Austin-designed Mini pioneered 10-inch wheels and rubber springs. It has also won many international rallies.

different. What it amounted to was to sit down and actually rethink the whole idea of what makes a car a car.

Three principles guided them towards the final design. First, light cars must have a forward weight bias to assure directional stability. That meant mounting the engine in front. Secondly, to obtain adequate traction with a front engine in a light car, empty or laden, it must have front wheel drive. Thirdly, there was no time to design, develop and tool up for a completely new engine so that car must be designed to use an existing BMC engine. The smallest was the A-series introduced in 1951 for the Austin A-30. An in-line four-cylinder unit, it would occupy the least space if placed transversely between the front wheels.

Out of this reasoning Issigonis began making sketches. There were no product planning committees, no market studies and no marketing strategy. There was no styling. Issigonis reported directly to Lord and Lord ran the corporation with an iron will. As a result, Issigonis had exceptional freedom to adopt unusual solutions and the full support of an autocratic leader who was himself an engineer.

For instance, Issigonis decided to use Moulton rubber springs for all four wheels and all-independent suspension. He drew up a boxy lightweight monocoque body with sub-frames for the front and rear suspension assemblies. In the original design, the fuel tank was mounted in the cowl and used as a stress-carrying member of the body. It was later moved to the back. Also, the radiator at first was mounted in the right front wheel housing but it was later moved to the left side and mounted on the front sub-frame.

Unusual ADO-15 Development

It was March, 1957, when ADO-15 was given top priority. Prototypes were built and testing began. The transverse engine installation gave some problems. At first, the engine was mounted with the carburetors in front and the electrical accessories behind the block. That led to carburetor icing, so the engine was turned around. Now the electrical parts needed protection, but that was more easily cured by shielding.

To make room for the gearbox, Issigonis put it inside the engine's oil sump with an extra idler gear to provide clearance for the crank throws. The engine was slightly offset to the right with a simple helical spur gear drive to the centrally located final drive unit and with equal-length drive shafts. Cardan-type universal joints were used for the inboard location but outer joints were of the Birfield-Rzeppa type.

Front suspension control arms were narrow-based with a stabilizer bar acting also as a drag strut for the lower arm. At the rear end, trailing arms were used. The wheels were set at a permanently negative camber to restrict the car's sensitivity to accelerator position changes during cornering. Wheel rims had only a 10-inch diameter which placed exceptional demand on the suspension system and the rubber elements did their job quite well.

Due to the small wheel size and the lack of installation space, the rubber springs were restricted to a 5.25-inch diameter. That in

Austin Mini had the BMC "A" series engine turned 90 degrees to the left with its transmission incorporated in the crankcase.

turn led to a lever-type linkage with a five-to-one ratio so that vertical wheel travel of 2 inches displaced only 0.4 inches of rubber. Rubber spring life turned out better than expected and the linkage was tough enough. But the hydraulic shock absorbers took a beating and needed frequent replacement.

The small wheels also imposed a severe limit on brake drum size but that was not viewed as a potential source of trouble for what was designed as an all-out economy car and when it later became a problem due to the car's amazing speed capacity, it was solved by using front disc brakes.

Steering was by rack and pinion, arranged to give 2½ turns lock to lock and a 32-feet turning diameter. The car was short and wide with an 80-inch wheelbase and tracks of 47.4 inches in front and 45.9 inches in the rear. With an overall length fractionally over 120 inches, the Mini was light with a curb weight of 1,250 pounds, distributed so that the front wheels carried 61 percent of the static weight.

Remarkable Performance of Mini

The 848-cc engine's 37.5-hp were enough to give it quite astonishing performance. With a 3.765:1 final drive ratio, it was geared to run 14.8 mph per 1,000 rpm and this held the top speed down to 73 mph. But this also made it very lively throughout its speed range with ability to cover the standing-start quarter-mile in 23.5 seconds. Going from standstill to 50 mph took 18.5 seconds. What's more, it could be driven fast on curves due to its amazing roadholding so that remarkably high average speeds could be turned in.

Production started in August, 1959, with one basic body style for both Austin and Morris versions, a two-door coupe chopped off behind the back seat. Early models were very noisy and some noise "leakage" was traced to the direct stick shift linkage through the floorboards. The car became quieter after it was redesigned with a remote-control floorshift.

Mini Variants for Utility and Performance

A van version was introduced in Junuary, 1960, and a station wagon in September of that year. The first Mini-Cooper came out in September, 1961, with a 997-cc engine supposedly developed jointly with Cooper Car Co. of Surbiton, builders of Grand Prix racing cars. Two new versions of the ADO-15 labeled Riley Elf and Wolseley Hornet were added in October, 1961. They were mechanically

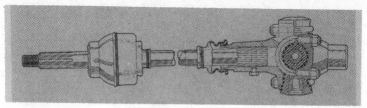

Mini drive shaft has Birdfield-Rzeppa outer joint but the inner joint was a special Cardan-type with hefty rubber bushings to cushion shock loadings both axially and rotationally.

identical with the Austin and Morris versions but different in cosmetic treatment.

Private owners began to compete in rallies and races with the Mini and soon the BMC competitions department was called upon to provide a sports-model ADO-15. That became the Mini-Cooper S which first appeared in April, 1963, with a 1,071-cc engine and a number of chassis modifications including larger-size constant-velocity joints, reinforced steering arms, stronger lower control arm pivot shaft, and metal couplings for the drive shafts instead of rubber. In April, 1964, a 1,275-cc engine replaced the 1,071-cc version. A smaller Mini-Cooper S with a 970-cc engine was built from April, 1964, to January, 1965.

Hydrolastic suspension (with water-and-alcohol connections between rubber spring units to replace the shock absorbers) was adopted for most ADO-15 cars in September, 1964. But in November, 1969, the basic Mini 850 and Mini 1000 reverted to rubber springs. Vans and wagons had never changed.

An automatic transmission option was added in October, 1965. The unit was developed and manufactured by Automotive Products and was unusual in that it used differential-type gear sets rather than planetary gearing. This was done because of the limited diameter in the lower crankcase where the unit had to be fitted. Here was a very long but also very narrow four-speed automatic which overcame a problem that had not even been envisaged by Issigonis in designing the car—the fact that the lack of an optional automatic drive hurts the potential demand for the car.

Mini Continuation and Upscaling

Later models of the Mini have retained the same technical specifications and differ mainly in body design and equipment. The Riley and Wolseley name plates were phased out after BMC came under Leyland management. The Mini lives on in the original Austin and Morris identities and also as the Italian-made Nuova Innocenti.

The Innocenti Company of Milano began to assemble the Mini in 1965 and in 1975 added a new series with a Bertone-designed body. This is the version that's still built in Italy.

A new Mini project code-named ADO-80, was started in 1975, and was shelved at the end of 1977. The old Mini will be kept in the lineup as long as the demand for it warrants continuation of its production and it will be supplemented by an enlarged version that's been on the drawing board since 1978.

Upscaling the Mini is not a new idea. Issigonis had it first and began working on the ADO-16 before the ADO-15 was even finished. This project went into production in October, 1962, as the Morris 1100, Austin 11, and MG 1100. It used a 1,098-cc edition of the A-series Austin engine with a Mini-type drive train. The same AP automatic transmission was offered as an option. Hydrolastic suspension was standard and the front wheels had disc brakes. It was built as a two-door or four-door sedan, the semi-fastback body design coming from Pininfarina. A station wagon was added two years later. With its 93.5-inch wheelbase and 147-inch overall length, the ADO-16 weighed 1,775 pounds and had a front/rear weight distribution of 62/38 percent. It used 12-inch wheels and had a 36-feet turning diameter (same as the VW Beetle), with rack and pinion steering geared for 3½ turns lock to lock.

Variants of the ADO-16 appeared in October, 1965, as the Riley Kestrel and Wolseley 1300, the latter featuring the 1,275 cc engine. Innocenti also built the ADO-16 from 1966 to 1973. The Morris line was confined to the wagon for the 1972 model year and then phased out. Austin continued the 1100 and 1300 sedans and wagons through 1974. The last survivor of the ADO-16 family was the Austin Apache built in Australia from 1970 to 1976.

Blowing up the Mini concept by using bigger and bigger engines, longer and heavier cars, kept Issigonis busy for years. The ADO-17 went into production in 1966 as Austin 1800 and Morris 1800. As the numbers indicate, engine displacement was 1.8 liters (an Austin B-series engine). These models were built on a 106-inch wheel-base and reached an overall length of 164.2 inches. Curb weight was 2,540 pounds with 63 percent resting on the front wheels. It was built as a four-door sedan with a short rear deck.

Rather than fitting power steering, Austin slowed down the gearing to 4.4 turns lock to lock. Turning diameter seemed excessive at 40.5 feet. Suspension was a hydrolastic system and front disc brakes were standard. With its 86-hp and 3.88:1 final drive ratio, the ADO-17 cars ran 17.7 mph per 1,000 rpm in top gear and had a top speed of 90 mph. Acceleration from standstill to 60 mph took 15 seconds and the standing-start quarter-mile 21 seconds.

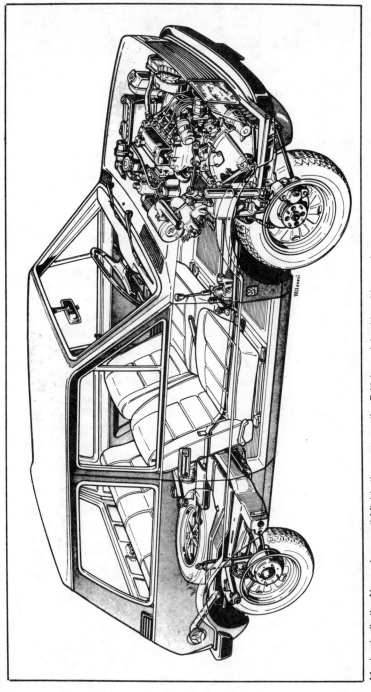

Mechanically the Nuova Innocenti Mini is the same as the British model, with rubber springs.

165

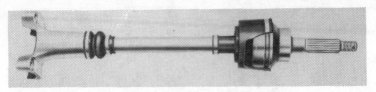

Morris 1100 drive shaft had Birdfield-Rzeppa outer joint but the inner joint was the same Cardan type used on the Mini with special rubber bushings.

Culmination of the ADO-17

In March, 1967, BMC began producing the Wolseley 18/85 which was a super-deluxe edition of the ADO-17 with Borg-Warner automatic transmission and power-assisted Burman rack and pinion steering. The steering cut the lock-to-lock wheel movement from 4.4 to 3.6 turns. The transmission was a design which placed a hydraulic torque converter at the end of the crankshaft with chain drive to the input shaft to a planetary gear train in the lower crankcase, whose output shaft turned the final drive spur gear. But the Wolseley was not the culmination of the ADO-17.

A variant known as the Austin X6 Tasman went into production in Australia in September, 1970, and was built there up to 1976. It had a slightly longer body and was powered by a six-cylinder overhead-camshaft engine mounted transversely. For this job, Austin could no longer use the Cardan-type BMC rubber-resilient inner joints but adopted a Delta type. Outer joints, as a matter of course, were Birfield-Rzeppa.

This was followed up with three six-cylinder cars made in England starting in the spring of 1972. They were called Austin 2200, Morris 2200, and Wolseley Six and continued in production until replaced by the Princess in September, 1975. They combined the Tasman engine with the 1800 and 18/85 vehicles. This engine was a six-cylinder version of a new E-series overhead-camshaft four designed for the Austin Maxi which had been introduced in April, 1969.

The Maxi had the ADO number 14 which normally indicates that the project antedated the Mini—and it does, but only with regard to the engine. The rest of the car is a newer creation. And the engine had a long gestation period since an overhead camshaft was a new departure for Austin.

Maxi Direct Mini Descendent

Charles Griffin was chief engineer for the ADO-14, Issigonis having been placed in charge of research and forward planning but removed from near-term production projects. Design work on the

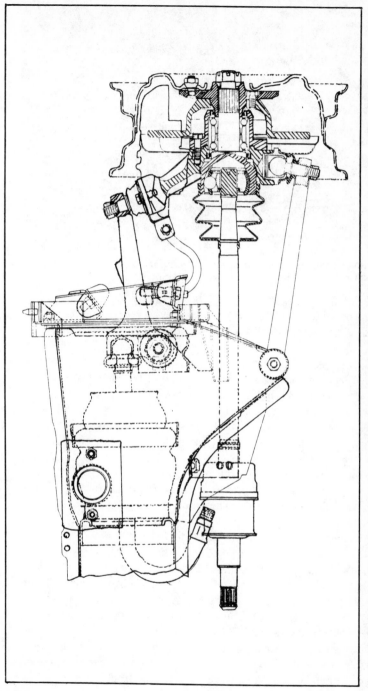

Austin Maxi abandoned the rubber-bushing Cardan-type inner joint in favor of a constant-velocity joint. Outer joint is Birfield-Rzeppa.

Austin Maxi had new overhead-camshaft engine and five-speed transmission in combination with f-w-d and Hydrolastic suspension.

Maxi began in the spring of 1965 and still has the hallmark of its Issigonis background. Though entirely new, engine and drive train follow the identical principles. But the gearbox got five speeds instead of four as in earlier models. It had hydrolastic suspension with a lower A-frame control arm and a straight lateral upper link and wide-based trailing links in the rear. The subframes had been replaced by reinforcements in the body shell.

The Maxi engine was a 1.5-liter of 75 hp so that the car occupied the space between the 1100/1300 models and the 1800/2200 cars. It was built as a four-door sedan and used the doors and door sills from the 1800/2200. It was built only as an Austin, without a Morris counterpart, for the Leyland management had decided that the Morris name was henceforth to be used only for cars of conventional layout and construction while Austin was to specialize in f-w-d models.

In dimensions also the Maxi fit between the ADO-16 and ADO-17 with a 104-inch wheelbase and 157.5 inches of overall length. Curb weight is 2,158 pounds with 63 percent on the front wheels. Griffin managed to get a tight turning diameter of 30.5 feet by using steering angles up to 39½ degrees on the inside wheel. The steering was geared for 4 turns lock to lock. The car had an exceptionally high swivel axis inclination of 12 degrees, but a modest 2.72-inch positive scrub radius. The roll axis was nose-up, tail down, with a ground-level roll center in the rear and a roll center height of 4.65 inches in front. As a result, there is no front stabilizer bar.

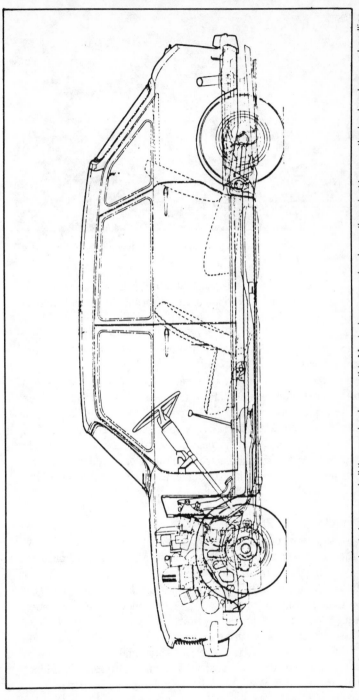

F-w-d permits rear suspension to be moved all the way back as on this Maxi, since rear wheels are there just to carry the load and assure handling stability but play no part in traction.

Austin Allegro was conceived as a replacement for the 1100 but the two were produced side by side for several years.

Top speed for the Maxi was about 90 mph and it was geared for economy rather than performance. In overdrive fifth it ran 19.6 mph per 1,000 rpm, which meant spinning the engine at 3,800 rpm for a road speed of 70 mph. Acceleration from standstill to 60 mph was a matter of 16.5 seconds. Overall fuel mileage centered around the 35-mpg mark.

In October, 1972, the Maxi became available with a four-speed Automotive Products automatic transmission, scaled up from the unit used in the Mini and 1100/1300 series. At the same time Austin offered a 1750 HL Maxi with a 1,748 cc engine and 96 hp. The Maxi is still in production, awaiting replacement by a new car known only as the C-10 (and which will also replace the Allegro and the Marina). The Marina is a Morris with front engine and rear axle drive but the Allegro is an Austin which started life as the ADO-67.

Austin Allegro and Princess

Design work on the ADO-67 began in 1969 immediately following the Leyland management's outline of a new product planning program. It went into production in May, 1973, as a more or less direct replacement for the ADO-16 models. The suspension design is very similar as far as geometry is concerned but a new spring system known as Hydragas has replaced Hydrolastic. It inherited the A-series engines and drive train, steering and brakes. The body has new lines, but dimensions are closely similar, with a 96-inch wheel-base and a curb weight of 1,990 pounds. An HL (High Line) version came out in September 1974, and a station wagon in May, 1975.

170

Harry Webster, creator of the Triumph Herald, Spitfire, TR-4, 2000 and 1300, had been appointed executive chief engineer for Leyland's Austin-Morris Division in 1969 and played a role at the tail end of the Maxi development. He took a more dominant position in the Allegro program. He was to direct the next one, ADO-71, a car we know today as the Princess. Webster joined Standard in Coventry as an apprentice in 1932 and was deputy chief inspector when Standard and Triumph merged in 1945. He became chief chassis engineer for both in 1948 and chief engineer in 1955.

The ADO-71 was started to prepare a replacement for the ADO-17 in 1971 and development continued unabated but in the direction of more efficiency rather than more power and speed during 1973 and 1974. It went into production in September, 1975.

Allegro introduced the Hydragas suspension, a lower-cost system than Hydrolastic, still retaining the principle of front/rear interconnection on each side.

Princess by British Leyland comes with a choice of four- and six-cylinder engines mounted transversely in a British-styled body shell.

Hydragas suspension replaced Hydrolastic and an all-new body, modern and streamlined, was designed. The 1800 cc four and 2200 cc six-cylinder engines were continued in the same position—or almost—with the same drive train.

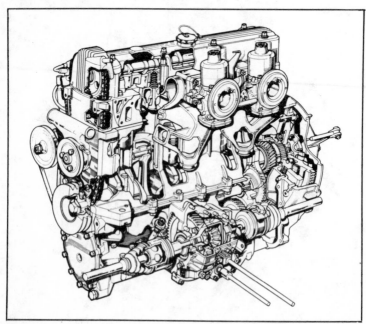

Six-cylinder E-series engine was short enough to fit inside Princess engine bay without hurting turning circle. Transmission was positioned to give equal-length drive shafts.

Princess front end had Hydragas units linked to upper control arms and mounted horizontally. Disc brakes were carried outboard.

173

The difference in engine mounting was not big. The whole power unit was moved about an inch forward. But the wheels remained where they were and no changes were made in the drive shafts. The result has been that overloaded shafts and joints, working at angles they are not intended for, make noise and finally break, sometimes after low mileages (under 10,000 miles).

In July, 1978, a new O-series four-cylinder engine replaced the B-series unit in the Princess. The O-series engine is an overhead-camshaft design, made in two sizes, 1,698 cc and 1,994 cc, with 88 or 94 hp. The 2,227-cc six is an E-series engine and about equally modern in its design.

The Princess represents the state of the art at the Austin Design Office and it can be assumed that the C-10 will be a scaled-down car of similar layout, shape and structure.

Chapter 10
Peugeot

Automobiles Peugeot acquired control of Automobiles Citroen at the start of 1975, but Peugeot did not do it to get access to Citroen f-w-d technology. The reasons for the merger were commercial and political and Peugeot had indeed been manufacturing f-w-d cars for nearly ten years.

The first f-w-d Peugeot car was designated 204 and dates from 1965. But Peugeot had been building f-w-d vans since the company took control of Chenard-Walcker in 1945 and inherited its f-w-d one-ton compact van designed in 1941 by Marcel Collette. It's still being built in more up-to-date form as the Peugeot J-7. But during all the years of making a f-w-d vehicle of this size, no one at Peugeot dared think of making f-w-d cars until...well, that story begins with the death of the Peugeot 203 in February, 1960.

THE MINI CONCEPT BUT LARGER

The 203 was a 1949 model looking very much like a scaled-down 1947 Dodge, with front engine and rear axle drive. It was a medium-priced car, competing with the Simca Aronde, but positioned well above the Renault Dauphine and well below the Citreon DS. When the 203 was discontinued, Peugeot lost a good part of its representation in this market, for the 403 was priced above the Aronde and the 404, going into production in May, 1960, was competing against the low end of the Citroen D-series. A replacement for the 203 was regarded as a very urgent matter but none was ready. The reason was not unpreparedness for the en-

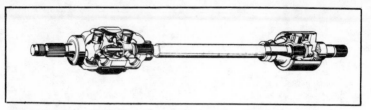

Peugeot 204 drive shaft had Delta-type inner joint with double-Cardan-type outer joint. Inner joint accepted axial movement.

gineering staff had been working on the task for years but the leaders kept rejecting their proposals. The 203 replacement has to be smaller, lighter, roomier, with higher performance and better fuel economy, all at the same time.

Gradually, it became apparent to technical director Marcel Dangauthier that the design could not be met with a car of conventional conception and layout. He asked for new ideas. About the same time, British Motor Coporation put the Mini in production. This was far smaller than anything Peugeot had in mind but some of its solutions could be applied to a vehicle corresponding to Peugeot's objectives. A young engineer named Claude de Forcrand made up some sketches to demonstrate how he would translate the Mini concept into a four-door family sedan in the under-2,000-pound weight class. That was the start of the 204.

OC ALUMINUM FOUR FOR THE 204

A design group led by Victor Dornier had completed work on an all-aluminum 1,130-cc four-cylinder overhead-camshaft engine. This unit was placed transversely and tilted 20 degrees to the front. The clutch was on the left side with an output shaft forming a sleeve on the crankshaft next to the final main bearing and carrying a spur gear drive to the gearbox primary shaft. The countershaft, directly below, was also the output shaft, with helical spur gear drive to the differential. All four gears were indirect, with a slight overdrive on fourth, combined with a 4.06:1 final drive ratio. All forward gears were synchromesh and the linkage led to a column shift. Drive shafts were of equal length and used Delta-type inner joints and double Cardan-type outer joints.

MACPHERSON AND TRAILING ARMS SUSPENSION

This power train was combined with a MacPherson-type front suspension permitting steering angles up to 45 degrees on the inside wheel and 35 degrees on the outside wheel. The steering axis was inclined at 9½ degrees and static wheel alignment called for ½

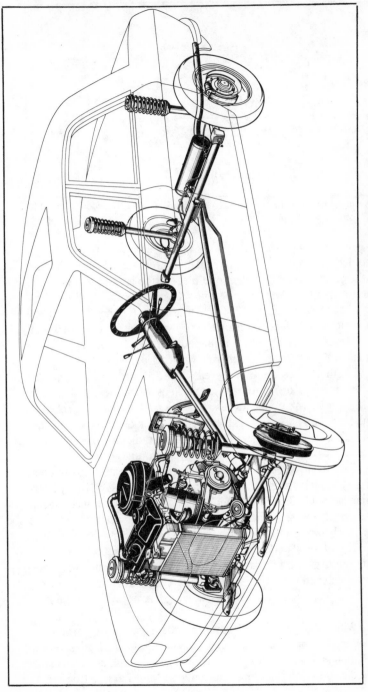

Peugeot 204 had traverse four-cylinder engine and all-coil suspension, disc/drum brakes and rack-and-pinion steering.

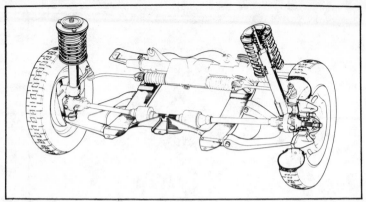

Front suspension on the Peugeot 204 had MacPherson spring legs standing on hub carriers directly above the center line.

degree negative camber. The spring leg was mounted on a boss extending from the hub carrier and its center line led into the center of the outer universal joint. A one-piece, wide-based A-frame lower control arm completed the design with no use of a stabilizer bar.

At the rear end, the 204 was fitted with trailing arms and coil spring legs. The rear wheels were set with zero camber and toe-in. Wheel rates were the same front and rear, 93.35 pounds per inch, intended to give an acceptable ride with four people on board as well as with the driver alone in the car. The front roll center was 5.2 inches above ground level, giving excellent roll stiffness and the rear roll center was at ground level so that the car had a nose-up roll axis. This tends to give roll oversteer with the rear-end geometry of the 204's rear suspension geometry—an effect sought by Peugeot to counteract the basic understeer of the front end.

The front wheels carried 58.5 percent of car's 1,874-pound curb weight assuring a majority of the weight on the driving wheels under all conditions of load and grade. With its 102.2-inch wheelbase, the 204 was 157 inches long overall. Front track was wider (52 inches) than rear (49.6 inches), and the car's turning diameter was 33.8 feet. Its rack and pinion steering was light and precise, with a 18.6:1 ratio giving 3.75 turns lock to lock. Ten-inch front disc brakes were combined with 9-inch rear drums. The hydraulic system incorporated a compensator valve for limiting line pressure to the rear wheels.

With its 53 hp at 5,800 rpm, the 204 engine was geared for a speed of 15.3 mph per 1,000 rpm in top gear, giving it a top speed of 85.5 mph and acceleration from standstill to 60 mph in 21 seconds. Fuel consumption in normal use ranged from 27.6 to 34.6 mpg.

The Peugeot 204 sedan went into production in May, 1965, and was followed by a station wagon in October of the same year. For 1967, two two-door models, a fastback coupe and a convertible, both built on a 91-inch wheelbase, were added. In 1969 a 1,255-cc diesel engine became optional for the 204 station wagon. It was good for speeds in excess of 5,000 rpm, and gave the car a top speed of 78 mph.

Farina 304 Development of 204

Peugeot discontinued production of the 403 in 1966, and Dangauthier decided to replace it with an enlarged and updated version of the 204. The result was the 304, which went into production in September, 1969. It weighed 2,017 pounds, with a front/rear weight distribution of 57.3/42.7 percent.

Wheelbase was unchanged, but overall length went to 163 inches. The 304 had a sleek new body designed by Pininfarina but was generally assumed to be a 204 under the skin. That was quite wrong for the 304 introduced several important chassis modifications. First, the outer universal joints were changed from double Cardan to Rzeppa-type (made by Glaenzer-Spicer). Secondly, spring rates were softened and stabilizer bars fitted both front and rear. Front ride rates dropped to 86 pounds per inch, and at the rear, to 81. The suspension members and geometry, however, were left unchanged with the roll axis. The entire steering system, simplified for lower cost, was adopted. Instead of the former three-pistion

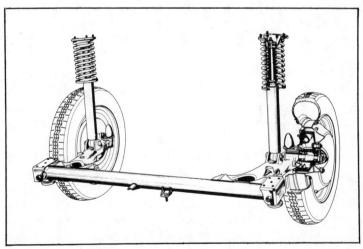

Rear suspension of the Peugeot 204 was independent with trailing arms and vertical coil-spring and shock-absorber legs.

calipers, a new two-piston type and hydrovac power booster were added.

At the same time, the 304 brake system was adopted for the 204 which remained in production. Despite its larger engine (1,288 cc) and higher power output (58.5 hp), the 304 retained the same 4.06:1 final drive ratio. It gained in both top speed and acceleration but suffered in fuel economy compared with the 204. Reaching 60 mph from a standing start took 15.5 seconds and top speed increased to an even 90 mph. Average fuel consumption worked out to a range from 25.5 to 32.2 mpg.

304 Variations Include Diesel

In April, 1970, new 304 coupe and convertible models replaced the 204s. They inherited the short-wheelbase concept using the standard running gear from the sedan but did not take over the 204 coupe and convertible bodies. Instead, Pininfarina created new designs for them. Mechanically, the 304 coupe and convertible were no longer quite identical with the sedan for they sported a new floorshift instead of the earlier console shift.

In October, 1970, a 304 station wagon was added but the 204 sedan and wagon remained in production through 1976. The 304 S was introduced in March, 1972, with a 69-hp version of the same 1.3-liter engine. At first it was only for the coupe and convertible, but starting in September of that year, the sedan also became available as a 304 S with a top speed of 100 mph. The coupe and convertible in the 304 series were discontinued at the end of the 1975 model run and a year later a larger 1,375 cc diesel became optional for the 304 sedan and station wagon that are still being built.

The 104—Family Minicar

In the meantime, Peugeot had gone into production with the 104, a minicar for the family, smaller than the 204. In comparison with Austin Design Office creations, it was smaller and lighter than the 1100 but bigger and roomier than a Mini. The 104 was launched in October, 1972—half a year after Renault had introduced its R5.

It was a four-door sedan of only 141 inches overall length built on a 95.4-inch wheelbase. It had a curb weight of 1,753 pounds of which the front wheels carried 1,058.5 pounds, or 60.4 percent. The engine was an overhead-camshaft unit in the 204-304 family, all aluminum, but the mounting differed in that for the 104, the engine was leaning back at 72 degrees from vertical—almost a transverse pancake installation.

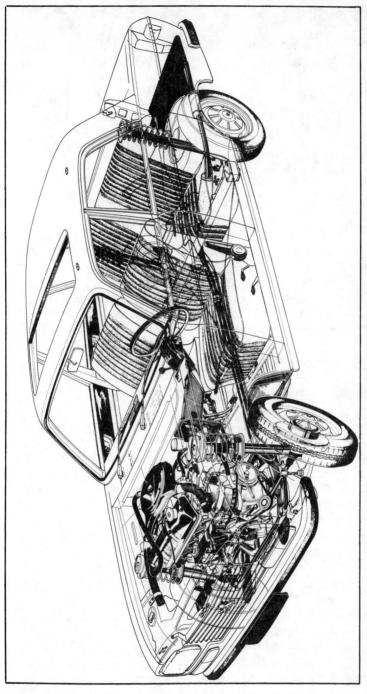

Peugeot 304 had purely conventional proportions with seating layout and trunk size and shape made possible by unified power package in front.

181

Peugeot 104 is an extremely compact four-door sedan and introduced transverse engine lying down at 18 degrees from horizontal.

The transmission followed the 204 layout and used a stickshift as standard. Inner and outer universal joints were of the Delta type with axial variations permitted by a sliding pot at the inner joint. Front suspension design evolved to a pure MacPherson, conforming to the original patent drawings where the stabililzer bar also served as drag struts for the lower control arm, linked to a single lateral arm for triangulation. The spring legs were mounted on brackets extending from the hub carriers and the steering arms pointed backwards to meet the rods from the rack and pinion steering gear. The steering was quick, light and precise despite its 18.38:1 ratio, for due to the very tight turning diameter of 31 feet its 3.33 turns lock to lock gave immediate response.

The 104 had front disc brakes and drum brakes in the rear wheels. Rear suspension followed previous Peugeot practice, with trailing arm and coil springs legs. The big difference from the 304 was that the spring legs on the 104 were mounted on the wheel spindle (compared with the semi-forward mounting of the 304) where the leverage necessitated much higher spring rates to obtain the desired ride rates. Also, the 104 rear spring legs stood upright whereas on the 304 they were tilted slightly backwards at the top. Wheel rates on the 104 were 53.3 pounds per inch in front and 80 in the rear.

The gearbox had all-indirect ratios and the final drive had a 4.06:1 ratio, which gave a theoretical top speed of 90 mph, except the little engine was incapable of revving out in top gear so that the car peaked out at 80-81 mph. The 954-cc power unit delivered 46 hp and gave the car zero-to-60 mph acceleration of 20 seconds flat.

A two-door 104 coupe with shortened body and wheelbase appeared the following year. In France, contrary to American practice, the two-door is more expensive than the sedan. Its sportier and less utilitarian styling is exploited to furnish it with a higher-grade interior which sort of justifies pushing the price up.

New 305 Really Develops 104 Features

The latest addition to the Peugeot f-w-d family is the 305, launched in November, 1977. It has the XL5 (1,290 cc) engine from the 304 installed in the same position, transverse and tilted forward at 20 degrees. The BB8 transmission from the 304 is used also but the drive shafts are larger versions of those on the 104 with Delta-type joints at both ends.

Nor has the 305 inherited the 304 front suspension with its A-frame lower control arms. Instead, it has an up-scaled version of the 104 suspension design with greater tilt on the MacPherson spring legs to lower the roll center, and with a sturdier stabilizer bar because of the greater weight. The same applied in the rear suspension design. Though the 305 is bigger and heavier than the 304, it does not follow its design principles, but uses an enlarged version of the 104 rear suspension.

The 305 is actually the replacement for the 404 since the two correspond closely in interior dimensions, carrying capacity and

Peugeot 104 power train had drive shafts no bigger than the stabilizer bar in diameter. Disc brakes were mounted outboard.

"Peugette" was the name chosen for Pininfarina's proposed roadster using 104 running gear. Interchangeable front and rear body panels indicated way to cut cost.

performance levels. But the 404 had rear axle drive and fell far short of the 305's fuel-efficiency, ride comfort, and ease of handling. The 305 has a curb weight of 2,040 pounds and an overall length of 166.8 inches. Front/rear weight distribution is 56.8/43.2 percent with a relatively long 103-inch wheelbase. Its steering is geared at 20.1:1 and gives 3.6 turns, lock to lock, which is quite sporty with its 33-feet turning diameter. The engine is geared for 16.7 mph per 1,000 rpm in top gear and gives the car a top speed of 91 mph. It can accelerate from standstill, to 60 mph in 17 seconds and do the standing-start quarter-mile in 20 seconds.

For those who require more performance, Peugeot offers a larger 1,472-cc version of the same engine, with power boosted from 65 to 74 hp at 6,000 rpm. It has the same final drive but different gear ratios, doing 17.8 mph per 1,000 rpm so that its top speed is an honest 95 mph. Acceleration from standstill to 60 mph becomes a

Peugeot 305 is designed for production with rear axle drive as well as with f-w-d. As a compromise, it's extremely successful.

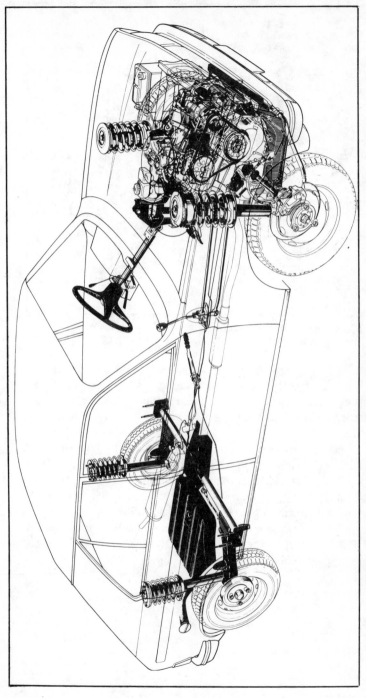

Peugeot 104 broke with earlier f-w-d techniques of the company and set the course for future development leading directly to the 305.

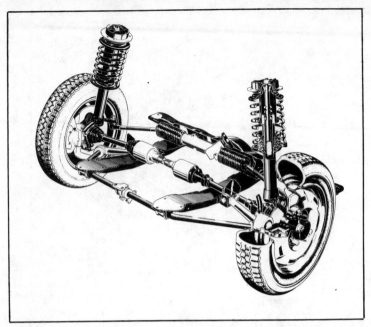

True MacPherson front suspension is used on the Peugeot 305 with the stabilizer bar also serving as a component of the lower control arms.

matter of 13 seconds and the quarter-mile time drops to 18.5 seconds. Because of the difference in gearing, it's more economical for cruising at 55 mph than the 305 with standard engine: 37.9 mpg compared with 36.15 mpg. At higher speed, the difference is even greater.

Since its experience with the 204, Peugeot has built larger as well as smaller cars with f-w-d. Does the 305 indicate that f-w-d will be used for increasingly large models, such as the coming replacement for the 504, for instance? As Peugeot sees it, the 305 size is the crossover point and larger cars will continue with rear wheel drive. The 305 will in fact later be produced in a rear-wheel-drive version for certain export markets (Iran, U.S.A.) while the f-w-d version alone is to be sold in Europe.

Chapter 11
General Motors

The recent history of General Motors' activity on front wheel drive vehicles began in 1954 when the Universelle experimental chassis for a forward-control panel truck was completed. It was built by the GMC Truck and Coach Division in Pontiac, Michigan, to designs by Maurice Thorne and Gil Rodewig. The V-8 engine was placed behind the front wheel center line and the front wheels were sprung by a system of short-and-long lateral control arms and longitudinal torsion bars. The Universelle was given a futuristic body by Harley J. Earl, Charles M. Jordan, and William Lange of GM Styling, went on a round of exhibitions, and was seemingly forgotten until 1965.

But on the inside, GM was busy with studies on the use of f-w-d for various types of production cars. As early as 1958 Jack Wolfram and Harold Metzel of Oldsmobile Division decided to explore the possibilities of converting one of their models to f-w-d. This was at the time they were preparing the compact F-85 and that was the vehicle they had in mind at first. Based on an early F-85, the first front wheel drive test car, built early in 1960, had a monocoque body with a front sub-frame. Performance and handling characteristics were said to be satisfactory but more work was needed on the transmission.

The test car was rebuilt in July, 1960, with many design changes. Design concepts for a production model were formulated by mid-1961. About 1963 they reversed themselves and decided to go ahead with a full-size six-seater Oldsmobile instead of the compact. Several test cars were built with standard Oldsmobile bodies while a completely new vehicle progressed on the drawing board.

Original Toronado was the largest and most powerful f-w-d production car ever built when it appeared as a 1966 model.

Many Attractions of Toronado Design

The final design was ready in the spring of 1964 and Oldsmobile began tooling up for production. The car was named Toronado and introduced in October, 1965, as a 1966 model.

Oldsmobile was motivated into its program by its desire for improvement in the following areas of car design: 1. interior space, 2. trunk space, 3. ride comfort, 4. wet traction, 5. directional stability, and 6. noise and vibration. F-w-d held high promise for improvements on all points and Oldsmobile's attraction to f-w-d was further compounded by its promise of greater styling freedom, possible savings in production costs, and last but not least, the need for doing something radical to maintain Oldsmobile's reputation for technogical leadership and pioneering.

By greater styling freedom I mean the possibility of lowering the roofline without losing interior space. By a possible cut in production costs, I am referring to the saving made by eliminating the live rear axle, the propeller shaft, and the rear suspension reinforcements needed to take up the torque and thrust of a live rear axle. Oldsmobile's reputation for advanced engineering rests solidly on this division's development of the first Hydra-matic transmission (1939) and the high-compression overhead-valve V-8 engine (1949).

Engineering Team for the Toronado

The f-w-d engineering team was headed by John Beltz (Wolfram had retired, and Metzel had succeeded him as general manager) who had worked for Packard and Reo before he joined Oldsmobile in 1947. Donald Perkins was executive engineer for the project and Andrew K. Watt, a veteran Oldsmobile engineer who had joined the division in 1931, coordinated all its various elements. The idea for the transmission layout came from Jim Lewis and was developed by Howard Kehrl with the aid of John D. Malloy at the GM Engineering Staff. W. A. Weldman was in charge of drive train design and James Diener was responsible for chassis design.

Oldsmobile chose its largest and most powerful engine for the Toronado, a 425 cubic-inch V-8 with a 10.5:1 compression ratio and enlarged valves delivering 385 SAE gross hp. Compression was lowered to 10.25:1 for 1968 with a loss of 5 hp. New emission-control devices for 1969 dropped output to 375 hp. With reduced compression ratio (to 8.5:1) for using regular-grade gasoline and the switch to SAE net hp for 1972 the rating came down to a realistic 190.

Cadillac Nixed Transverse Engine

Since Oldsmobile produced nothing but V-8 engines, no other type was considered for the f-w-d car but they tried several ways of

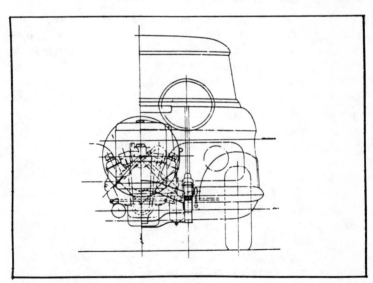

Experimentation with f-w-d at General Motors in preparation for the Toronado began with the GMC Universelle in 1956.

mounting it including a transverse position. That was discarded for reasons concerning another division: Cadillac. Oldsmobile claimed it was due to problems with torque reactions in the fore-and-aft plane but that was only a pretext. The real reason was that Cadillac was interested in building its own version of XP-784, as the project was code-named. And Cadillac was developing a V-12 engine which due to its length could not be installed transversely. And because of the need to keep production costs low, Cadillac and Oldsmobile had to share a maximum of body and chassis parts which dictated their use of the same engine position. Later on, however, Cadillac shelved the V-12 project.

In its final form, the XP-784 had the engine in its usual position centered on the front wheel axis with a hydraulic torque converter on the rear end of the crankshaft. Behind the converter was a chain drive to the three-speed planetary transmission which was located alongside the crankcase, taking the drive forward to a planetary differential. The main factor that made this drive train possible was the mounting of the torque converter *ahead of* (in the power flow sense) the chain, so as to cushion power pulsations and other engine vibrations. There was no manual transmission system available for the Toronado. The torque converter and planetary gears were standard mass-produced HydraMatic components.

Drive Train Elements Turned 180°

The planetary gear sets were turned at 180 degrees to the torque converter so that the power flowed back to front. Space considerations made the use of a conventional differential impractical so Oldsmobile went to a planetary differential made by Buick. The chain drive between the torque converter and the planetary gears was enclosed in a sheet metal cover at the back of the engine. Both sprockets rotated at torque converter output shaft speed and there was no tensioner.

The chain was of the Hy-Vo type manufactured by Morse Division of Borg-Warner. The chain was a link type designed to provide smooth engagement on the sprockets and allow the links to assume the load gradually. This reduced impact forces as well as the rise and fall of each chain pitch as it engaged the sprocket. A link never carried load across its tips. The load was transmitted through pins and rockers into the next link.

Because the power flow was turned around by the chain cross-drive, all of the rotating parts in the planetary transmission turned in the opposite direction of their rotation when installed in a rear-wheel-drive car. All gears for Toronado transmissions had helix

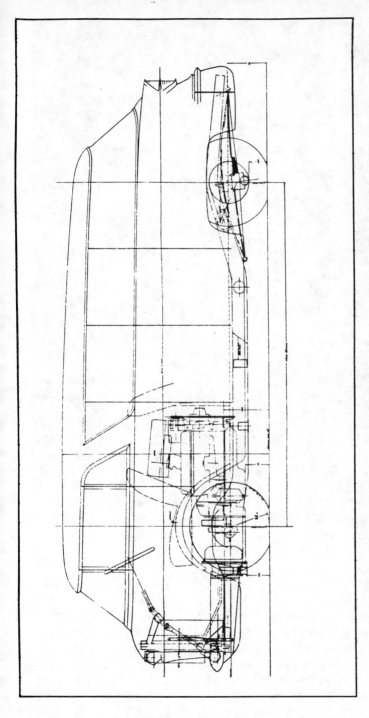

Mounting the V-8 engine inside the wheelbase in the Universelle van cost a lot of cargo space and stretched the overall length of the vehicle to make room for driver and controls.

Toronado ladder-type frame shows lack of mechanical connection between front and rear ends, giving a low and flat floor.

angles leading the other way to maintain proper direction of end thrust. All brake band apply servos were moved to the opposite side of the case. All one-way clutches were reversed to energize and free-wheel in the opposite-to-normal direction. The pressure regulator valve and variable stator blade angle control solenoid and valve were moved from the pump body to other locations so as to be accessible for service.

The transaxle was located on the lower left hand side of the engine. Pinion and ring gear were of the spiral bevel type (not hypoid) because of the need for adequate ground clearance. Instead of a differential cage, the ring gear had an internal ring gear (annulus) which provided a circular track for six planet gears. The planet gears ran in three pairs mounted in a planet carrier. The sun gear was splined to the right-hand drive shaft. The planet carrier had a splined sleeve which engaged the left-hand drive shaft. With the car traveling straight ahead, the sun gear rotated at ring gear speed, planet gears merely orbiting but not revolving.

Rzeppa Joints for Drive Shafts

The engine was positioned 1.82 inches right of center in the car with the final drive unit offset on the left. A short drive shaft with Rzeppa-type constant-velocity inner and outer joints went to the left front wheel. The inner part of the two-piece right wheel drive shaft passed closely under the engine oil pan and had no angular variations. It was held in place by the differential on one side and a support bearing on the other. The right-hand shaft was really a three-piece

Toronado engine straddled the front wheel axis with the HydraMatic transmission split in two parts at the back end.

design, for the outer shaft was split in the middle where a biscuit coupling held it together. The rubber biscuits worked as a torsional damper and allowed up to 7½ degrees of torsional deflection due to variation in rotational speed; thus keeping wheel vibrations from being fed back through the transmission.

A short, splined shaft with Rzeppa-type constant-velocity universal joints at both ends took the drive to the right front wheel hub. The drive shafts are arranged to run at an angle of about 3 degrees. This assures absence of concentrated wear (brinnelling) in the ball-type inner joints.

On full lock, the inside wheel moved up to a 36-degree steering angle but the angle at the outer joint was only 33 degrees. The outside wheel turned up to 28 degrees while its maximum joint angle was 31 degrees. This gave the 119-inch wheelbase car a turning diameter of 43 feet. The inner joints allowed axial variations during wheel deflection by the use of six rows of small balls (30 balls per joint) located around the outside diameter of the outer race, giving a frictionless slip joint.

Strong Torsion Bar Front Suspension

The front suspension layout was based on that of the GMC Universelle with transverse control arms and longitudinal torsion bars. The bars were made of SAE 5160H steel and had a twist rate of 540 inch-pounds per degree, giving a wheel rate of 162 pounds per inch. That's 89 percent higher than on the Starfire, a rear wheel drive model in the same weight class. The bars were 58.95 inches long and 1.112 inches in diameter. Wheel travel was average for a large car, with 4.75 inches rebound and 4.00 inches in jounce. A one-inch diameter stabilizer bar of SAE 1070 steel was installed to add roll stiffness and the upper control arm was tilted back to give 50 percent anti-dive effect on braking. No front suspension changes were made until the 1969 model, when new torsion bars were introduced. Shorter (58.05 inches) and narrower (1.071 inches) they had a twist rate of 465 inch-pounds per degree, which maintained the same wheel rate.

Static wheel alignment called for ⅛ degree of positive camber and 2 degrees of negative caster. The design also specified a negative scrub radius of ½ inch. The U-shaped "dead" beam rear axle was carried by two tapered single-leaf springs made by Rockwell-Standard, 64 inches long and 3.0 inches wide. They had a deflection rate of 152 pounds per inch, giving a wheel rate of 157 pounds per inch. That's 57 percent higher than on the Starfire. They gave only 3.3 inches of rebound travel but allowed 5.5 inches in jounce.

Drive shaft to the right front wheel carried a flexible torsional vibration damper but none was needed on the left side.

Damping was taken care of by two shock absorbers on each side: one vertical and one horizontal. No stabilizer bar was included and Oldsmobile claimed that roll oversteer was limited to ½ percent. The first change in this design came on the 1969 model. Spring rates were lowered to 125 pounds per inch (corresponding to a wheel rate of 139 pounds per inch).

The steering, made by GM's Saginaw division, was a typical GM parallellogram linkage. Unique to the Toronado, however, was this feature: The tie rod was connected to a hydraulic shock absorber to reduce vibrations that might be transmitted to the steering wheel. Static wheel alignment called for zero to 1/16 inch toe-in. The recirculating-ball type steering gear had a 17.5 to one ratio giving an overall steering ratio of 17.8 to one (3.4 turns lock to lock). The power steering pump was driven by belt from the crankshaft.

Much Concern with Braking

The production model weighed 4,496 pounds with 60.3 percent carried on the front wheels and had a top speed of over 125 mph. The brakes were cast iron drums with integral heat rejection fins, cooled through openings in the wheel spider. The front drums were 11 inches in diameter and 2.75 inches wide. Rear drums had the same diameter but were only 2.0 inches wide. Brake force distribution was set for 64 to 72 percent on the front wheels.

A Bendix vacuum booster was integral with the master cylinder. Disc brakes were not optional the first year. They became available on the front wheels as an extra-cost option in 1967 with cast-iron vented rotors and two pistons per caliper. The discs (rotors) were 11.3 inches in diameter and increased the swept area on the front brakes from 190 square inches with the drums to 222 square inches. Rear wheel brake swept area remained at 138.2 square inches. A proportioning valve to prevent premature locking of the rear wheels was added.

With front wheel discs brakes, effectiveness was set at 64 to 72 percent on the front wheels. No brake improvements came in 1968 but new discs became available on the 1969 model. Drums on all four wheels were still listed as standard equipment. The new discs were of 10.94-inches diameter and gave 217.63 square inches of swept area. The proportioning valve was abandoned and 69.03 percent of the brake force was applied to the front wheels, regardless of circumstances. The following year (1970), front discs were standardized and front wheel swept area rose to 226.2 square inches. Brake force on the front was increased to 71.5 percent.

In Feburary, 1970, the Toronado got a new brake option called "True-Track." It was an anti-locking device built by GM's Delco-Moraine and AC Spark Plug Divisions and had been under development for about five years. True-Track braking was composed of three main elements. These included a pair of electronic sensors (one at each rear wheel); a control unit to monitor rear wheel braking performance as reported by the sensors; and a modulator capable of regulating rear wheel brake pressure on command from the computer. When an impending wheel lockup was detected, an electronic signal from the computer activated the modulator which, by means of a solenoid valve, instantly reduced the brake pressure being applied to the rear wheels. A fraction of a second later, pressure was reapplied, and if locking persisted it was again momentarily reduced. The cycle could be repeated up to 5 times a second.

Cost Considerations Cut Components

The 1966 planetary differential had a 3.21:1 ratio. It went unchanged for 1967. The 1968 model, however, acquired a spiral bevel differential. The space considerations that had dictated the move to a planetary differential two years earlier were no longer

By 1972 the Toronado had been converted into a luxury car and the merits of f-w-d were well disguised.

allowed to overrule the cost considerations of using a unique differential on the Toronado. Standard ratio was 3.07:1 that year, with a 3.36:1 option. For 1969 and 1970 only the 3.07:1 ratio had been offered. Concurrently with the economy move on the differential, Oldsmobile decided to economize on the universal joints. The 1968 model, was equipped with Delta-type joints inboard (retaining the Rzeppa-type constant velocity joints nearest the wheel hubs).

The initial production model had 15 × 6K wheels and a two-ply 8.85-15 TFD tire developed in conjunction with Uniroyal and Firestone. Radial-ply tires were tested extensively during the development period and for a while Oldsmobile meant to adopt them as standard equipment. At the last minute that was vetoed for cost reasons. A 9.15-15 oversize option was listed but the tire was the same basic two-ply TFD. The 1967-69 models have had 15 × 6JK rims as standard equipment and a J78-15 fiberglass-belted bias-ply tire became standard equipment on the 1970 model.

For 1971 the Toronado gained over 4 inches in wheelbase (now 122.3 inches)and overall length was stretched to 219.9 inches. Turning diameter went to nearly 47 feet. The car gained weight to 4,557 pounds (2,754 on the front and 1,823 on the rear). For the first time, the Toronado was built on a full frame rather than the abbreviated stub frame of 1966-70. The frame was basically the same as for the 98 series. Oldsmobile engineers claim that the new frame allowed the installation of six extra body mounts, improving ride characteristics and reducing road noise transfer and vibration.

Because of the new rear frame section, the rear suspension system was brought closer to other Oldsmobiles. It is a four-link and coil spring design with a "dead" beam axle. The rear coil springs are made of SAE 5160 H or 9260 M steel. Spring size and rates were computer-selected in accordance with vehicle weight and suspension option fitted. This design change was introduced because it helped cut production cost. A revised front suspension utilized a nodular iron steering knuckle for improved durability. No steering or brake system modifications were made for 1971.

New Steering New Engines and Downsizing

New power steering with a 20.4:1 ratio giving 3.25 turns lock to lock was adopted for the 1972 Toronado. At the same time, spring rates were lowered in order to improve ride comfort and reduce noise and vibration. The front brakes were equipped with a pad wear sensor giving audible warning when the friction material had worn down beyond safe conditions. Engine cooling was improved by adopting a venturi fan shroud. Final drive ratio was lowered to 2.73:1 to give better fuel economy and quieter high-speed cruising.

For 1973 the Toronado was given a 215-hp 455 cubic-inch engine and steel-belted radial-ply tires were offered as an option. No important modifications were made for 1974, 1975 or 1976. For 1977, the engine size was reduced to 400 cubic inches and the following year a new 403-cubic inch V-8 was standardized. The 1979 model was downsized in parallel with Cadillac's Eldorado and at the same time Buick's Riviera was redesigned with the Toronado power train.

Cadillac Eldorado Nearly All Different

While the Oldsmobile engineers were toying with the f-w-d F-85 and produced designs for a front-wheel-drive "98" limousine, the top management of General Motors decided that Cadillac should be given full use of the Toronado design for its 1967-model Eldorado. It shared the entire design concept with the Toronado but the two had practically no interchangeable parts other than for the transmission. Cadillac's chief engineer Carlton Rasmussen led a design team that produced a true Cadillac front-wheel-drive car, adding several refinements not available in the Toronado such as automatic level control and variable-ratio steering. Robert J. Templin was assistant chief engineer for chassis design with F. H. Cowin working on suspension and steering. Bruce Edsall adapted the transmission to the Cadillac V-8 engine designed by J. B. Richardson and his team.

Last of the full-size Toronados was the 1978-model. Potential for using f-w-d to gain useful space was completely ignored, extra cost of f-w-d wasted.

The 429 cubic-inch V-8 used in the 1967 model gave way to a new and even larger 472 cubic-inch unit for 1968.

The 1967 Eldorado was built on a 120-inch wheelbase with a front rack of 63.5 inches and a 63-inch rear track. It had an overall length of 221 inches and weighed 4,790 pounds with a front/rear weight distribution of 60.9/39.1 percent. Compared with conventional Cadillacs, the Eldorado had stiffer front springs, with a ride rate of 140 pounds-per-inch compared with 86 for the Calais. At the rear end, the Eldorado had softer springs, with a 105-pounds-per-inch ride rate compared with 110 for the Calais. The Eldorado had the same 125-mph top speed as the Toronado but was slower in acceleration due to its greater weight. The Cadillac took 9.2 seconds to go from zero to 60 mph while the Oldsmobile did it in 8.8 seconds.

Power disc brakes were standardized for 1969 and the following year the Cadillac engine was enlarged to a full 500 cubic inches. The 1971 Eldorado was given the full frame of the Toronado and a convertible was added. At the same time, wheelbase was stretched to 126.3 inches, and the curb weight rose to 4,965 pounds. Engine size was reduced to 425 cubic inches for 1977 and 1978. The 1979 model is an all-new design of a smaller size with engine size reduced to 350 cubic inches.

Drastic Downsizing and IRS

For 1979 the Toronado, Eldorado and Riviera share the Fisher A-body with the two-door intermediates and have the same 114-inch wheelbase. Buick has the 350 cubic-inch V-8 only in the luxury version of the Riviera but has outfitted the Riviera S with the turbocharged V-six from the Century Regal. The power flow is similar to the Toronado design.

All three divisions have gone to four-wheel independent suspension, dropping the "dead" beam rear axle in favor of a system

1979-model Riviera introduced f-w-d to Buick's specialty car, now downsized to share the two door A-body with the Century.

comprised of semi-trailing arms, coil springs, and a stabilizer bar. The front end is based on the Toronado/Eldorado design with upper and lower A-frame control arms and longitudinal torsion bars extending backwards from the lower control arm pivot shaft. Something new is added in the form of a torque reaction member which applies spring pressure against the lower control arm through a friction pad. Curb weight for the 1979 Riviera had been brought down to 3,762 pounds, distributed so that the driving wheels carry 65 percent of the static weight.

Riviera transmission followed Toronado layout. Smaller size of Buick's V-six moved center of gravity for the unified power package inside the wheelbase.

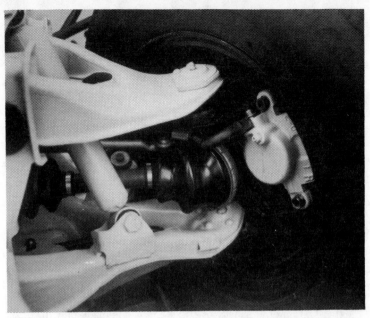

Front suspension uses upper and lower A-frame control arms with torsion bars linked to rear control arm pivot shaft.

Compacts Next GM FWDs

Where is GM going with front wheel drive? The next group to make the switch will be the new compacts for 1980. A totally new drive train will be used with transversely mounted four-cylinder and V-six engines. And a Chevette replacement now on test is said to be an f-w-d design, also with a transverse engine installation.

It's unlikely that the B-body cars (Caprice, Catalina, Delta 88 and Le Sabre/Electra) will deviate from their present configuration. The variations on the A-body, accommodating three f-w-d models into a family of cars with conventional layout, show the possibilities of going either way with the same basic vehicle—at least in that size and weight class. It may not be the best way to exploit the potential advantages of f-w-d but it does open the way for greater choice for the customer with limited additional investment and cost for the manufacturer.

Chapter 12
Ford

Ford has two front wheel drive cars in production today. One is the Fiesta. The other is usually overlooked for it is made only in Brazil and not exported. It's the Corcel. Neither can be called the first production-model f-w-d Ford for that was the Taunus 12M of 1963, a car that Ford seemingly would be just as happy to forget.

Its story began in 1957 with a research program known as "Project A" or "Cardinal." As time went on, it had other titles, too. Its aim alternated between a "world car" concept, something that could be manufactured in a globe-spanning production scheme involving all or most of Ford's overseas subsidiaries, and a car that would put the Volkswagen in its place, particularly in the North American market—or ideally, out of that market.

Twisted Path of the Taunus 12M

Several things happened in the Ford organization in 1957 that directly concerns the Cardinal. First, the advance-design offices in England and Germany were asked to submit their ideas for an ideal "world car" concept. Secondly, Henry Ford II made the decision to produce a compact car in America.

The US-built compact became the Falcon, a 2,500-pound sedan with a six-cylinder engine. A proposal that lost out was for a 2,200-pound subcompact with a four-cylinder engine. While Ford was tooling up for the Falcon, nervous product planners and marketing exports were beginning to wonder if they had made the wrong decision. The subcompact idea was not allowed to stay on the shelf.

As the "world car" designs from Europe were completed, they were forwarded to Dearborn where it was seen that Fred Hart at Dagenham had gone the conventional route and drawn up a small box with front engine and rear wheel drive that would be economical to produce and reliable in operation, while August Momberger at the Cologne works had come up with a most interesting f-w-d proposal. Momberger had come to Ford from the Borgward organization where he had been responsible for f-w-d cars with Lloyd, Goliath and Hansa name plates.

Now the Cardinal, and Sudden Priority

At this time, it was 1960. The Falcon had gone into production and was a big success, but as Ford's product planners saw it, a four-cylinder subcompact would be needed by 1965.

There was no urgency on going ahead with the "world car" so the European designs were handed over to the group in charge of the American economy car project. Engineers Jack Collins, Roy Lunn, and Fred Bloom were influential in picking the Cologne design over the one from Dagenham. This group developed the complete package and sold it to the board of directors. Henry Ford II insisted it

Taunus 12M power train shows overhanging position of V-4 engine and use of transverse leaf spring as upper control arm.

must be ready by 1963, not '65, and the Cardinal was given top priority. It was to be built in the Lousiville, Kentucky, plant that now manufactures heavy trucks.

Now a full redesign for production was undertaken by an engineering team led by Bertil Andren and Jack Prendergast. In March, 1962, Ford announced it expected to introduce the Cardinal as a 1963 model but in April Henry Ford II, "as a result of market conditions and other factors", canceled the plan.

The real reason was that the production costs calculated for the Cardinal were higher than the proven costs of building the Falcon. And the Cardinal, seating four while the Falcon could carry six, had to have a lower list price!

Back to Germany, Cardinal= Taunus

Still, there was so much momentum in the Cardinal that it refused to die. It was handed over to Ford of Germany where Jules Gutzeit directed its redesign and Bernhard Osswald, Hans Kling and August Momberger took charge of its development. Incidentally, the British "world car" proposal was returned to Dagenham, where Fred Hart readied it for production. It became famous as the Cortina.

The Cardinal in final production form, now renamed Taunus 12M, was powered by a 1.2-liter V-4 engine stuck out ahead of the front wheel axis with the gearbox behind the final drive. It used a hypoid bevel pinion and ring gear and the mainshaft for the four-speed transmission was hollow, giving coaxial input and output shafts, so that top gear was direct drive. The splined drive shafts carried simple Cardan-type joints at the inner ends and Rzeppa-type constant-velocity joints at the outer ends.

The front suspension consisted of a transverse leaf spring crossing above the final drive unit and serving as an upper control arm, plus A-frame lower control arms. The spring had eight leaves, three inches wide, so that it was quite capable of handling torque loads due to braking, acceleration and roadway uneveness. The lower arms were widely splayed and absorbed the main thrust loads from braking and accleration. Their pivot shaft was carried on the transaxle casing so that the whole power-pack was well insulated from the body shell. Shock absorbers were mounted directly on the upper ball joint socket.

Front suspension geometry was designed to provide progressively greater negative camber in jounce and stay very close to zero in rebound. The power pack had three mounts, large-size rubber insulators, one on each side in front and a single central block behind

204

In 1968 the Taunus was converted to MacPherson front suspension and outboard-mounted front disc brakes.

the transmission. The rear suspension used a "dead" beam axle and semi-elliptic leaf springs plus a stabilizer bar and telescopic shock absorbers. Its geometry was designed for zero roll steer effect.

With a wheelbase of 99.5 inches, the 12M had a curb weight of 1,863 pounds, carrying 61 percent on the front wheels. Front and rear track were identical at 49 inches. Tires were 5.60-13 and the turn diameter 33.8 feet. The recirculating-ball steering took four turns lock to lock. The engine delivered 40 hp at 4,500 rpm and the final drive ratio was 3.78:1, giving it a top speed of 76 mph. Acceleration from standstill to 60 mph took 28.5 seconds.

The two-door sedan was introduced first, in September, 1962. Before the end of the year came the 12M/TS with 55-hp 1.5-liter engine and 3.56:1 final drive. Four-door sedan and station wagon followed in March, 1963. A two-door coupe went into production in September, 1963, and Ford arranged with Karosseriewerk Deutsch to produce a convertible. In September, 1964, a 65-hp version of the 1.5-liter engine became available.

Redesigned 12M and 15M Quite Different

A redesigned 12M with 3 inches longer body and 2 inches wider track appeared in September, 1966, along with a 15M companion model. Engineering changes on the newcomers were quite significant. The transverse leaf spring front suspension was discarded in

205

favor of a MacPherson type due to excessive pitching and body roll. The lower control arms were retained and a stabilizer bar added. Front disc brakes (which had been optional since 1964) were standardized. And rack and pinion steering was adopted with a faster ratio giving 3.5 turns lock to lock.

The new models were heavier, too, reaching 2,215 pounds for the 15M. It had a top speed of 85 mph. These cars remained in production through 1970 when they were replaced by a new generation of Taunus cars with rear axle drive. Ford's experience with f-w-d had not been a happy one and no one in Cologne could think in 1971 that another f-w-d car would ever again be built there.

Fiesta Development Also Complex

But in July, 1976, Ford was again producing f-w-d cars in Germany. This time it was called Fiesta and was a 1,545-pound minicar with an overall length of 140.4 inches. Why did Ford choose f-w-d for the Fiesta? Partly because of example and partly because of market research. The example was set by the Fiat 127, which served as a pattern for the Ford designers, and the market research showed that people generally expected or demanded f-w-d in a vehicle of that size.

It was no "world car" concept nor was there great emphasis on the American market. It started as a car for Europe's crowded streets, poor secondary roads, steep hills and high gasoline prices. The basic design originated in the mind of Jim Donaldson, a product planner at Ford's technical center at Dunton, England, probably as early as 1967. He began design work in 1969, sending long reports to support his sketches. He built a full-scale body shell on wheels which was shown to Ford management as easly as 1970.

Worldwide Team Behind Fiesta

Ford executives began to take the idea seriously. Other economy-car programs were started—one was a small car built in Dearborn under the code name Nevada. Ghia was assigned to make styling studies and built an f-w-d prototype in 1972. By June, 1972, the framework for the design was established: The car was to be built on a 90-inch wheelbase, with a curb weight of 1,540 pounds. Overall length was to be under 12 feet and all interior dimensions were planned to give it class leadership in terms of roominess.

In September, 1972, Henry Ford II gave the green light to develop the car and arrange for its production using plants in Spain, France, Britain and Germany. The project was then named Bobcat.

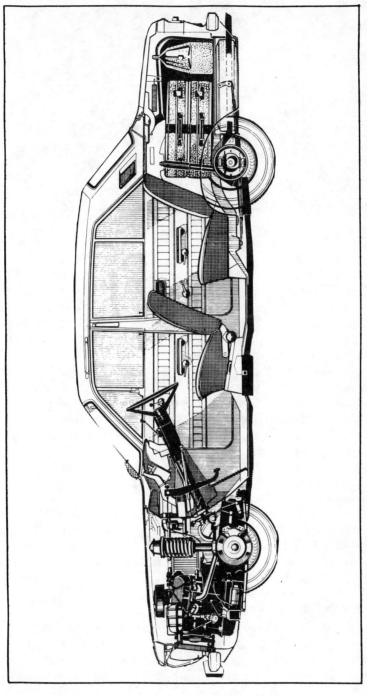

Side section of Taunus 15M shows outstanding space utilization. Fairly high roofline helped keep overall length within compact size.

Fiesta took nearly 7 years from idea to production. The Ford car shows influence from both Fiat 127 and VW Golf.

Over the next three years, the engineering elements were fixed and a body shape gradually emerged.

No one man can be credited with the engineering and design of the Fiesta. It was a teamwork effort with Dearborn-based product planners and cost-control experts taking up residence in the Cologne area and American, British and German engineers and technicians collaborating. Overall coordination for the engineering rested with John L. Hooven, who had come to Ford as an hourly employee at the River Rouge plant about 1942 and rose through the ranks to assistant chief engineer for light vehicles by the mid-Fifties. He supervised the design of the Falcon and in 1964 was transferred to Cologne as product engineering director. By 1967, he was vice president for product development for Ford of Europe and in August, 1973, was given the title of vice president for special product and manufacturing programs.

It was very important to combine product design and manufacturing responsibility for the Fiesta in one office, first because of the cost-control pressure, and secondly because Ford had never before planned to build a car this way with multi-point assembly and multinational sourcing of components.

Simplicity Main Aim for Components

Engine development costs were kept low by using the familiar Kent unit as a basis, though the Fiesta engines have no interchangeable parts with the UK versions of the same four-cylinder mill. In the drive train, Ford has accepted the theoretical problem of unequal-length drive shafts (as on the Fiat 127) in the interest of simplified design and lower cost.

The engine is installed transversely and it took Ford a long time to develop a suitable mounting system. But no other position could be adopted without breaking the framework specifications in terms of overall length vs. interior room, or going beyond the target weight. It was also reported that an advanced type of front suspension design was being developed for the Fiesta but was ditched in favor of a simple MacPherson spring-leg system with low cost and well-known behavioral characteristics.

The design was developed for maximum lightness and simplicity. The hub carrier takes the form of a semi-leading arm that also makes up the rear half of the lower control arm whose forward portion consists of a simple drag strut. The drag strut could easily have been incorporated in a stabilizer bar but the idea was to avoid its use. The basic Fiesta comes without a front stabilizer.

An extra saving accrued from the use of the Transit van front wheel bearings on the Fiesta. As for the rear end, Ford was looking at the very clever independent rear suspension systems of the Polo, Golf, R-5 and Fiat 127 but finally decided that both weight and money could be saved by using a dead axle. The result is a simple tube that carries the hubs, located laterally by a track rod and in the fore-and-aft plane by two pressed-steel radius arms and two splayed telescopic dampers. Rear hubs were adapted from the Escort front wheels.

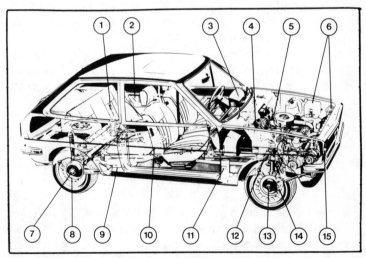

Fiesta has MacPherson front suspension but a "dead" beam axle at the rear with trailing arms and coil springs.

Cost control for the body shell cannot be separated from normal advances in production engineering. Ford had taken no shortcuts that would detract from torsional rigidity, fatigue life or the supression of noise and vibration, but had developed a precision shell, totally avoiding soldered joints, using 40 percent fewer parts than the Escort body.

The transmission is positioned on the left side of the flywheel and consists of an all-synchromesh four-speed gearbox with all-indirect ratios. Final drive is by helical spur gears and final drive ratios vary according to engine size: 4.056:1 with 957-cc and 1117-cc engines, and 3.842:1 with the 1,297 cc engine. That's equivalent to 15.8 and 16.7 mph per 1,000 rpm, respectively. The two smaller engines were available at the start of production in October, 1976, and the 1.3-liter was added in September, 1977.

Spring Options and Unusual Brakes

Standard springs are quite soft and suitable for the average customer. Two types of stiffer springing are offered in the form of Sport and Heavy Duty suspension. Basic wheel rates are 109 pounds-per-inch in front and 126 pounds-per-inch in the rear. The sport and Heavy Duty springs are 13.5 percent stiffer in the rear and 14 percent stiffer in front. Differences between Sport and Heavy Duty do not show up in the front suspension, only in the rear, where the Sport has more restricted wheel travel (6.5 inches instead of 7) and the Heavy Duty setup has extended wheel travel (7.2 inches). Sport versions also have a front stabilizer bar. Heavy-Duty suspension gives an extra inch of ground clearance.

Rack and pinion steering was adopted as a matter of course, with an overall ratio of 18.62:1, giving 3.4 turns lock to lock with a 32.2-foot turning diameter. Front wheels are set with a negative scrub radius (because of the diagonally split hydraulic brake circuits). Front wheels have disc brakes of 8.7-inch diameter with 7-inch drums in the rear wheels. The unusual feature about the discs is that the rotors are mounted outboard of the hubs, retained by the wheel bolts. This simplifies assembly and relining.

Hub and outer universal joint are set very deep inside the wheel (to provide the negative scrub radius desired). The splined joint is made with a helix angle of only 8 minutes to eliminate drive line "clunk." The right-hand drive shaft (the longer of the two) has a harmonic damper clamped to its middle point to minimize the effect of torsional nodes. Outer universal joints are of the Rzeppa-type while inner joints are of the Delta type.

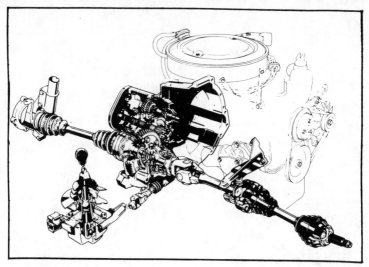

Fiesta power package has transverse engine with gearbox off to the side and helical spur gear final drive. Split shaft to right wheel gives equal length on outer shaft sections.

With the 957 cc engine the Fiesta has a top speed of 84 mph and can go from standstill to 50 mph in 14.2 seconds. Top speed goes to 90 mph with the 1,117-cc unit which also shortens the 0-50 mph acceleration time to 10.8 seconds. The Fiesta 1.3 S (1,297 cc) reaches 50 mph from standstill in 8.9 seconds and has a top speed of 97.5 mph.

Whatever Ford's specific cost targets were for the Fiesta, it is unlikely that they have been met. For one thing, the Fiesta is not the lowest-priced car in the range of European Fords. That's the Escort, a light car of straightforward engineering with a front-mounted engine and rear axle drive.

Will the Fiesta make Ford shy away from switching to f-w-d on other models? There are no signs that Ford is planning f-w-d cars for production anywhere in Europe or the U.S. and it would be unnatural if the Fiesta experience were not taken into account in the planning of new Ford products.

Chapter 13
Chrysler

In recent times, Chrysler Corporation has become an important producer of f-w-d cars on both sides of the Atlantic with the Dodge Omni and Plymouth Horizon in the U.S. and the Simca 1100, Rancho, Horizon, and 1307/1308 in France. The last-named is also assembled in England as the Chrysler Alpine. But it was not Chrysler's initiative that produced this range of f-w-d models. At the time the first f-w-d Simca was being designed, Chrysler held only a minority stake in Simca. The company was more or less a French branch of Fiat.

Simca Project 928 Out of Fiat

As we have seen in another chapter, Fiat was taking steps to build its own f-w-d cars in the early Sixties, and naturally, a program was started at Simca so that it would not be left behind. Project 928 was started in 1963 by Vittorio Montanari, a top-level Fiat engineer then on loan to Simca. Since his best design engineer, Rudolf Hruska, had returned to Italy (to help with the preparation of the Fiat 124), Simca needed some truly creative engineering talent in a hurry and an offer was made to Peugeot's leading f-w-d expert, Claude de Forcrand, who was just putting the finishing touches on the 204. He accepted and left Peugeot for Simca to take charge of Project 928.

This was to be a replacement for the Simca Aronde and a car to fill the gap between the Simca 1000 and the 1300/1500 series. The

Aronde was basically a French version of the Fiat 1100. Project 928 can be regarded, on the other hand, as a precursor of the Fiat 128.

Project 928 developed into the Simca 1100 and went into production in September, 1967. Two models were offered, two-door and four-door sedan, both with hatchback bodies. A station wagon was added later, and after some years, a van and a pickup truck. Finally, in 1976, a recreational vehicle was built in collaboration with Matra and marketed as the Rancho.

Logical, Fault-free Simca 1100

Built on a 99.2-inch wheelbase, the Simca 1100 had a front track of 53.8 inches and a rear track of 51.6 inches. The four-door sedan weighed 1,984 pounds and had a front/rear weight distribution of 58.4/41.6 percent. The two-door version was 44 pounds lighter, carrying less weight on the rear wheels, so that the weight distribution changed to 59/41 percent.

The engine was a new design based on the rev-happy 944 cc unit of the Simca-Mille with 1,118 cc displacement. Two versions were provided, a 53-hp low-compression job and a high-compression engine with 56 hp. As for the Peugeot 204, and the Autobianchi Primula, Montanari and de Forcrand chose a transverse engine installation. For the Simca, the cylinder block was pushed as far to the right as possible and tilted back at 41 degrees from vertical. The drive line layout departed from Peugeot practice and followed along Primula principles.

The Simca 1100 had a two-shaft gearbox with the main-shaft extending axially from the engine crankshaft and the countershaft carrying one of the final drive spur gears. This layout tends to place

F-w-d came to Chrysler in the form of this Simca 1100 which combined Peugeot and Fiat influence in engineering and design.

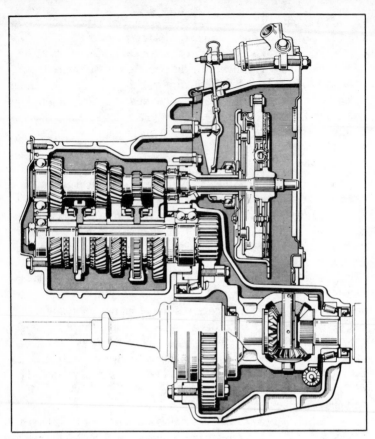

Four-speed synchromesh gearbox lined up with the clutch and fly-wheel on the Simca 1100 and the countershaft carried the final drive input gear.

the final drive in an offset position so that one drive shaft is longer than the other. But with this design Simca got the final drive within 3.35 inches of the car's center line—such a small dimension that the shafts could be considered—for all practical purposes—as being of equal length.

The transmission was a four-speed all-synchromesh unit with all-indirect ratios and its final drive ratio of 3.94:1 gave a 15-mph road speed in top gear per 1,000 rpm. Top speed was 88 mph and acceleration from standstill to 60 mph took 18 seconds.

Delta and Cardan Joints Used

Delta-type inner joints had sliding pots to accommodate axial movement. The outer ends of the shafts were splined into the

214

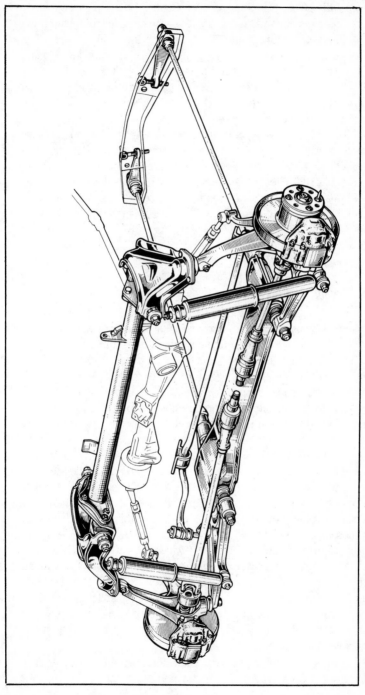

Unusually great distance between upper and lower control arms was a feature of the Simca 1100 front suspension.

driving members of double Cardan joints of very high angularity limits. The maximum steering angle on the outside front wheel was 31 degrees 45 minutess and 43 degrees on the inside wheel. Rack and pinion steering was used with an 18.5:1 overall ratio giving a fast 3.15 turns lock to lock for a turning diameter of 33.8 feet. The front wheels carried disc brakes with 9.17-inch solid rotors, while 8.5-inch drums were fitted at the rear. Seventy percent of the total brake force went to the front wheels.

Torsion bars were used at both ends. At front, a fairly typical Chrysler design with A-frame control arms of unequal length and a longitudinal torsion bar extending backwards from the lower control arm pivot shaft. The front suspension control arms were designed to avoid positive camber in both jounce and rebound and the steering axis was set at 13 degrees, which gave a positive scrub radius of about 0.65 inches. The stabilizer bar was 0.787 inches in diameter carried in two rubber bushings in the front body shell extension with its ends linked to the lower control arms.

Rear Suspension Also Torsion Bars

Rear suspension was independent with trailing arms and transverse torsion bars (each tilted forwards or backwards to avoid going to different wheelbase for left and right sides). A bracket welded to each trailing arm held the ends of a half-inch diameter stabilizer bar.

Springs were selected to give acceptable ride comfort throughout the vehicle's load range. Wheel rates were lower in front than in the rear (82 pounds per inch compared with 91). Yet it was the rear suspension that had the longest wheel travel: 9 inches, against only 6.8 in front.

Simca chose suspension geometry with a nose-up tail-down roll axis. The rear roll center was located at ground level while the front roll center was one inch higher up. Front and rear stabilizer bars were fitted, with two-thirds of the roll stiffness coming from the front end. Stabilizer bars accounted for one-third of the front roll stiffness and one-eighth of the rear roll stiffness. The front end was designed for zero roll steer effect, which was accomplished.

For 1969, a 1,204-cc version of the same engine was made available and for 1972, a still larger version with 1,254 cc displacement. The evolution of the Simca 1100, which is still in production, has been remarkably uneventful. The original design had no bugs in it and no technical modifications affecting the drive train or suspension principles have been made.

Automobiles Simca became Chrysler-France in 1970. At that time Project C6 was instituted to develop a new series of f-w-d cars to replace the antiquated Simca 1300/1500 which dated from 1963. As the C6 program progressed, it became apparent that the new cars would also have to replace the unfortunate 160-180 series introduced as 1972 models, with front-mounted engines and rear axle drive and looking like scaled-down versions of the contemporary Plymouth Fury. As a result, the new models had to cover a wide market spread. Claude de Forcrand was the principal engineer on the project, reporting now to a new engineering director, Joe Farnham, who came from Chrysler-UK (the former Rootes Group, makers of Hillman and Sunbeam cars).

Broad Project C6 Under Chrysler

Two new engine sizes were readied, 1,294 cc and 1,442 cc, to power the new models, designated 1307 and 1308. Their layout was basically similar to the Simca 1100 with wheelbase stretched to 102.5 inches and overall length to 167 inches.

The base-model C6 weighed 2,315 pounds and had a front/rear weight distribution of 58/42 percent. Engines were installed transversely and tilted back at 41 degrees, just as in the 1100. The drive line was adapted from the 1100 with final drive ratios of 3.71:1 for the 1.3-liter and 3.59:1 for the 1.44-liter engine.

The front suspension was based on that of the 1100 with the major change being the elimination of the scrub radius in an attempt at center-point steering. At the rear end, a totally new design was developed with trailing arms and coil springs. The coil springs were short and mounted ahead of the shock absorbers. Spring rates were

Simca 1308 S broke new ground for Chrysler-France when it went into production in September, 1975. Half a million were built in less than three years.

arranged to give a 24-percent greater ride frequency in the rear suspension, with 3.6 inches of front wheel jounce travel and 5.5 inches in the rear.

The C6 cars went into production in September, 1975, labeled 1307 and 1308, with only one common body style, a four-door hatchback sedan. The 1308 had the most powerful engine and a top speed of 102.5 mph. It could go from standstill to 50 mph in 9 seconds and to 60 mph in 14, with ability to cover the standing-start quarter-mile in 19 seconds flat.

International Omni-Horizon Team

The 1307 was chosen as the basis for a Chrysler "world car" concept known as Project C2—a model to be built in both Europe and America. For the American market, the idea was to offer a truly modern car of Vega/Pinto exterior size and weight with ample interior room and none of the drawbacks of the Ford and GM subcompacts (which were obsolete at the time of their introduction). For the European market, the idea was to prepare a successor to the 1100 but since the 1100 remains as popular as ever, Chrysler now contends that the intention was simply to bridge the gap between the 1100 and the 1307.

The planning and engineering of the C2 became an international affair almost on the scale of Ford's Bobcat (Fiesta) program. The key figures at the Detroit end were Leo Walsh, chief engineer for advance engineering, and Don Gschwind, director of chassis engineering. On the European side, a new engineering team was formed under Burt Bouwkamp. He had been chief engineer of product planning until his assignment as director of engineering for both Chrysler-UK and Chrysler-France. De Forcrand was not on the team as he had left the corporation by this time.

French and American Horizons Differ

The green light for the C2 was given in April, 1975, and production began in France in November, 1977, and one month later, in the U.S.A. The four-door hatchback bodies are identical but the French and American version show a lot of difference in their mechanical specifications.

The Simca Horizon could rely on off-the-shelf components and sub-assemblies from either the 1100 or the 1307 while the parent organization did not even have four-cylinder engines in production. Consequently, Chrysler arranged to purchase engines from Volkswagen (as used for the Pennsylvania-built Rabbit) and developed a new MacPherson-type front suspension.

French-built Horizon uses unified power packages from either Simca 1100 or Simca 1307 and is not available with automatic transmission.

Compared with the Ford Pinto and Chevrolet Monza, the Dodge Omni and Plymouth Horizon are far roomier. First off, the Pinto/Vega/Monza bodies were always two-door sedans or coupes. Next, the Omni measures 100.2 cubic feet of useful volume, far more than the 83 cubic feet of the Pinto or the 88 cubic feet of the Monza. In addition, the Omni has more cargo space—35.8 cubic feet compared with 29 in the Pinto and 26.5 in the Monza. And the Omni contains all this useful space in a lighter vehicle. It has a curb weight of 2,137 pounds, vs. 2,472 for the Pinto and 2,665 for the Monza. Because of its lighter weight, it needs less power and therefore runs more economically. With its 75-hp 1.7-liter engine the Omni beats the 88-hp 2.3-liter Pinto from standstill to 60 mph, 13 seconds flat to 13.8.

The U.S. bumper laws have caused an extra deviation between the American and European C2 versions. Omni bumpers add 75 pounds to the curb weight and alter the weight distribution from 59.3/40.7 percent to 62/38 percent. The made-in-U.S.A. cars are known to have odd behavior in critical handling situations such as a peculiar maneuver that's part of the test routine of *Consumer Reports*. The French-built Horizon has no handling problems whatever and the altered behavior of the Omni is not due to the difference in front suspension systems but to the American bumpers.

The Omni/Horizon are offered with a Chrysler-made automatic transmission as an extra-cost option while the Simca version is strictly manual with four-speed gearboxes shared with the 1100 and 1307. The U.S. models are also offered with power steering while none is available on the Simca. The gearshift linkage on the Simca uses rods and levers but the Omni/Horizon have only a cable lin-

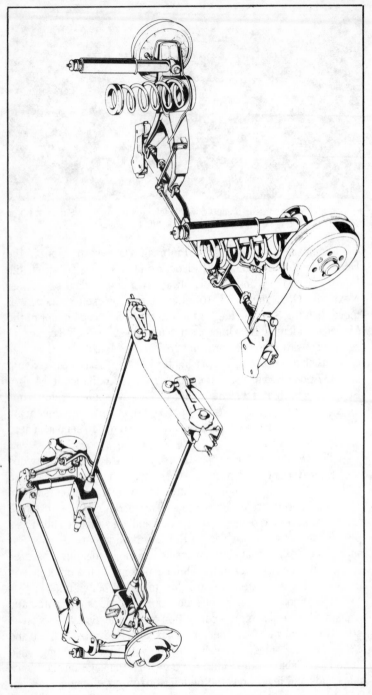

Simca Horizon differs from Plymouth version in having torsion bar front suspension (apart from difference in the power train).

kage. The Simca gets somewhat better fuel mileage, as you would expect with smaller-displacement engines and lower curb weight. The EPA rates the Omni at 25 mpg in simulated city driving and 39 mpg on the highway for a 30-mpg composite rating while owners average about 28 mpg in normal use.

At a steady speed of 55 mph the Simca burns its gasoline at a slow rate of 36.7 mpg which drops to 27.6 at 75 mph. In urban traffic, it averages about 27.5 mpg. It's also faster than the Omni with a 97-mph top speed (from the 1.3-liter engine) and acceleration capability of a 19.5-second standing-start quarter-mile.

What about the future? Chrysler's European branches are now going under control of PSA Peugeot-Citroen and it's that group's top management that will decide how long the Simca and Sunbeam name plates will be continued and direct any future products carrying these ex-Chrysler labels. American models? Chrysler Corporation wants to put f-w-d on its compacts but the difficulty lies in the fact that the 225-cubic-inch slant-six is not easily adaptable to transverse installation . . Any other f-w-d installation is unthinkable. What this means is that six-cylinder and V-8-powered Chrysler cars with f-w-d will not be made until the corporation has developed a new engine family—and that may be some time away.

Chapter 14
Alfa Romeo

To an American car company it would be unthinkable to design a new car for the 1970s without thorough market research. But in Italy, a car that's in far greater demand than the production volume can hope to satisfy for a long time was created without any market research at all. And it was created not in order to exploit a particular gap in the market, or because the manufacturer had found a special niche for his new product. It was simply brought into existence because Alfa Romeo, a state-owned corporation, had been told by the government to put up a factory in the southern part of the country and the factory needed a product to make.

The government wanted a factory in the south to alleviate the unemployment situation there and turn the region's economy around from agriculture to industry. That meant the plant would be manned by unskilled labor—men who had no previous experience of factory work. It was unthinkable to try to produce any existing model of Alfa Romeo under such conditions.

Unusual Design Motives for Alfasud

In addition, the government wanted a big plant giving jobs to about 15,000 men. It may be a unique case in history where the size of the work force dictated the type of car any auto plant was to build! And that's in fact what happened, for with the number of workers as the basic factor, an equation was established where production volume was balanced against unit cost. The more cars turned out, the less each one would cost.

Alfa Romeo's involvement with f-w-d began in 1958 with the Romeo van. The Giulietta engine was carried as front overhang, opening up the full interior for cargo.

Considerations of purchasing, materials flow, production methods, distribution and merchandising brought the target volume out of infinity and down to a practical ceiling of 1,000 cars a day. To sell 1,000 cars a day, the product had to belong in the most popular market segment, that is to say a family sedan in the 1,750 to 1,900-pounds weight class with an engine in the 1,100-cc to 1,500-cc category. And the final product must be competitive not only on price but on quality, performance, ride and handling, durability, and resale value.

So far, the question of f-w-d had not even come up. Alfa Romeo had never built an f-w-d car (though it begain building the f-w-d Romeo van as early as 1958). The fact that the Alfasud does have front wheel drive stems from the reasoning of the chief engineer, Rudolf Hruska.

Hruska's Remarkable Opportunity

He saw in the Alfasud project an equivalent to the opportunity that Hitler had given Porsche with the Volkswagen some 35 years earlier. The situations were similar. In both cases, the projects were government-sponsored. In both cases, factories had yet to be built to produce cars that were not designed or developed. In both cases, minimum lead time was essential. Porsche's Volkswagen took six years from Hitler's go ahead to get into production. Hruska said he could do it in four.

It is significant that it was Hruska that made the commitment, and not Alfa Romeo. Hruska was working for Fiat at the time he was approached about the Alfasud project. Alfasud was a new subsidiary organization that barely existed even on paper in 1967. And Hruska had one year to go on his contract with Fiat. He went to Rome to discuss the plan with Alfa Romeo and government officials. Here was the chance of a lifetime and one that's only given to one engineer in a million.

All his career Hruska had been a "backroom" engineer, one of those giant brains that is often kept anonymous. A native of Vienna, Austria,he had gone to work for Porsche in 1938, shortly after getting his engineering degree. After the war he worked on the Cisitalia, assisted Porsche on some projects, and was loaned to Alfa Romeo where he set up the company's first assembly line. He went to Fiat about 1957 and worked most of the time with Deutsche Fiat and Simca.

He wanted to do the Alfasud and Fiat agreed to overlook the remaining time on the contract. Now he had to make up a detailed plan and "sell" it to the government and Alfa Romeo. He had, of course, no help from Alfa Romeo but worked strictly as an outside vendor, a private agent.

Independently, he formed a group of 27 men in November, 1967. Where did he get his assistants? Not from Alfa Romeo. He got some out of the engineering schools. He got some out of other industries. But for the most part he got them out of retirement! Seasoned engineers that he knew well, who were overjoyed to tackle an all-new car instead of modifying an old one. They were not all product engineers but also production engineers, for the car and the plant went together; "you can't have one without the other" was clear to all parties.

Commitment to Build Factory and Car

In February, 1968, Hruska presented the complete package and engaged himself to start production in four years from the word "go." The contract was signed. Alfa Romeo already had the land, a tract on flat ground inland from Naples, and the cornerstone was laid in April, 1968.

To meet the target date for production, factory construction had to proceed side by side with the design and development of the car. But Hruska never blinked. He was so sure the car was right as it

Alfasud combines a flat-four engine with four- or five-speed manual transmissions and f-w-d. The car has all-coil suspension.

came from his drawing board that no basic changes would need to be made. Consequently, there was no hesitation about signing tooling orders long before the car had been fully tested.

The first engine ran in June, 1968. Hruska test-drove the first prototype in October of that year. He contacted Giorgetto Giugiaro of Ital Design to handle the styling for the production model. The factory was built and equipped on time and came on stream with only three months' delay in the summer of 1972. The Alfasud had made its official debut in November, 1971, as two-door and four-door fast-back sedans with a curb weight of 1,830 pounds. Built on a 96.65-inch wheelbase, it was 153.15 inches long overall, 62.6 inches wide, and 54 inches high.

Hruska Team's Design Features

Of Hruska's assistants some who deserve particular mention are Luigi Vincenti as design director, Giovanni Lo Coco for chassis design, D. Chirico and C. Bossaglia for the engine and drive train, and M. Manfrino for the factory layout, methods, and tooling.

The engine was a flat-four mounted ahead of the front wheel axis, with the transaxle behind. It looked very much like Citroen's solution for the GS except that the Alfasud had a water-cooled engine and the GS used air cooling. The four-speed all-synchromesh transmission was a two-shaft design with the countershaft serving also as pinion shaft for the hypoid bevel final drive. The shift rods and forks were located at the bottom with positive connection to a remote-control floorshift.

Inner universal joints were of the Delta-type while Rzeppa-type joints were fitted at the outer ends. The steering was limited to a maximum angle of 33½ degrees on the outside wheel due to space restrictions caused by the front suspension design. That gave a larger turning diameter of 34.8 feet than is normal for f-w-d cars of its size but it was accepted as the penalty for the optimized front suspension.

A MacPherson-type design was chosen mainly because of Hruska's desire to distribute the suspension loads into the body shell at three points as widely spaced as possible. The lower control arm is a two-part assembly with the forward member semi-trailing at about 20 degrees from longitudinal, reaching far ahead to a rubber-hushing mount on a cross member in the very nose of the body shell.

The second member was semi-leading at about 65 degrees from longitudinal, anchored in a rubber bushing on a bracket extending from the transaxle and corresponding very closely in its length and arc to those of the drive shaft. This setup gave considerable anti-dive effect.

The MacPherson spring legs extended below the hub carrier base and had pronounced inward (sea-legs) tilt. The idea was to get the lower ends of the struts as far apart as possible and that in turn necessitated tilting them to clear the tire at the top end. The wheel spindle was fixed to the outer element of the spring strut to achieve maximum bending resistance and the steering arms extended from the cylindrical struts just below the coil spring bases, linked to a rack and pinion steering gear.

Zero Scrub Radius & High Roll Center Achieved

The tilting of the spring legs also enabled them to gain length, giving reduced friction and improved wear resistance. The legs contain Bilstein telescopic shock absorbers and carry coil springs on top, their upper abutments being welded into the body shell at points where the loads are fed into the cowl structure. The swivel axis does not coincide with the spring leg but runs from its upper mounting to the ball joint on the rear control arm, coinciding with the center of the tire contact patch. That gives zero scrub radius.

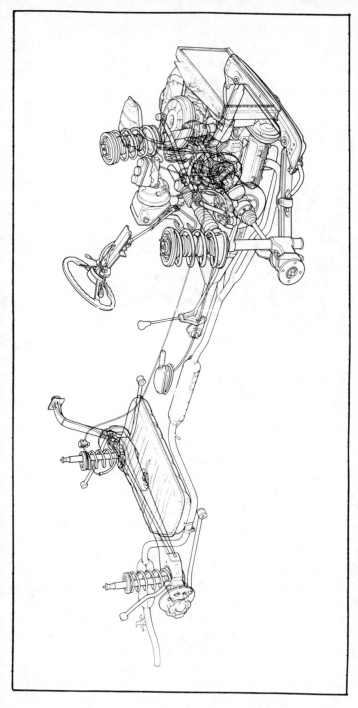

Alfasud chassis features MacPherson front suspension with particularly wide-splayed lower control arms, inboard disc brakes, and non-independent rear suspension with a Watt linkage.

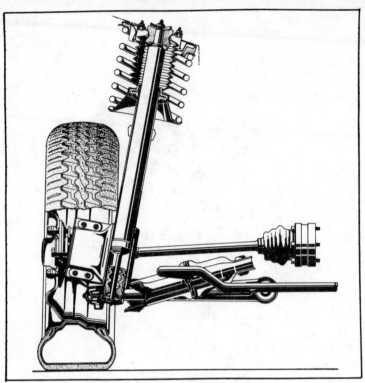

Alfasud front suspension is designed with zero scrub radius and static wheel alignment calls for pronounced negative camber.

The suspension geometry provides a high roll center, 3.36 inches above ground level and a heavy stabilizer bar adds extra roll stiffness to assure flat cornering under abnormally high side forces. Also, the front wheels are set with a static negative camber of 2 degrees 12 minutes which assures a total absence of positive camber, relative to the roadway, even with maximum body roll.

Disc brakes with solid rotors of 10.5-inch diameter are mounted inboard on the shafts to minimize unsprung weight. Disc brakes are used also at the rear. They are mounted in the wheels and have a diameter of 9.2 inches. The hydraulic systems has two circuits, one operating on all four wheels and the second operating both front wheels only. The second circuit is claimed to give 70-percent of full braking efficiency. The handbrake works mechanically on the front calipers. Brake lines to the rear calipers are fitted with a load-sensitive valve to prevent premature wheel locking.

At the rear end, the Alfasud has a "dead" beam axle located via a Watt linkage on each side (as close to the wheels as practical) with

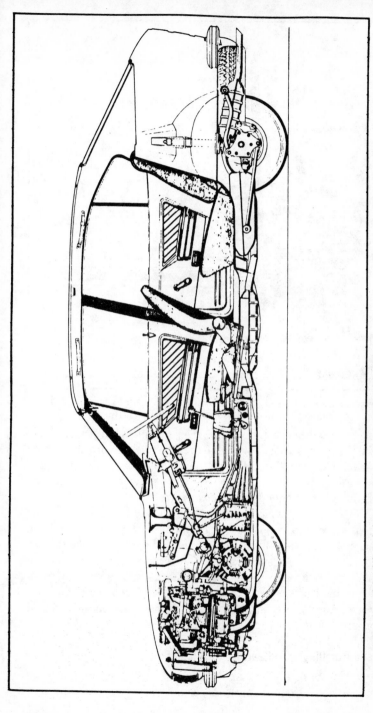

Sectioned side view of the Alfasud shows well thought-out layout with particular attention to safety as well as comfort and practicality.

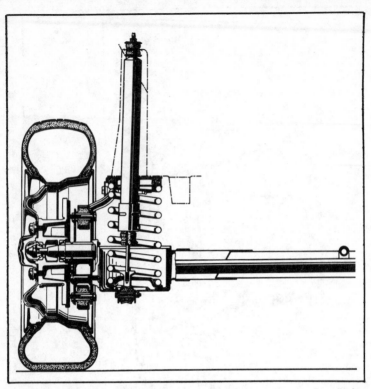

Horizontal track bar on Alfasud rear axle assures lateral location. Disc brake rotors are carried close to center line of the wheel.

coil springs. Telescopic shock absorbers are mounted concentrically with the springs and extend above them. A track bar provides lateral location of the axle and the Watt linkage is arranged to provide a strong anti-dive effect. Rear wheels were set with zero camber and toe-in, helping to keep roll steer at zero.

The "dead" beam rear axle was chosen because it was the simplest way to keep the wheels vertical at all times, and the execution does not involve much more unsprung weight than an independent rear suspension system. It takes up very little space and has permitted excellent rear seating as well as a roomy trunk with a low flat floor. It gives a very high roll center (9.16 inches above ground level) with sufficient roll stiffness to eliminate the need for a rear stabilizer bar.

Good Handling and Steering No Accident

With its high roll axis, running down towards the nose, the extraordinary front suspension geometry, and its 57/43-percent static front/rear weight distribution, the Alfasud has remarkable handling characteristics. A slight initial understeer gives way to neutral steer with exemplary stability in S-curves and an almost complete absence of throttle-steer phenomena. If anything, there's stronger understeer in power-off situations than when cornering power-on.

The steering remains uniformly light and precise regardless of speed though the effort does increase on very sharp turns calling for extreme steering angles. Its rack-and-pinion steering gear was somewhat slow-geared at 3.75 turns lock to lock; but the car gives such quick response that the overall impression is very sports-car-like and entirely worthy of Alfa Romeo traditions.

The Alfasud engine delivered 63 hp at 6,000 rpm from 1,186 cc and the all-indirect four-speed gearbox had 3.3 percent overdrive on top. With a final drive ratio of 4.11:1, the car ran 16.1 mph per 1,000 rpm in top gear and had a top speed of 93 mph. Performance levels are highly creditable for a car that averages 30 mpg in normal use, with acceleration capability of covering the standing-start quarter-mile in 20 seconds flat and going from zero to 50 mph in 12.5 seconds.

Derivations Confirm Outstanding Design

In November, 1973, The Alfasud ti was introduced. It was basically the two-door sedan equipped with a partial front air dam and

The Italian racing fraternity was not slow in discovering the sporting qualities of the Alfasud which provided the basis for a whole new class of production-car racing.

a rear-end spoiler. Mechanically, it had the benefit of a five-speed transmission with a 1.11:1 reduction on fourth and 7 percent overdrive on fifth. Final drive ratio remained at 4.11:1. The two-door baseline sedan was discontinued.

The Alfasud L appeared in January, 1975, as a deluxe version of the four-door sedan incorporating as standard equipment a selection of items that had formerly been optional. Three months later came the Giardinetta station wagon with a straight roofline and top-hinged tailgate on the basic two-door body, sharing the running gear of the Alfasud N. This was followed by the Alfasud Sprint in October, 1976. It had a newly designed two-door coupe body by Giugiaro and mechanically it was the same as the ti. At the same time, the Alfasud L became available with the 5-speed gearbox.

The Alfasud Super was announced in January, 1978. It was available with a 1,286-cc version of the same basic engine and the five-speed transmission was standard. The Super was followed in May, 1978, by the Sprint 1.5 and ti 1.5 with a new 1,490-cc edition of the overhead camshaft flat-four power unit. It delivers 85 hp and gives the cars a top speed of 107 mph. Final drive ratio has been lowered to 3.89:1 for these models which raises the road speed per 1,000 rpm in overdrive fifth to 17.9 mph. They will cruise at 55 mph with a fuel economy of 39.5 mpg, and even at a steady 75 mph the gasoline mileage does not drop below 27 mpg.

The Alfasud range has earned unreserved praise from the quarter where it counts most—its competitors, including Fiat and Lancia. The Alfasud ti has given birth to a separate stock-car racing category in Italy, and the Super 1.3 and Sprint 1.5 have become the yardstick against which any new pretenders must be measured.

Chapter 15
Front Wheel Drive in Japan

Automotive engineering in Japan was a joke until about 15 years ago. The industry got its start by copying American and European designs. The change from copiers to innovators took place gradually. First, one company would find new detail solutions in an existing model. Then another company would produce a power unit of entirely original design. Finally, a car maker would introduce a complete car of his own creation.

This process was well under way before any modern f-w-d Japanese car had been thought of. The explanation may be historical, at least in part. The cars the Japanese industry bought the rights to produce in 1948 were the rear-engined Renault 4 CV and the conventional Hillman Minx and Austin A-40.

What would have happened if Japan had instead secured licenses for the Citroen 2 CV, Auto-Union DKW, and Dyna-Panhard makes for fascinating speculation. But reality is no less interesting, for when the Japanese auto manufacturers eventually did turn to f-w-d, they had their own good reasons for doing so and they had to go through research and development programs that owed nothing to European practice but showed full independence of thought and an impressive clarity of purpose.

Honda Innovation with a Mini

It began with Honda, the giant motorcycle manufacturer, who started sports car production with its S-600 and made a splash in Grand Prix auto racing in 1964. In mid-1963, a Honda design team had started a new project for a four-seater f-w-d minicar to compete in the lowest price and tax class in Japan—cars with under 360 cc engine displacement and certain maximum dimensions.

This market segment was dominated by Mitsubishi, Suzuki, Mazda, Daihatusu and Subaru with cars that differed greatly in their technical makeup but had an odd resemblance in overall shape. Some had rear engines and others carried the power units in the front, but all had driving rear wheels and the packaging invariably ended up as a little box, from quite square to eggshell-shaped, with a short hood in front and a wagon-type rear end.

This design formula evolved before BMC had shown its Mini and was caused more by Japanese regulations for maximum length and weight than the designers' desire for maximum compactness. Honda's reasons for choosing f-w-d were simple. A rear engine would steal too much useful space from the interior and push the back seat too far forward. Consequently, the engine had to be in front. Honda was a mass-producer of engines—transversely mounted—with integral gearboxes for its motorcycles and it was more logical to stick with that layout, adding only a jointed shaft to each front wheel, than to rig up a long and clumsy drive line to the rear wheels.

The Honda N-360 made its debut at the Tokyo auto show in November, 1966, powered by a 354-cc air-cooled parallel-twin engine developed from an existing motorcycle unit. It was built on a 78.75-inch wheelbase and weighed only 1,091 pounds but could seat four persons. It was geared for a road speed of 8.7 mph per 1,000 rpm in top gear which seems incredibly low until you realize that the Honda delivered its peak power of 31 hp at a crankshaft speed of 8,500 rpm! The N-360 had a top speed of 71.5 mph.

Chain-Driven Non-Synchromesh

The engine stood vertically in the nose of the car with chain drive giving a 2.05:1 reduction from the crankshaft to the gearbox mainshaft (which carried a outrigger clutch). The four-speed non-synchromesh unit featured a top gear that gave a 28.6-percent overdrive, and chevron-type helical spur gearing to the final drive which had a 3.54:1 ratio. The gearbox shafts were arranged horizontally behind the crankcase below the crankshaft center line with the differential at the rear end of the transaxle. Delta-type universal joints were used at the inner ends and double Cardan joints at the outer ends.

For the front suspension, Honda chose a MacPherson-type design with the lower control arm being a two-piece member made

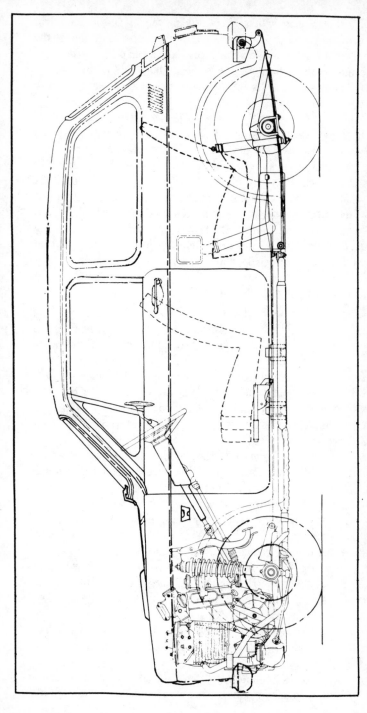

Built on a 78.8-inch wheelbase, the Honda N-360 and N-600 were only 122 inches long overall yet they were full four-seaters (for Japanese-size occupants).

up of a lateral arm with a slight leading angle, and a drag strut anchored in a rubber bushing at the extreme front corner of the engine cradle, and tilted down towards the hub at an 11-degree angle at design height. The spring legs were sharply tilted in order to eliminate any scrub radius and the swivel axis ended up at a radial 16 degrees from vertical.

The front wheel had 2.44 inches of jounce travel and 3.07 inches of rebound with a static camber angle of half a degree negative, going increasingly negative in jounce but to positive camber in rebound. The front coil springs were fairly soft, giving a wheel rate of 73 pounds per inch. Rack and pinion steering was used with a 17.4:1 ratio that gave 3 turns lock to lock and a tight turning diameter of 28.8 feet. Front track was 44.9 inches compared with only 43.3 inches at the rear. The outside front wheel had a maximum steering angle of 27 degrees 33 minutes while the inside wheel could be turned up to 35 degrees 12 minutes.

Variable-Rate Springing at Rear

For the rear end, Honda chose a "dead" beam axle and variable-rate leaf springs. The axle was a lightweight steel tube and the semi-elliptic springs had two leaves of 2-inch width, the lower one 38 inches long and the upper one 25 inches long. The upper leaf is tapered towards the ends and that's what gives the variable spring rate (33.6 to 129 pounds per inch). Why the variable rate? Because of the tremendous load variations relative to net vehicle weight. The static weight on each rear wheel increased from 396 pounds unladen to 930 pounds with a full load.

No stabilizer bars were fitted at either end. The rear roll center was located 7.87 inches above ground level and the front roll center 2 inches above the ground. The front suspension provided 58 percent of the car's total roll stiffness, however. With 67/33-percent front/rear weight distribution, it had firm understeer all the way, increasing at an alarming rate with higher side forces. And it was terribly sensitive to accelerator position changes, darting instantly to a new course with a tighter arc when going from power-on to power-off.

At the end of 1967, Honda offered a larger engine of 600 cc in the same car for export. The N-600 engine delivered 42 hp at 6,600 rpm and the gearing was reworked with a 3.36:1 final drive that gave a road speed of 13 mph per 1,000 rpm in fourth gear. Because of the higher torque, Honda went to Rzeppa-type outer joints in the drive shafts.

As an option, semi-automatic drive (Honda-Matic) was introduced with a hydraulic torque converter mounted at the end of the crankshaft, engaged or disengaged by a lockup clutch facing the flywheel. The drive was taken via the standard chain reduction to a three-speed two-shaft gearbox forming a transaxle with the final drive and differential.

The N-600 with manual transmission had a top speed of 80 mph and could accelerate from zero to 50 mph in 12.7 seconds, reach 60 mph from zero in 19, and cover the standing-start quarter-mile in 21.3 seconds. Its average fuel consumption in normal use was 31 mpg.

Mini Success Led to Bigger Challenge

The N-360 immediately took sales leadership in its class and began to push its competitors into extinction. But the N-600 never enjoyed much success in Europe or America. In a separate program that started shortly before the N-360 went into production, a Honda engineering team was looking at a bigger car, a four-door subcompact in the 2,000-pound category with an engine size between 1,000 and 1,500 cc. This resulted in the Honda N-1300 which was first revealed to the public in November, 1968.

It was a challenge to Japan's traditional representatives in that segment of the market. It was also Honda's first attempt to make a

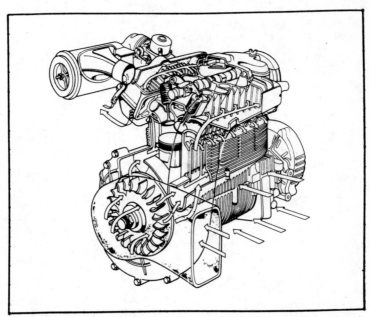

Crankshaft on Honda N-1300 engine drives transmission left side and cooling air fan on the right. Primary chain drive was inherited from N-600.

car for world markets (instead of exporting cars designed for Japanese conditions).

The framework for the design specified an interior as roomy as a typical Japanese 1.5-liter family car (Datsun 510, Toyota Corona) with a 1.3-liter engine as powerful as a normal 2-liter unit and fuel economy comparable with a car of 1-liter engine displacement. And it must be a car that presented its own unique appeal to the clientele. It was unique all right. Honda produced a four-cylinder, in-line, air-cooled engine, installed transversely, and mated with a transmission that looked very much like a grown-up version of the N-360 setup.

The engine was installed vertically in the nose of the car. In order to get it low enough, it was built with dry-sump lubrication. The timing gear was placed on the right and the flywheel on the left and the whole unit offset to the right as far as needed to get a centrally located differential. Two versions existed, Type 77 with a single carburetor and 96 hp, and Type 99 with four carburetors and 110 hp. Both has separate exhaust pipes for each cylinder on the front side and carburetors and ignition on the back.

Still Chain-Drive but New Rear Suspension

The primary-reduction chain drive had a ratio of 1,667:1 and the final drive ratio was 3.50:1 so that the car ran at a road speed of 14.6 mph per 1,000 rpm in top gear. A synchromesh four-speed gearbox was adopted with direct-drive top gear. Shortly after production got under way, the primary reduction ratio was lowered to 1.24:1, raising the speed per 1,000 rpm to 19.6 mph. The drive shafts had Delta-type joints next to the differential and Rzeppa-type joints near the wheel hubs.

A MacPherson-type front suspension was retained for the N-1300 but instead of the "dead" beam axle at the back was a setup best described as a twin I-beam layout. Each wheel was carried on a hub at the end of an axle that ended just short of the other wheel. They were pendulum-type swing axles with the pivot points removed in opposite directions—fully independent yet with near-parallel wheels and a high roll center. The twin I-beam layout was first used on Unic cars from the mid-Twenties for the *front* suspension to combat shimmy and was taken up for Ford pickup trucks in 1965. The leaf spring design from the Honda N-360 was suitably redesigned and the rear hubs carried a base for the telescopic shock absorbers.

Rare Failure for Honda

Steering was by rack and pinion with a 17.6:1 ratio giving 3.25 turns lock to lock and a 31.9-feet turning diameter. While the N-360 and N-600 had drum brakes on all four wheels, the N-1300 used discs in front. Surprisingly, the discs were only 6.9 inches in diameter compared with 8 inches for the rear drums.

The car was built on an 88.5-inch wheelbase and had an overall length of 151 inches. With a front track of 49 inches, it had a 48.5-inch rear track. Curb weight was only 1,725 pounds with a front/rear weight distribution of 59.8/40.2 percent.

What Honda had intended to be a world-beater turned out to be—not a sheep in wolf's clothing, for it did not have the styling for that—but sort of a dog. It did not have 2-liter peroformance though it enjoyed parity with some European 1,600-cc cars. It went from zero to 50 mph in 9.9 seconds and from zero to 60 mph in 15.8 seconds. Top speed was 97.5 mph, far below the 110-mph target. And its fuel economy was far below 1-liter standards, giving only 23.7 mpg at a steady speed of 55 mph and 18.5 mpg at a constant 70 mph. The steering was lacking in precision, demanded high effort, and the car's cornering behavior was upset by abnormally strong throttle-change reactions. The N-1300 was a failure and was quietly withdrawn from production in 1972.

Honda Life Led to Civic

Another engineering team had made considerable progress with the idea of developing the N-360 into a four-door sedan pow-

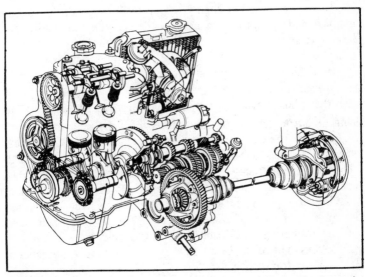

Life engine was mounted on the left with the radiator on the right. New transmission eliminated the primary chain drive.

Honda Civic made the start of Honda as a mass producer of cars as well as motorcycles. The clean-air stratified-charge CVCC engine made it known around the world.

ered by a water-cooled engine. It began life in June, 1971, as the Honda Life. Wheelbase was stretched at 82 inches and overall length to 118 inches. Weight increased to 1,125 pounds with the driving wheels carrying 61 percent of the static load.

Along with the new engine design and the addition of a radiator came a new transmission. The primary-reduction chain drive was dispensed with and a simple 3-speed transmission replaced the four-speed unit.

The N-360 was renamed N-III and a Z-coupe on the same chassis added. All of these minicars were phased out in 1976-77 so Honda could divert its factory capacity to newer and more successful models.

Honda's success in the car market began with the Civic which appeared in July of 1972. It was "larger than Life" in the sense that it shared the basic layout of the Life with transverse water-cooled engine and front wheel drive and nearly the same silhouette. In its original form, the Civic was a two-door hatchback of 1,825 pounds curb weight built on an 86.6-inch wheelbase with a front track of 51.2 inches and a rear track of 50.4 inches. It had 60/40-percent front/rear weight distribution and all-independent suspension with a MacPherson-type in front and coil spring legs in the rear, with lateral control arms and semi-trailing radius rods. Predictably, it had rack-and-pinion steering and disc/drum brakes. Engine size was 1,169 cc and buyers had a choice of four-speed manual or two-speed Honda-Matic transmission.

Here was a Honda that had very nice road manners, the power-on, power-off steering problems finally having been licked.

The chassis was so good, in fact, that it could obviously handle a lot more power and speed. The next step was to raise engine displacement to 1.5-liters, then to 1.6 liters.

Accord Culmination of Civic

In 1974 Honda added a four-door Civic and the following year a station wagon. The four-door sedan was longer (146 inches overall) and 220 pounds heavier at 2,045 pounds curb weight. Front/rear weight distribution changed to 60.8/39.2 percent. Spring rates were increased by 18 percent front and rear to handle the additional load. The 1.5-liter Civic four-door sedan had a top speed of 93 mph and claimed to give 40 mph at a steady speed of 40 mph. The engine was tuned to deliver 63 hp at 5,500 rpm and, in combination with a final drive ratio of 4.73:1, gave the car a road speed of 21.4 mph at 1,000 rpm in top gear.

Honda's next f-w-d car was the Accord first shown in November, 1976. In its initial version, it was a two-door coupe, looking like nothing more than a bigger brother to the Civic. And that, in a nutshell, is what it is. Wheelbase was stretched to 93.7-inches and overall length to 162.4 inches. It was wider, too, with a

Honda Accord layout followed the principles laid down with the Life, transverse engine offset to the left, slanting forward, with transaxle behind, MacPherson front suspension, outboard front disc brakes, and rack-and-pinion steering.

Four-door sedan version of Nissan Cherry used B-210 engine installed transversely, driving the front wheels.

track of 55.1 inches in front and 54.7 in the rear. Curb weight increased to 1,930 pounds.

A four-door notchback sedan followed in November, 1977, weighing 2,166 pounds and having a front/rear weight distribution of 58/42 percent. Its 1.6-liter engine delivered 80 hp at 5,300 rpm and coupled to a five-speed transmission. Final drive ratio was 4.117:1 which gave the car a road speed of 18.1 mph per 1,000 rpm in top gear. Fifth gear was a 28.6-percent overdrive and fourth was a 14.6-percent overdrive.

This power train gave an excellent compromise between performance and economy, with a top speed of 102 mph and a standstill-to-60 mph acceleration time of 14.2 seconds, and an average fuel consumption of 27 mpg. The optional Honda-Matic for the Accord had a three-speed planetary gear train combined with the usual torque converter, and gave about 25 percent higher fuel consumption and 10 percent longer acceleration times, with a 5-percent loss in top speed.

Datsun/Nissan Try FWD

The second Japanese auto maker to begin production of f-w-d cars was Nissan Motor Company, the nation's number two producer (behind Toyota). About 1965 the company decided to develop a new small car the size of the Sunny (B-210) with the same carrying capacity, maneuverability, and low running costs but offering different styling, improved comfort and greater versatility. Such a car was needed to meet the demands of the younger generation also in terms of pricing, the marketing experts concluded. In pursuing these objectives, the Nissan engineers were naturally led to an f-w-d concept.

The engine was taken from the Sunny, a 1-liter to 1.2-liter unit. It was turned sideways and combined with the transmission and final drive. Since it would be the company's first f-w-d production car and a mass-producer like Nissan could ill afford any kind of failure in product engineering, a large amount of money and manpower was put into testing and development. A fleet of experimental cars covered nearly 3 million miles before production got under way.

The car went on the market in September, 1970, with two labels, Datsun 100A and Nissan Cherry. It was built as a two-door and four-door sedan with a fastback roofline, weighing 1,622 and 1,645 pounds respectively. Front/rear weight distribution was 62/38 percent. There was also a van and station wagon body.

Wheelbase was 92 inches and front and rear track 50 and 48.6 inches. Overall length was kept down to 142.2 inches. The 988-cc engine delivered 58 hp and the 1,171-cc unit 70 hp. Cars equipped with the former had a three-speed transmission and a 4.43:1 final drive ratio. The larger power unit was matched with a four-speed transmission and a 4.067:1 final drive ratio. Later, the four-speed was extended also to cars with the smaller engine and the final drive was altered to 4.266:1, which gave a road speed of 14.5 mph per 1,000 rpm.

Rack and pinion steering was used, geared at 3.25 turns lock to lock for a very tight turning circle of 31.3 feet. Front disc brakes were fitted on cars with the 1.2-liter engine while the baseline model had drum brakes on all four wheels.

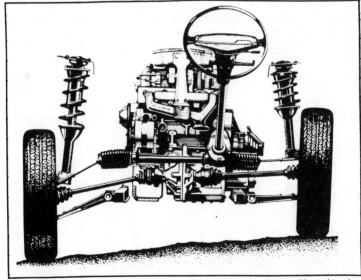

Nissan Cherry engine was centrally located with transmission positioned to give equal-length drive shafts. Suspension geometry was intended to keep wheels vertical (but permitted positive camber in roll).

Nissan Pulsar was introduced in the summer of 1978 as an upgrade companion model (and probably future replacement) to the Cherry. It is known as the Datsun 310 in the U.S.

A MacPherson-type front suspension was chosen with an A-frame lower control arm and spring legs inclined to give center-point steering (no scrub radius). The roll center was located 2.75 inches above ground level and with high spring rates of 101 pounds per inch, the car had enough roll stiffness in the front end to eliminate the need for a stabilizer bar.

At the rear end, trailing arms and coil springs gave independent suspension with even higher spring rates (121 pounds per inch) and a roll center at ground level. The result was a car with slight initial understeer and quite neutral handling except on sudden release of the accelerator while cornering, which caused a definite, but not violent, change of helm to a shorter turning radius.

F-11/Cherry Joined by Pulsar

The 4-speed 1-liter Cherry had a top speed of 87 mph and could reach 50 mph from standstill in 12 seconds. Fuel mileage in normal driving was 28-29 mpg. In 1974, Nissan redesigned the Cherry/100A/120A for improved safety, lower exhaust emissions, and greater fuel economy. Weight increased to 1,710 pounds and overall length grew to 150.8 inches. In some markets, including North America, the new models were sold as the Datsun F-11. In June, 1978, Nissan added the Pulsar series to its f-w-d model lineup. It was designed as a replacement for the Cherry but the two are being built side by side since they are not aimed at exactly the same market.

Mechanically, the two are very similar. The Pulsar could be described as a wide-track Cherry, with a 54-inch track in front and 52.75 in the rear. Pulsar engines were the 1.2-liter from the Cherry plus a more powerful (80 hp) 1.4-liter unit.

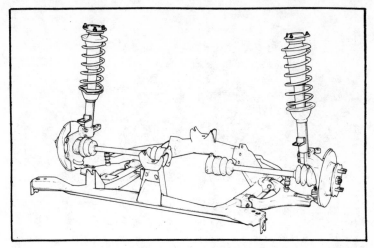

Pulsar front suspension has MacPherson spring legs mounted behind the front wheel axis and an absence of a stabilizer bar.

Now the question is whether Nissan will continue to increase the size of its f-w-d cars. In other words, whether the models that are next in size, Nissan Violet (Datsun 710) and Datsun Bluebird (810), will be replaced by f-w-d designs. If so (and it's likely), the door is open to introduce f-w-d replacements for the Skyline and Laurel, Cedric and Gloria.

Subaru Design from 1966

Until October, 1966, the car production of Fuji Heavy Industries consisted solely of minicars with two-stroke, rear-mounted

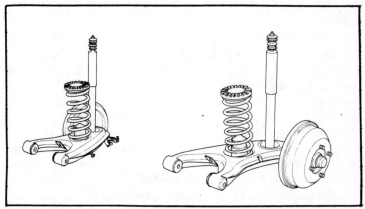

Rear suspension for the Pulsar has coil springs located halfway between wheel axis and trailing arm pivot shaft while shock absorbers stand vertically, further back.

Subaru FF-1 featured flat-four engine placed as front overhang and torsion bar all-independent suspension. Spare wheel was carried under the hood.

engines and rear wheel drive. Then the company launched the Subaru FE-type with f-w-d. In 1968, it was replaced by the FF-1 (known as Leone in some markets).

The FF-1 first appeared only as a two-door coupe with a 95.3-inch wheelbase and a curb weight of 1,532 pounds. A four-door sedan and station wagon soon followed. The engineers at Fuji Heavy Industries chose a flat-four engine positioned ahead of the front wheel axis, citing advantages for this layout in terms of vibration, cornering ability, stability, crashworthiness, safety for pedestrians, and greater design freedom for the rest of the car.

Design work had begun in 1961. Two problem areas were given top priority. One was the universal joints and the other was gradeability.

Birfield in England was consulted about the constant-velocity universal joints and the usual Birfield-Rzeppa type was chosen for the outer ends. For the inner joints, Birfield developed a new design known as a double-offset joint. It belongs in the Delta-type family and had special features to permit a wider downward angle than usual and additional freedom of axial travel without resorting to splines.

Gradeability problems centered on climbing hills with a full load in the car, a condition where the front wheels carry the lowest proportion of the gross vehicle weight. Testing on the steep slopes of Hakone and Rokko, in all types of weather and with surfaces including gravel, concrete and asphalt, provided information for a lot of mathematical work, which led to the conclusion that a front/rear weight distribution of 61/39 percent would be necessary to assure restarting gradeability in practical use.

Subaru DL coupe contained numerous refinements over FF-1 specifications but remained similar in overall layout.

With the entire engine carried as front overhang, a forward weight bias came naturally and the rest of the design fell in line to provide a static, unladen, weight distribution of 65.5/34.5 percent. With the driver alone aboard, the weight carried by the front wheels rose to 68 percent. With five occupants, it dropped to 60 percent. This was deemed satisfactory.

A-Arms and IRS for First Subaru

The first FE prototypes were built with a front suspension system consisting of upper and lower A-frame control arms, with

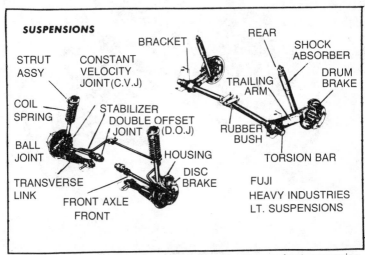

With the arrival of the DL, Subaru switched to MacPherson front suspension, added a front stabilizer bar, and went to outboard front disc brakes.

longitudinal torsion bars. This design was later discarded in favor of MacPherson-type front suspension, providing a higher roll center. At the rear end, an independent layout with trailing arms was drawn up. The arms were not purely trailing, however, for their pivot shafts were turned backwards (towards the center line of the car) so as to provide a measure of roll understeer.

The arms were connected to short torsion bars enclosed in tubes and ending short of the vehicle center line. Thus the bars did not cross or cause any Renault-type wheelbase difference between left and right sides.

All models had rack and pinion steering. The FF-1 had drum brake on all four wheels but the Leone introduced front disc brakes in 1972. Engine size started out as 1,088 cc and a 1.3-liter version was added in 1972 with a 1.6-liter becoming available in 1977. From 1976 onwards, Fuji Heavy Industries also offered a four-wheel-drive version of the same car.

Daihatsu Charade Is Three-Cylinder

Daihatsu Motor Company of Osaka has a long history of building minicars with rear-mounted, two-stroke engines and since the mid-1960s has also been producing small family cars with front engines

Lower control arms on Charade are extremely wide-based and suspension geometry arranged to give center-point steering.

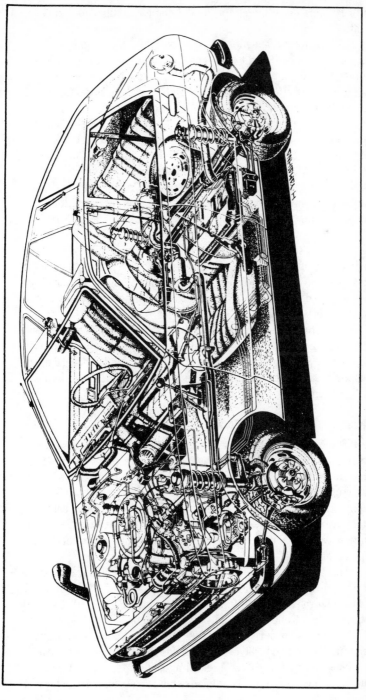

Daihatsu Charade has three-cylinder four-stroke transverse engine and all-coil suspension with a "dead" beam rear axle.

and rear axle drive under the model names Compagno and Charmant.

The company launches its first f-w-d car in November, 1977. It's called Charade, and it's unusual in having a three-cylinder, four-stroke engine. The power unit is mounted transversely, slightly offset to the right (just enough to get the differential on the vehicle center line).

The 993-cc engine delivers 55 hp at 5,500 rpm and the Charade gives buyers a choice of 4-speed and 5-speed transmissions, both with the same final drive ratio of 4.588:1. Both fourth and fifth are overdrives, 2.9 percent in fourth and 21.5 percent in fifth, which means that cars with four-speed transmission run 14 mph per 1,000 rpm in top gear compared with 17.2 mph for five-speed models. Top speed is claimed to be 88 mph and average fuel economy 35 mpg.

MacPherson front suspension was chosen for the Charade with a one-piece stamped lower control arm reaching far forward but having only a slight leading angle to the rear pivot point. Rear suspension is by a "dead" beam axle located by dual radius rods on each side and a track bar, with vertical coil spring legs enclosing the shock absorbers.

The Charade is equipped with rack and pinion steering and power brakes with discs on the front wheels. Built on a 90.55-inch wheelbase, it weighs from 1,390 to 1,455 pounds, according to equipment and trim level. Front/rear weight distribution is 55.5/44.5 percent.

Mitsubishi Mirage Has 8 Forward Gears

The latest Japanese newcomer to the ranks of f-w-d car manufacturers is Mitsubishi. Its Mirage was introduced in March, 1978. Since 1971 Mitsubishi Motors has been conducting market studies, planning and developing a small car in the Toyota Corolla/Datsun Sunny price class. In a complete break with its own technical traditions, the company rejected the conventional layout and chose front wheel drive with a transverse engine for its advantages of packaging, traction and handling stability.

The Mirage exists only as a two-door hatchback built on a 90.55-inch wheelbase with front and rear tracks of 53.9 and 52.75 inches. Overall length is 149.2 inches and curb weight 1,800 to 1,850 pounds with a front/rear weight distribution of 57.5/42.5 percent.

The engine is derived from the Mitsubishi Lancer series and is an in-line four with overhead camshaft and five-bearing crankshaft. It is offered in two sizes for the Mirage, 1,244 cc and 1,411 cc, delivering 55 and 68 hp. The engines stand up straight in the nose of the body shell and have no offset to left or right but are neatly centered.

By far the most intriguing aspect of its technical makeup is the drive line with its eight-speed transmission. The transmission is combined with the crankcase and is a unique four-speed design with integral overdrive, manually engaged and disengaged, for third and top gears. This has been obtained by having a dual connection from the input shaft to the countershaft, giving two different speed ranges. The driver chooses the range by a separate stick next to the floorshift lever—push forward for power, pull back for economy. The main shift lever operate selector forks on the output shaft which has five gears in constant mesh with gears on the countershaft and drives the differential unit via a helical-spur gear set. Mitsubishi calls it Super Shift. With the stick in its "power" position, there is a reduction of 1.526:1, while the "economy" position gives a reduction of 1.181:1.

MacPherson front suspension is used with a geometry that minimizes camber changes during wheel deflections. A stabilizer bar is attached to the drag struts. The static wheel alignment includes a negative scrub radius of 5 mm which is said to contribute to wet-road braking stability. Steering is by rack and pinion with an articulated steering column.

The Mirage has independent rear suspension with tubular trailing arms connected to a stabilizer bar and vertical coil springs to carry the load. The fuel tank is located in the space between the rear wheels for protection in a rear-end collision.

The brake system has a double master cylinder and twin circuits with disc brakes on the front and drums on the rear wheels. The parking brake acts on the rear wheel brakes. Standard tire size is 6.00-12 for cars with the 1.2-liter engine and 155SR-13 for cars with the larger power unit.

All current Mitsubishi cars are of a size where standardization on one basic theme can bring tremendous economies of scale and the introduction of the Mirage serves to hint that when standardization comes, it will be with an f-w-d layout instead of the Colt-Lancer type.

Toyota's Big Jump Forward

Only two Japanese manufacturers remain without an f-w-d car in the present lineup: Toyo Kogyo (Mazda) and Suzuki. Suzuki has considerable experience with f-w-d cars (as detailed in the historical review) and Toyo Kogyo had an f-w-d car in limited production in the late 1960s. There will be a new f-w-d Mazda production car by 1980.

Toyota went into production with its first f-w-d cars, Tercel and Corsa, in August, 1978. Development work began in November, 1973, and involved a complete car including a new engine. After investigation of all possible drive train configurations, the Toyota engineers opted for a longitudinal engine installation. The power unit stands vertically on the car's center line with the rear end of the block coinciding with the front wheel axis so that the engine is in fact carried as front overhang.

The clutch faces the flywheel and carries a short output shaft with gear drive to a two-shaft gearbox laid on its side below and behind the bell-housing. Two types are available, a four-speed and a five-speed, both with full synchromesh. The output shaft doubles as the final drive pinion shaft with a differential located ahead of and below the front wheel centers, forcing the drive shafts to run permanently pointing upwards and backwards to the wheel hubs, like the wings of a light airplane. Constant-velocity inner and outer joints have no difficulty in accepting this angularity, however.

Front suspension is of the MacPherson type with spring legs mounted on the drive shaft line and tilted to give a slight positive scrub radius. There is a single lateral control arm on each side with compression struts to form the necessary triangulation. Front wheel geometry is designed for minimal camber variations during wheel deflection. Steering is by rack and pinion. Independent rear suspension was chosen, the design using semi-trailing arms with coil springs mounted vertically inboard and ahead of the shock absorber mounting which is as close to the wheel hub as possible. The control arm pivot axis is almost transverse which assures minimal camber changes during spring deflection.

The engine location poses no problem in terms of either weight distribution or hood length for it is a lightweight construction with an aluminum cylinder head and weighs just 224 pounds and is only 22 inches long. Toyota's reasons for using this configuration (instead of a transverse engine, for instance) are found in considerations of accessibility, vibrations and torque reactions, and gearshift inkage precision.

Overhead camshaft drive via cogged belt is a first for Toyota on the Tercel and Corsa engine which has 1,452 cc displacement and puts out 80 hp at 5,600 rpm. That's enough to give the cars a top speed just over 100 mph with final drive ratios of 3.583:1 or 3.727:1 (available with either gearbox).

The Tercel and Corsa are sister series that differ only in frontal appearance and interior equipment. Both are offered in three body styles, two-door sedan, four-door sedan, and two-door hatchback coupe. Exterior dimensions are similar to those of the Corolla, but with its longer wheelbase of 98.5 inches, the Tercel/Corsa series has better interior space.

The f-w-d models will be restricted to the home market for the first year's production and Tercel exports are planned to begin in 1980. Toyota is scheduling output of 85,000 Tercel and 60,000 Corsa in 1979—fairly low volume by Toyota's mass-production standards. If the arrival of the Tercel and Corsa signals the start of a large-scale switch to f-w-d at Toyota, it is clear that the company is not forcing the pace but intends to act slowly and deliberately with all due consideration of public preference and free market forces.

Chapter 16
Birth of a Technology

Front wheel drive is as old as the car itself. The first motor vehicle, Cugnot's "Fardier" steam tractor of 1769, had front wheel drive. This machine was a three-wheeler with a single front wheel. An enormous steam boiler overhung the wheel with two vertical cylinders standing ahead of the wheel center. Connecting rods from the pistons drove the wheel via a ratchet arrangement.

Nicholas Joseph Cugnot was a military engineer from Lorraine who intended his vehicle as a prime mover to haul heavy cannon. Nowadays such a machine would have three or more axles and all-wheel-drive. Cugnot probably understood the need to weight down the driving wheel to assure traction and the heavy steam boiler provided a considerable load. But it was attached so that it also had to turn with the wheel. The wheel had a 50.5-inch diameter and the Fardier's wheelbase was 121 inches. To steer, the driver turned a handlebar on top of a vertical shaft with a rack and pinion gear at the bottom. The vehicle ended its active life by running into a stone wall during a test drive in Paris. Cugnot might have been more successful if he had also invented power steering!

Selden and Porsche Firsts Were FWD

It is remarkable that the man who built the first of all self-propelled road vehicles as well as the man who sought to hold a monopoly on the right to make automobiles chose *front wheel drive*.

The latter was a patent lawyer from Rochester, N.Y. named George Baldwin Selden. His patent drawing from 1879 shows a

Model of Cugnot's Fardier shows steam boiler and cylinders with drive to single front wheel.

three-cylinder horizontal gas engine mounted transversely on the front axle, which was pivoted on its center. By clever manipulation he delayed the granting of the patent until 1895 and then began issuing licenses to the companies that made up America's fledgling auto industry, against payment of royalties. Ford was the first to fight the Selden patent, beginning 1903, but it took until 1911 for a district court of appeals to settle the case with a verdict against Selden.

Strangely, the f-w-d aspect of Selden's patent played no part in the litigation. That's perhaps not the most surprising fact in f-w-d pre-history, however. None can be more surprised than Porsche owners and enthusiasts of the rear-engined cars from Stuttgart-Zuffenhausen to learn that Dr. Porsche's first cars had front wheel drive! The 1899 Lohner-Porsche was driven by electric motors mounted in the front wheel hubs.

In the works of the pioneers of car-making we are treated to surprises in abundance. A striking example is the fact that before the turn of the century, two groups of pioneers (who had no idea that the other existed) each produced f-w-d cars with transverse engines and advanced suspension systems: Graf in Austria and Latil in France. These are really the forerunners of the modern f-w-d automobile. Along the way, brilliant engineers such as Robert Schwenke, John Christie and others less famous took steps that remain milestones of progress. It's also important to realize that many of the early f-w-d vehicles built around the world did nothing to advance the state of the art.

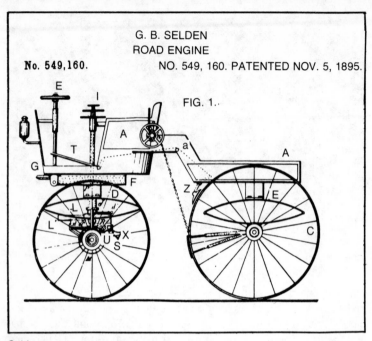

G. B. SELDEN
ROAD ENGINE

No. 549,160.

NO. 549, 160. PATENTED NOV. 5, 1895.

FIG. 1.

Selden patent drawing shows fore-carriage vehicle with horizontal, three-cylinder, transverse engine.

Single-Wheelers and Electrics Had Roles

Vehicles with a single (driving) front wheel can be dismissed as creations of engineering convenience—a refusal to face the technical complications of driving two front wheels. Vehicles with front bogies or fore-carriages that turned as a unit fall into the same category. The fore-carriage axle had fixed hubs without kingpins. It was connected to the vehicle by a "fifth wheel" arrangement inherited from horse-drawn semi-trailer attachments. They came into being as a logical way to motorize existing horse-drawn carriages and were of great commercial significance for many years. But such designs involved installation packages that were seen as unacceptable when the car became a mass-produced article.

Far from lacking merit were the electric and hybrid-electric f-w-d vehicles of the industry's formative stages. They have been kept alive in specialized transport equipment (and may come into use on future cars) but disappeared from the mainstream of the technical evolution of the popular f-w-d passenger car.

There have been f-w-d cars with chain drive to the wheels. There have been f-w-d cars with live axles and other dead-end proposals. The fact is that all modern f-w-d cars have independent

256

front suspension and this review has the creation and development of this type of f-w-d car as its primary focus.

Front-wheel Electrics

For the record, a brief discussion of defunct f-w-d systems is in order to discourage and prevent misunderstandings about the origins of things. For instance, Porsche was not the first to use electric motors attached to the wheels. It was the invention of Louis Krieger who designed an electric vehicle with f-w-d on the fore-carriage principle in 1894 and got a patent for it in 1895. He built a number of prototype vehicles with battery-electric power from 1895 to 1900 and then started production at Courbevoie near Paris. Krieger fore-carriages were built under license by Namag in Bremen and Krieger Italina in Torino up to 1907. His business failed in 1908. We last hear of Krieger working for Peugeot in 1926 on the design of an electric taxicab.

But Porsche was the first to integrate the motors with the wheel hub. In the Krieger system, the motor was mounted on the axle, adjacent to the wheel hub, and driving an external ring gear on the hub from a small pinion to provide the desired reduction gearing.

Porsche used larger-diameter armatures and did not need gearing. The motors were mounted outboard to make room for kingpins

German-made Namag fore-carriage (Krieger license) from 1907 had motor next to hub and single spur-gear reduction.

257

in a conventional arrangement. Instead of battery power, Porsche used a gasoline engine to run an electric generator which fed current to the motors. Lohner-Porsche cars using this drive system were in production from 1899 to 1905. The following year Jacob Lohner sold the patents to Austro-Daimler who then built a little-known car, the Mercedes-Electrique (but it was not an f-w-d car, for the motors were placed in the rear wheel hubs).

Charles Jeantaud had built his first battery-electric car in Paris in 1881. Having seen the Lohner-Porsche, he produced several battery-electric f-w-d cars with hub-mounted motors from 1900 to 1906 (his company died when he committed suicide that year).

J.J. Heilman patented his "motor bogie" in 1899. He was a railroad engineer who applied an electrical drive system to a road-vehicle fore-carriage. It was built in considerable numbers. A similar design, the Solignac electric fore-carriage, based on an 1898 patent, was used for a Paris taxi fleet. Cantono Avantreni S.A. in Rome built electrical vehicles of the same type from 1904 to 1906.

European Use of Fore-Carriage Idea

As we have seen, Selden's idea was to have a gas engine drive the fore-carriage axle by mechanical means. His design included a clutch and a reduction gear but no provision for stepped gearing. More practical executions based on the same idea came into extensive use in Europe where the leading fore-carriage was the Kuhlstein-Vollmer, manufactured by the Kuhlstein Wagenbau-Gesellschaft in Berlin-Charlottenburg to designs by Joseph Vollmer.

Vollmer was an engineer from Baden-Baden who had formerly designed the Orient Express for Theodor Bergmann's Industrie-Werke Gaggenau. The Kuhlstein-Vollmer fore-carriage had a frame, semi-ellipitic leaf springs and carried its gasoline engine as sprung weight. The axle had a differential and the drive chain used a complicated system of automatic tensioning. The German Post Office became an important customer, converting many of its horse-drawn delivery vans to fore-carriage trucks. The Auto Fore Carriage Company was formed in New York City in 1900 to exploit the Vollmer patents but did not succeed.

No better fortune befell the Tractomobile built from 1900 to 1902 by the Pennsylvania Steam Vehicle Co. of Carlisle. Another steam-powered fore-carriage was designed in France by Turgan & Foy in 1899 but it is doubtful that a prototype was completed. But the gasoline-powered fore-carriage was common in France. The first patent was taken out in 1896 by an engineer named Drapson who built several different versions up to about 1900.

One of the best known was the two-cylinder Riancey from Levallois-Perret, built in considerable numbers from 1898 onwards, followed by the Pretot, Gevin, Gauthier-Wehrle and the impressive design of the Compagnie Francaise des Ponts Moteurs of Levallois whose design included a V-twin air-cooled engine, brakes, and wide-section solid rubber tires. In Britain, large numbers of Lawson Motor Wheel fore-carriages were produced by Dougill & Co. of Leeds.

Long Life for Single Front Wheel

About 1905 the limitations of horse-drawn vehicles and motorized fore-carriages made it apparent that this form of construction was nothing but a blind alley and it quietly disappeared from the market. F-w-d cars with a single front wheel lived on a little longer.

Though restricted to very compact and lightweight engines, this form of construction was alive well into the 1930s. I remember riding in a Framo van built about 1937 that had a motorcycle engine suspended on the front wheel fork and driving it via chain. This design was directly related to the principle behind Cugnot's Fardier and it made sense for certain types of vehicles.

The first was the Cyklon designed by the German engineer Franz Huttel from Erlau in Saxony. He first tried this f-w-d principle on a motorcycle he built in 1900. A small air-cooled single-cylinder engine rode on top of the front wheel, and a belt drive turned the wheel. This motorcycle was produced from 1902 to 1904. It was in 1902 that Huttel built his first Cyklonette three-wheeler with the same system. The Cyklonette went into production in 1904 with a 3½-horsepower 450 cc engine. The first model had the same primitive belt drive used on the motorcycle but Huttel later developed a two-speed belt drive for the Cyklonette.

When Cyklon entered a cartel with Gustav Hiller's Phanomen-Werke of Zittau in Saxony in 1907, the Cyklonette design evolved into a Phanomobil, whose specifications showed somewhat more ambitious engineering. The 1908 Phanomobil had an air-cooled V-twin 880 cc engine of 7-8 horsepower with a two-speed-and-reverse planetary transmission and chain drive to the single front wheel. By 1912 the phanomobil received a four-cylinder 1,536 cc engine of 12 horsepower, still carried in the traditional position above the front wheel. It remained in production until about 1920.

In France, the same ideas were realized by Denis de Boisse who in 1902 commissioned Panhard & Levassor to build a three-

Single front wheel carrying single-cylinder engine was used for Cyklon three-wheelers from 1903 to 1922. This is a 1907 model.

wheeled front wheel drive car with a single front wheel. The engine was a small air-cooled unit carried above the wheel. Apparently only one was built for the personal use of Denis de Boisse.

Many years later, in the Twenties, Villard revived the idea for a light van. A number of Villard vans were built for the Felix Potin restaurant chain and became a familiar sight on the streets of Paris. The last model appeared in 1931 with a 500 cc Chaise narrow-angle V-4 engine made under Lancia license. Similar vehicles were built in Paris by Etablissements Caffort from 1923 to 1927 and by Automobiles Regina from 1920 to 1923. The Framo from Hainichen in Saxony was the last survivor of this school.

FWD—Thanks to de Dion Axle

The advent of scientifically designed, two-wheel, f-w-d systems was moved into the realm of reality by an invention which was originally intended for rear-wheel-drive steam vehicles: the de Dion axle. Though it is believed to have been the idea of a third-ranking partner in the business, M. Trepardoux, it was patented in 1894 by Count Albert de Dion and his chief engineer, Georges-Thadee Bouton. In this design, the driving wheels were united by a tube which kept them both constantly upright on the road and at a constant track. The drive shafts were open, separate from the tube, and fitted with inner and outer universal joints (inner joints next to the final drive housing, and outer joints next to the wheel hubs) to allow uninterrupted drive during spring deflections. The final drive unit was bolted to the frame. This relieved the axle shafts, wheel hubs and spokes of driving stresses and the axle shafts had no locating duties. The de Dion tube was attached to leaf springs which located tube and wheels both laterally and longitudinally.

Why was the de Dion axle so attractive to f-w-d pioneers? Because it separated the axle suspension from the drive train in a manner that did not necessitate new inventions to provide proper steering geometry or mechanisms. It made possible the realization of f-w-d layouts existing in the minds of people like Carl Graf, Georges Latil, and Robert Schwenke.

What Carl Graf and his associates did was to move the de Dion design up front and turn it around. A single-cylinder 3½ hp de Dion-Bouton engine was placed vertically in the nose of the car, offset to the left. The crank-shaft ran in the transverse plane. The 3-speed gearbox was offset to the right and the final drive was

First of the "modern" f-w-d cars was this Viennese vehicle built between 1897 and 1899 by Carl Graf and associates. It had a single-cylinder engine mounted transversely and a de Dion axle.

located on the chassis center line to give equal-length drive shafts. The outer joints were combined with the kingpins and both outer and inner joints were of the straight-forward Cardan type.

Graf and Letil Designs Unproductive

Carl Graf was born in Vienna in 1871 and educated as a technician. He had made several automotive inventions before building his first car, such as a carburetor with variable air admission and pre-heating of the fresh air, a motor brake, a four-speed gearbox, and a beltless fan drive.

He began design work on his front wheel drive car in 1895 and engaged an engineer named Kainz to take charge of detail design. He also hired a young engineering student named Hans Ledwinka to assist in both drafting and construction. Ledwinka went on to a most distinguished carreer with Tatra. But the car was never developed and never reached production. In 1902, when Graf & Stift started to build cars in series, they had rear wheel drive.

Auguste Georges Latil and his partner, Alois Korn, were working on a similar approach. Latil was born in Marseille in 1878 as the son of a lawyer who liked to tinker with mechanical things and learned to handle tools and macinery in his father's hobby shop.

In 1895 Korn and Latil showed their plans to a rich industrialist, Charles Blum, and got the funds to go ahead and build their f-w-d car. The first test vehicle was ready in 1899. It is impossible to know which came first, the axle or the engine. Most likely, Latil chose the single-cylinder de Dion engine because of the de Dion tube, rather than discovering the tube as a result of buying the engine. The engine was mounted transversely at the extreme front end, offset to the right, with belt drive to the differential. Twin belts provided two ratios so there was no gearbox. The drive shafts had Cardan joints at both ends. The de Dion tube ran behind the shafts and was held to the chassis by semi-elliptic springs.

The following year Latil built a truck with a similar power train, using a two-cylinder engine. Being more interested in freight-carrying vehicles than in touring cars, Latit drifted away from f-w-d principles when getting into heavier and heavier equipment. He became one of France's leading proponents of all-wheel drive trucks and the Latil company lived on until 1956 when it was swallowed up in a Renault-dominated merger.

Important Schwenke and Christie Designs

Latil's ideas, along with those of Graf, had been noticed by Robert Schwenke, the former chief engineer of the Watt

Akkumulator-Werke in Berlin and the designer of an electrically powered f-w-d car for the firm of N. Israel, also in Berlin. Schwenke began taking out f-w-d patents in 1902. In 1905 he made a complete car with an air-cooled V-4 engine installed transversely behind the front wheel axis. It had a belt-drive transmission giving two forward speeds. A de Dion tube connected the front wheels ahead of the drive shafts. But Schwenke failed to get auto manufacturers interested in building his car and he returned to electrical work, becoming chief engineer of the Siemens-Schuckert works in Berlin.

Even more advanced than the Schwenke prototype was a car built in the U.S. in 1904, the Christie. John Walter Christie of New York was perhaps the most scientific of all f-w-d pioneers. A 35-year-old naval engineer when he became interested in cars about 1902, he worked alone and broke new ground in f-w-d technology. His 1904 prototype had a four-cylinder engine mounted transversely with independent front suspension on the sliding pillar principle.

This principle was first used by Ing. Cornilleau on the 1899 Decauville. The wheel hub was free to move up and down on the kingpin and a vertical coil spring controlled deflections. Christie's ultra-short drive shafts, of course, had inner and outer universal joints.

Christie built a second car in 1905 on identical principles but with a more powerful four-cylinder engine. With this car he covered the flying mile in 40 seconds! The following year he built another car, still bigger and more powerful. It reached 102.08 mph. The fourth Christie was a scaled-down version of the third one but it had a real passenger car body whereas the first three had been racing cars. His fifth car built in 1907 was another racer. The engine was an enorm-

John Walter Christie at the wheel of his 1904 f-w-d racer. Transverse V-4 is mounted on front wheel axis.

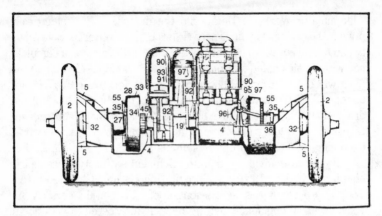

Christie patent drawings from 1904 show vertical transverse four. Drive shafts are two-jointed and front wheels have independent suspension with sliding pillars and coil springs.

ous V-4 tilted backwards in the chassis with the crankcase and drive gear at the forward end. A Christie taxicab followed in 1908, using a relatively small 18-hp engine. The seventh and last Christie was a huge 135-hp V-4 racing car.

About 1910 Christie was working full time on military vehicles and thus disappears from the f-w-d annals. But as we shall see later, his example led directly to the creation of other American f-w-d cars that were to have great influence on the trends of things to come. Christie may even have inspired the construction of an obscure English prototype of 1911 called the F.D.

Like the Christie, it had a four-cylinder in-line engine set across the chassis between the front wheels. The gearbox was mounted directly below with chain drive from the engine flywheel to a sprocket wheel on the gearbox main shaft. Spur gears took the drive to the centrally located final drive unit and the open shafts on either side. The wheel nuts were located by leaf springs without the benefit of a de Dion tube to keep them in a proper relationship. This may have been the cause of the F.D.'s failure.

Despite the state of the art having been pushed a long way forward by this time, front wheel drive cars were not to be produced for sale for many years. George Iden, operating as the Iden Motor Car Company, Ltd. in Fleet Street,Parkside, Coventry, built several front wheel drive cars between 1904 and 1907, but this business was closed when Iden was engaged to succeed J.S. Critchley as chief engineer of Crossley in 1907.

Emile Pilain in Lyon experimented with f-w-d in 1913. Pilain was a reputable manufacturer who would have known how to make a quality car with f-w-d but the outbreak of the war in 1914 put an end to his development work.

An experimental high-grade f-w-d vehicle was built about 1912/13 by Joseph Laviolette, famous for engineering the Spijker and Omnia cars. It never reached production but the prototype was sold and placed in service. The exact technical specification is not known but Laviolette was a true innovator (he designed the 1903 four-wheel-drive Spikjer) and the front wheel drive experiment must have been spectacular if it showed anything near ten years' advance on the Spijker.

Air-cooled V-4 mounted transversely with belt drive forms a unique combination. It's Robert Schwenke's 1906 prototype.

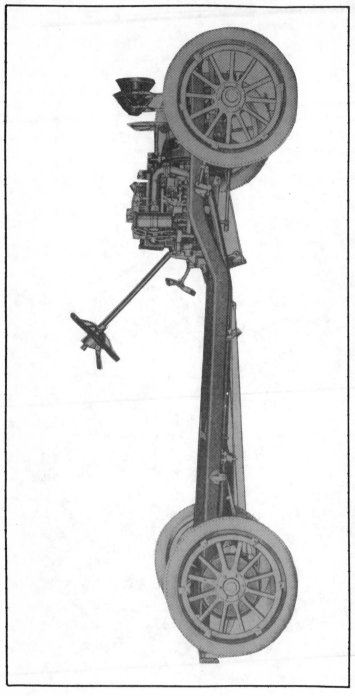

Side view of Frontmobile chassis shows Blomstrom's awareness of opportunity to lower the frame and hence the floor of the passenger compartment.

Charles Blomstrom's Frontmobile had a worm-drive differential and a de Dion front axle carried on leaf springs.

U.S. Failures Matched Europe's

Some unsuccessful examples from the U.S. include the Frontmobile, Homer-Laughlin, and Hamlin-Holmes. In 1916, the experimental car called Homer-Laughlin appeared in Los Angeles, California. It had a 25 hp V-8 engine and a most unusual drive train with chain cases to each front wheel (not unlike the rear drive chain cases on the 1964 Honda S-600). A jackshaft running transversely in back of the engine drove chain sprockets with chains taking the drive to larger sprockets on the front stub axles. The chain cases were located outboard of the semi-elliptic springs. The short stub axles had universal joints to keep the chains aligned regardless of steering angles. The project was abandoned after two years of trials and evaluation.

Charles H. Blomstrom had earlier built f-w-d prototypes in California and Michigan but the first production model of his creation was the Frontmobile, built in the 1917-20 period by the Bateman Manufacturing Co. at Grenloch, New Jersey, makers of a line of farm equipment. Frontmobile used a four-cylinder LeRoi engine installed longitudinally in the chassis well inside the wheelbase with worm drive to the transversely mounted 3-speed transaxle. Short drive shafts with simple Cardan joints at each end turned the front wheels connected by a de Dion tube.

An industrialist named Trinckle financed the f-w-d experiments of two engineers named Hamlin and Holmes working in a small shop in Harvey, Illinois, in 1918. About seven different experimental cars were completed between 1923 and 1926 but the Hamlin-Holmes never reached production.

Chapter 17
From Laboratory to Mass Production

During the decade and a half from 1920 to 1935 f-w-d progressed from the laboratory stage and reached the assembly line. Still, only a few brave manufacturers had the courage to invest in mass-production tooling for cars that were so completely different. The first mass-producers were French and German but the American influence that led to their adoption of f-w-d is astonishing in its strength and pervasiveness. As a matter of fact, it all goes back to Christie.

Great American Gregory-Miller Contribution

Ben F. Gregory began to experiment with front wheel drive in Kansas City in 1918. He had been a racing driver and had actually driven a Christie at Cleveland in 1913. During his military service, he managed to be assigned to Christie's tank and track-laying vehicle establishment in New York. Greogory became well acquainted with the inventor and earned a unique background in front wheel drive engineering. Gregory built his first front wheel drive car in 1919 using a 4-cylinder Saxon engine.

He patented his suspension design which used an upper and a lower transverse leaf spring to give fully independent suspension. The next year he built a racing car using a Curtiss OX-5 aircraft engine and a de Dion type suspension system. He was granted a patent for the front end design in 1921. Gregory then built a racing car with a 180-hp Hispano-Suiza aircraft engine—a combination for which he claimed a top speed of 143 mph. After this experience, he went into production with front-wheel drive touring cars in 1922. Sadly, Gregory can out of money before many had been completed and—happily—sold his front wheel drive patents to Harry Miller in 1923.

Normally, that would have been the last of Ben F. Gregory's work on front wheel drive. But he was no ordinary man. As late as 1947, now aging and possibly senile, he designed a small front wheel drive car with a *rear-mounted* air-cooled 4-cylinder 40-hp engine driving the front wheels via a torque tube. The design was taken over by Hoppenstand Motors of Greenville, Pennsylvania, who tried to make it work but finally scrapped the design in 1949.

Only one other f-w-d car with rear-mounted engine has come to my attention. It was built in 1932 by Harleigh Holmes and was a very low-built sedan with a Pontiac V-8 engine positioned immediately above the rear axle. It was not the first Holmes prototype. He had invented a steerable driving axle as early as 1919 and started a company to produce it for converting trucks to four wheel drive. This business was taken over by Coleman Motors in 1922 and George L. Coleman backed Holmes in constructing f-w-d racing cars cars and passenger cars for a number of years. In 1929 Holmes built some hill-climb specials for Pikes Peak with front-mounted Graham-Paige engines and f-w-d. But he used his live axle design and the cars did not have independent front suspension.

Racer Jimmy Murphy Inspired Miller Feats

That was a digression. Miller was to represent the mainstream of f-w-d developments and relied, it is true, more on Gregory's work than on Christie's. Harry Miller, whose work did more to advance the theory of front wheel drive than anybody else, originally had no ambition to build f-w-d racing cars. The whole thing was Jimmy Murphy's idea. Murphy was a leading racing driver, famous for winning the French Grand Prix at Le Mans in 1921 with a Duesenberg. Murphy's mechanic, Riley Brett, was an old Christie fan, who convinced Murphy of the advantages of "pulling a car around the turns instead of pushing it".

One day in 1923 Murphy placed an order for a front wheel drive car with Miller who was then even more famous than Duesenberg as a racing car constructor. Miller had long been a successful manufacturer of carburetors; then began to build racing engines; and, finally, complete cars. Murphy's order led to Miller's purchase of the Gregory patents. Then he built a car with a straight-eight Miller engine driving the front wheels via a de Dion axle. It was raced in 1925—and it was successful.

For the drive line, Miller began to take out f-w-d patents himself. He wanted the transmission to be as light and compact as possible thereby allowing the engine to be mounted further forward in the chassis. This kept overall length down while also placing more weight on the driving wheels.

Miller designed a transverse gearbox built into the side of the final drive casing. Dimensions were quite modest and weight was low but running the mainshaft coaxially with the differential ring gear meant slowing down the rotational speeds of the gearbox pinions. This increased the torque on the gears, reducing gear life and making gear-shifting difficult. This "drive mechanism" was patented in 1927, the same year that the Detroit Special appeared using a Miller engine but its own two-speed gearbox aligned with the crankshaft.

This front-wheel-drive car was built for Cliff Durant in the Hyatt bearing laboratory in the basement of the General Motors building in Detroit to designs by Tommy Milton and C. W. Van Ranst, both of whom were to be connected with later front-wheel-drive projects. Miller, at the same time, was encouraged by the success of his front-wheel-drive cars and built an important number of them between 1926 and 1931.

Rzeppa Joints Solution and Imitators Flocked

The de Dion tube on the Miller ran in front of the drive shafts which had Cardan-type inner and outer joints. With an engine that delivered 200 hp at 7,800 rpm, these joints gave a lot of trouble. Then Alfred H. Rzeppa invented a ball-type constant-velocity universal joint. The Rzeppa joints were heavy and bulky but Miller found they did not break. Miller mounted the brake drums inboard, that is, on the drive shafts, close to the final drive casing, so as to avoid interference between brakes and steering and drive train parts near the wheels. The de Dion tube was located by two quarter-elliptic leaf springs extending forward from the frame.

Without the racing career of the front-wheel-drive Miller, it is probable that the American automobile industry would never have been attracted to the idea of introducing sporty-looking, low-slung expensive front wheel drive models. But several did, notably Cord, Ruxton and Gardner. And though it is not commonly known that Oldsmobile, Packard and Chrysler thought seriously about it, these makers actually constructed experimental front-wheel-drive cars—but discarded them before they came anywhere near the production stage.

F-w-d Millers won many races at Indianapolis. This is the 1930 winner. De Dion axle runs in front of final drive unit and brake drums are carried inboard. Indianapolis Motor Speedway Official Photo.

Miller-Fords and the Way to Cord

Harry Miller's involvement with front wheel drive did not end in 1927. About 1932 he built a small number of road cars with the same drive train configuration as the racing car. He went bankrupt in 1933 but was back building cars again in 1935, this time in connection with Ford. He used Ford V-8 engines and Ford parts wherever possible but retained the Miller front wheel drive design with the transverse gearbox. On the other hand, he discarded the de Dion suspension in favor of a fully independent system with transverse leaf springs and parallel control arms. The Miller-Fords were a failure, imputable to lack of testing and development work, and Miller never built another front wheel drive vehicle.

Miller had been connected with the Cord as a consultant and the original prototype was built in his shops in California. The Cord L-29 was introduced in August, 1930, and production was suspended in 1932 after about 4,000 cars had been completed. The chief engineer for the L-29 was Cornelius W. Van Ranst, who had produced the Detroit Special, an experienced racing car designer formerly associated with the Chevrolet brothers. He had engineered the Frontenac, Monroe and Cornelian cars for Chevrolet. He came to Cord via Duesenberg, another division of the group of companies owned by self-made millionaire Errett Lobban Cord.

The L-29 followed Miller practice in using a de Dion axle but used Auburn parts wherever possible to keep manufacturing costs down. The engine was a straight-eight 125-hp 4.8-liter Lycoming unit (Lycoming was also part of Cord's empire). The transmission was a stock item made by Detroit Gear, a conventional gearbox laid on its side, interposed between the engine and the hypoid final drive.

The inner joints were of the simple Cardan type and the outer joints were a special constant-velocity type patented and manufactured by Auburn. The design looks like two Cardan joints mounted back to back with a center bearing. Inner joints were recessed into the brake drums. These joints allowed sufficient steering angles to make a 42-foot turning circle with a car that was built on a 137½-inch wheelbase. The front brake drums were mounted inboard as on the Miller. Front springs were quarter-elliptics, two on each side, coming forward from the frame. The front ends of the springs were anchored to a bracket attached to the de Dion tube and the ends of the tube were forked to accommodate steering swivels. The steering gear was positioned alongside the engine with drop arm and drag link connected to a steering arm running below the outer universal joint.

Cord L-29 helped build f-w-d fame in America. The L-29 was powered by a Lycoming straight-eight mounted within the wheelbase.

Budd Experimental Led to Ruxton

The Ruxton was Cord's contemporary but failed to reach anything like the same sales figures. Only about 500 were completed. The Ruxton stemmed from a Budd experimental job dating back to 1926. This famous maker of steel bodies was almost alone among supplier firms to the auto makers to get involved with the whole vehicle and actually initiate new-car projects. Some of the most important Budd cars have been front-wheel-drive models.

The 1926 Budd prototype that led to the Ruxton has a small Studebaker Six engine and the same Detroit Gear transmission that Cord used. The suspension system was of the de Dion type. Inner universal joints were of a new constant-velocity design patented by Carl W. Weiss of Brooklyn, New York. The engineering design was the work of William J. Muller, who had built racing cars for Ralph Mulford about 1915. He came to Budd late in 1921 after a year or two with Willys. Budd sold the front-wheel-drive package to Archie Andrews of New Era Motors and Muller redesigned the car for production. New Era Motors' production facilities included the plants of Moon in St. Louis, Missouri, and Kissel in Hartford, Wisconsin.

The production-model Ruxton had Spicer's dual-Cardan constant-velocity outer joints. They were far heavier than the Weiss joints on the prototype but also more durable. Muller also revised the transmission layout to improve weight distribution. He split the gearbox in two, moved most of the gears ahead of the final drive and inserted a worm gear in the middle to drive the differential ring gear. This enabled Muller to move the Ruxton's straight-eight Continental engine forward. Production began at the Kissel factory in 1930 but after the first 25 cars, Ruxton assembly was moved to Moon. Ruxton production was suspended in 1930, when New Era Motors fell too deep in legal trouble in St. Louis, merged with Moon in 1930, and Russell R. Gardner was offered the Ruxton design.

His chief engineer, E. A. Webber, went to work on it and reverted to a six-cylinder engine as in the Budd prototype and dispensed with Muller's split gearbox. The de Dion tube was attached to semi-elliptic leaf springs. The engine gave only 80 hp and the universal joints appeared to stand up well. But the f-w-d Gardner never went on sale, for the company collapsed before production could get under way.

After the failure of New Era Motors, Archie Andrews tried to sell the Ruxton design to Hupmobile. An experimental car with Ruxton drive train components was actually built in 1935 with sleek modern coachwork by Raymond Loewy. But that car never made it to the assembly line.

Abortive Oldsmobile, Packard, Chrysler Projects

A tradition at General Motors developed under Alfred P. Sloan's leadership that nothing must go by without some of its engineers making a study of it. Front wheel drive was no exception. The study was assigned to Oldsmobile and chief engineer Charles L. McCuen assigned a group of assistants to put together an experimental front wheel drive car in 1931. It had a Viking V-8 engine with a gearbox interposed between the engine and the final drive. Oldsmobile rejected it after a brief series of tests because of poor traction.

Packard's f-w-d project began in 1929 when chief engineer Jesse G. Vincent was preparing a new V-12 engine for production. This power plant delivered 175 hp and was to give the car a top speed above 100 mph. Vincent was a highly intelligent man and an engineer of wide experience but he did not want to jump into f-w-d without expert assistance. Therefore, he contracted with C. W. Van Ranst and Tommy Milton to have them prepare the design and take charge of its development.

The prototype built in 1931 had a two-speed transmission and a double-reduction final drive, so that a four-step gearing combination was possible. Because of the tremendous torque, there were double sets of pinion and ring gears and a twin-plate clutch. Packard's experimental department built the chassis and had it outfitted with an elegant four-door sedan body designed by Alexis de Sakhoffsky. It ran well but any hope of production was killed when Packard had to cut back its spending plans in order to survive.

Carl Breer, who had joined Walter P. Chrysler in 1923 after working with Studebaker, Acme Electrical Auto Works, Moreland Truck Company and Allis-Chalmers, had been toying with plans for a small car for some time. In 1935 he completed his designs and Chrysler built a front-wheel-drive prototype with streamlined body work and a five-cylinder air-cooled radial engine!

European Developments Led by Tracta

Wonderfully interesting as these American experimental cars were, it was nonetheless on the European continent that front wheel drive first enjoyed true commercial success. About 1920, Nemorin Causan, famous designer of Clement-Bayard, Gregoire, Delage, Bignan and La Licorne racing cars, patented a new type of universal joint giving uniform rotation velocity at all angles.

Tracta sports convertible from 1934 used Tracta joints and never had drive train failures. Engine was mounted within the wheelbase.

Another inventor was Rene Retel, brother of Jean Retel, then manager of Chenard-Walcker. Retel was the first to place two Cardan joints back to back on an f-w-d car so as to obtain true constant-velocity action, and he was granted two patents in 1922. Retel built an electric van called AEM in 1924 and this was the first vehicular application of the new joints. But the AEM never got into series production.

About the same time Pierre Fenaille patented a novel form of constant-velocity universal joint called Tracta. The drive shafts had forked ends, each straddling a central ball. One ball carried a key; the other had a slot. The key-and-slot ran in a perpendicular plane to that of the forks. The Tracta joint had large contact surfaces, no lubrication problems, proved to wear well, and manufacturing costs were low. Pierre Fenaille and his partner, J.A. Gregoire decided to make a front-wheel-drive Tracta car to promote the Tracta joint.

The first Tracta car ran in the summer of 1926. It was a light sports two-seater with a SCAP engine and Cozette supercharger. Lancia-type sliding pillar front suspension was used, with coil springs on the kingpins, and steering gear from de Dion-Bouton. The inner joints were Cardan-type (made by Spicer); only the outer ones were Tracta. The brake drums were mounted inboard. Several hundred Tracta cars were made between 1927 and 1932. Racing successes led to increased power, going from the 1100 cc SCAP via a 1600 cc SCAP and a six-cylinder Continental unit to a 3-liter Hotchkiss engine. A Tracta copy called Astra appeared in Belgium in 1929. Financed by Albert Dewandre, it was built in small numbers by De Mey, Coene, Delfosse and Dimon at Herstal near Liege.

Jean-Albert Gregoire was called in as consultant to Jerome Donnet when he and Leonel Mallard were designing a front wheel drive car in 1932. The six-cylinder 11 CV Donnet prototype appeared in 1933 with Tracta outer joints and Spicer inner joints. The front suspension was more modern, using upper and lower transverse leaf springs with shock absorbers linked to the lower spring. But Donnet was in financial trouble. Only a few experimental cars were completed before Donnet sold out to an Italian-born industrialist named Henri-Theodore Pigozzi who started to make Simca-Fiats in the old Donnet plant in 1936. They, of course, had rear axle drive.

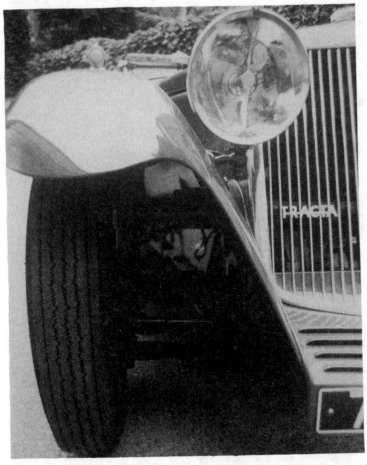

Tracta drive shaft carried torsional vibration damper next to outer universal joint which was not much bulkier than contemporary Weiss or Rzeppa joints.

Keystone Was CV Joint Production

Fiat's own experimentation with f-w-d began in 1929 when O. Lardone, a capable engineer who had formerly worked for Itala, presented a design for an f-w-d van. His design was patented in 1931. It has a V-twin air-cooled engine located in the nose of the chassis and independent front suspension with a transverse leaf spring. Fiat never put it into production because of high universal-joint wear and high production cost.

The availability of constant-velocity universal joints as regular production items from large producers of automotive components did a lot to make production of f-w-d cars on an industrial scale possible. Spicer adopted both the double Cardan joint and the Rzeppa joint, licensing Glaenzer to make them in Europe. Bendix bought the rights to the Weiss ball-type joint. The Tracta joint? J.A. Gregoire tried to sell it direct to the car makers (with some success) and among the supplier industries Bendix bought the rights and manufactured it in England. Despite steadily improving parts and an easier supply situation, many more cars, some failures and some near-successes, preceded the first true mass-production f-w-d models.

Considerable Success for England's Alvis

One of the technically most successful examples was the Alvis from Coventry. The prototype was designed in 1925 by G. T. Smith-Clarke and W. Michael Dunn. The power unit was a well-tried four-cylinder production engine known as the 12/50 placed back to front in the chassis. Two parallel de Dion tubes held the two front wheels and were located by two longitudinal quarter-elliptic springs on each side. The gearbox was placed between the engine and the final drive, giving the car a very long hood.

The following year, Alvis built an eight-cylinder Grand Prix racing car using the same drive train and suspension systems. It was completely redesigned for 1927. The gearbox was placed ahead of the final drive and de Dion suspension was discarded for a fully independent type, using four quarter-elliptic leaf springs mounted transversely on each side, carrying the front wheels and allowing them to deflect in a parallellogram action. Brake drums were mounted inboard of the inner universal joints. The steering gear was centrally located with a cross-shaft carrying worms at both ends. Each worm was connected to a drop arm and each wheel had its own steering arm and drag link. The engine was a supercharged twin-overhead-camshaft straight-eight of about 125 hp, giving the car a top speed of 125 mph.

Experience with this racing car encouraged Smith-Clarke to introduce a front-wheel-drive production model in 1928. It had a special high-performance version of the 12/50 engine and the running gear was based on the 1927 design. The car did well and continued practically unchanged through 1930. In 1929, Alvis produced more f-w-d cars than conventional 12/50s and six-cylinder Silver Eagle models.

For 1929, Alvis also added a straight-eight sports model, stretching the 1928 sports car chassis and installing the 1927 supercharged racing engine in it. The cars were fairly successful but Alvis was in financial trouble in 1931 and production was concentrated on two new rear-wheel-drive cars, the 12/60 and the 16/95.

In Germany, Voran and Adler Led

Concurrently, Germany had produced a crop of f-w-d cars such as the Voran, Rohr, DKW, Adler and Stoewer. In 1926, Richard Bussien had designed a front wheel drive prototype for the Gesellschaft fur Maschinen, Handel und Industrie in Berlin. This project blossomed into Voran Automobilbau A/G with a factory in Berlin. The Voran was a light car with the gearbox interposed between engine and final drive. It had independent front suspension with upper and lower transverse leaf springs stayed by drag struts on both sides. The outer joints were of the double-Cardan type. Bussien sold a Voran license to Brown & Sons in England, who apparently failed to make any cars.

The Voran Company lived on until 1933 when it was taken over by the Neue Automobil-Gesellschaft and the car was renamed NAG-Voran. From then on, Bussien worked together with NAG's chief engineer Paul Henze on new models. The first NAG-Voran 212 used the 100-hp 4½-liter V-8 engine from the NAG type 218 and a drive train adapted from the Voran. Front suspension was fully independent with two lower transverse leaf springs and triangular upper control arms.

A smaller companion model called the 220 was planned but never developed. The design called for a flat-four air-cooled engine at the front of the chassis. When the Nazi government empowered Oberst von Schell to "rationalize" the product lineup of the private automobile companies in 1933, the Voran was quietly purged from the NAG range.

One of the firms that von Schell's plan allowed to continue its production of f-w-d cars was Adler in Frankfurt. Adler had placed its excellent f-w-d Trumpf in production in 1932. The car was designed by a 35-year-old genius named Hans-Gustav Rohr who had formerly

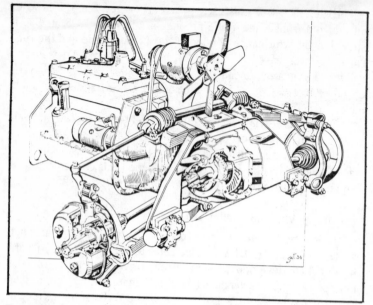

Trumpf Junior drive train had spiral bevel final drive and double-Cardan outer universal joints. Rack and pinion steering was used.

built the Rohr car on his own account but lost control of the business in 1929. Adler hired him as chief engineer in 1930.

Great Success of Rohr's Trumpf

The Rohr cars had not used f-w-d but their design dated from about 1926. In the meantime, Rohr the engineer had become enthusiastic about f-w-d and he sold the f-w-d idea to Adler's management. The Trumpf was a light car with a 1.7-liter 40-hp four-cylinder engine. The gearbox was interposed between the engine and the final drive unit. The front wheels were carried by upper and lower transverse leaf springs. Outer joints were Tracta type on the first 25,000 cars. Adler switched to a German-made constant-velocity joint as soon as it became available. The Trumpf was followed by a smaller companion model, the Trumpf Junior, in 1935. The engine was a 1000-cc four-cylinder unit and the drive train was a scaled-down version of that used on the Trumpf.

The Trumpf won immediate acclaim and Adler sold a manufacturing license to Lucien Rosengart who produced it in his factory at Neuilly from 1932 to 1935. Mattheus van Roggen of Automobiles Imperia at Nessonvaux near Liege acquired the Adler license in 1935 and produced both Trumpf and Trumpf Junior models in Belgium.

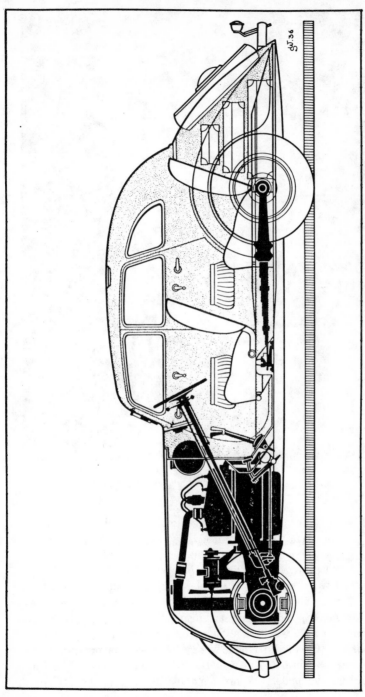

Adler Trumpf exemplifies the primitive approach to f-w-d though the vehicle itself is quite advanced in both chassis engineering and body design.

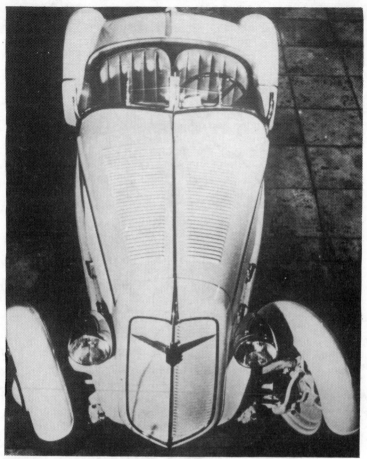

Roadster version of Adler Trumpf Junior had a successful carreer in trials and rallies. Cycle fenders were carried as unsprung weight but caused no handling problem.

Between 1936 and 1939 van Roggen also designed and built three experimental f-w-d cars with V-8 engines placed transversely in the chassis.

The last stage in the short and brilliant career of H. G. Rohr was reached when he came to Daimler-Benz as technical director in 1935. He did not like the conventional Nibel-designed 170-V and was even more opposed to the rear-engined Sailer-designed 170-H. He wanted to build f-w-d cars! Some experimental f-w-d Mercedes-Benz cars with the 170 engine were actually built and tested in 1936. Who knows if his company would not have gone into production with a line of f-w-d models if Rohr had not died on his way to the German

Grand Prix at Nurburgring in 1937? An acute case of lung inflammation took his life in Koblenz.

Simple and Successful DKW

Germany's largest producer of front-wheel-drive cars during the Hitler regime was DKW. These initials originally meant "Dampf Kraft Wagen" and were the trade mark of J. S. Rasmussen's factory in Zschopau in Saxony. Rasmussen built rear wheel drive cars from 1928 to 1931. Then his chief designer, Rudolf Slaby, got two f-w-d models (F-1 and F-2) ready with the same two-cylinder two-stroke 584 cc engine that was used in the earlier models. The DKW enterprise became part of Auto-Union in 1932 (along with Horch, Audi and Wanderer) and the management decided on f-w-d for the mainstay of DKW car production.

The drive train was beautifully simple. The engine, a vertical parallel-twin, was mounted transversely. A duplex chain drive connected one end of the crank-shaft with the gearbox mainshaft and a helical ring gear on the front wheel center line meshed with a pinion on the gearbox output shaft. Front suspension layout was equally simple: a lower control arm and an upper transverse leaf spring. No drive train changes were made when the all-new 1934 models appeared; a 584 cc 18-hp Reichsklasse and a 684 cc 20-hp Meisterklasse. Some production figures show the enormous success of the f-w-d DKW. From 16,991 cars in 1934, output increased to 24,776 cars in 1935, 37,702 in 1936 and 39,353 in 1937.

Strange Line From Budd to Spectacular Citroen

Both Adler and DKW were major producers but nothing shook the automotive world like the arrival of the *Traction Avant* Citroen in

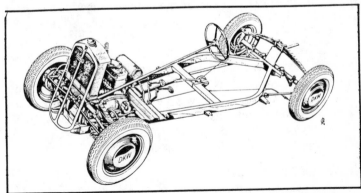

DKW chassis had independent front suspension and a straight tube rear axle with transverse leaf springs at both ends. In this era, the engine was mounted behind the front wheel axis.

1934. Citroen was France's most important car manufacturer, bigger than Renault, bigger than Peugeot. And now Citroen was not only introducing an f-w-d car, but proposing to make nothing but f-w-d cars! For the origin of the *Traction Avant* we must go back to the U.S.

After the Budd/Ruxton/Gardner affair, Budd made some sensational advances in monocoque body construction. This resulted in a new experimental f-w-d car being built in 1931 as a demonstration of how unit-construction could be applied to a truly modern car. The design was due to Joseph Ledwinka (no relation to the young engineering student who had assisted Carl Graf in building his front wheel drive car in 1897). William J. Muller acted as engineering consultant and few men in America had more experience with f-w-d. The Budd prototype was smaller than most U.S.-built cars of its time and considerably lower. The engine was an all-alloy V-8 designed by William Taylor (formerly of Scripps Motor Co. and Kermath Marine Engine Co.).

The Budd car's road to the production line is far from straight and the production model was really not the same car at all. Normally, no sane auto executive would think of Budd's car as anything but a far-out experiment. But a number of far from normal conditions existed—at the right time. First, there was Hans-Gustav Rohr whose Adler was a success. There was Lucien Rosengart who built Adler cars under license in France. Then there was Andre Citroen, shrewd businessman, forever seeking supremacy over his arch-rival Louis Renault. Rosengart knew Citroen socially and was responsible for sparking Citroen's interest in f-w-d. Andre Citroen had been to America. He had seen Detroit's assembly lines and he was aware of the Budd company's importance in the auto industry. This fact no doubt made him more receptive to the advanced experimental car of 1931 than he would have been without such an educated background.

Citroen had produced its steel bodies under Budd license since 1926 and there was an open flow of technical communication between the two companies. Now Citroen got the drawings for Budd's f-w-d car and Andre Citroen was determined to redesign it for French conditions and make the biggest possible waves in the market place. But he did not entrust the project to his normal engineering staff. He had to smuggle it in.

The Secret Citroen 7 CV

Louis Broglie was nominally Citroen's technical director, but he was a man of little imagination and in complete opposition to any f-w-d project. He had joined Citroen after leaving Renault in 1925.

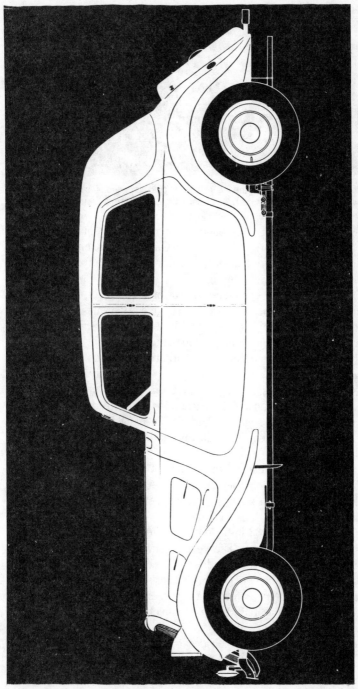

F-w-d Citroen introduced torsion-bar independent front suspension and unit body construction. Four-cylinder engine was mounted in-line behind front wheel axis.

Detachable power package of the 7 CV Citroen could be pulled off complete with front wheels. Four studs on body shell bolted into front cross-member.

Instead, Citroen engaged an engineer of superior talent from outside: Andre Lefebvre, right-hand man to Gabriel Voisin for 12 years. Voisin agreed to let him go, for he understood what a tremendous opportunity Citroen was offering him.

Lefebvre was in complete control of the project, reporting directly to Andre Citroen. Two parallel engine programs were instituted, one designed by Maurice Sainturat (formerly of Delaunay-Belleville, Hotchkiss and Donnet); and the other by Maurice Jouffret who had come to Citroen from Solex carburetors. It was Sainturat's engine that was picked for production.

Maurice Julien designed the suspension systems and Alphonse Foreau the transmission and drive train. Pierre Lemaire and Paul d' Aubarede handled the engine and drive train installation in coordination with body engineer Raoul Cuinet and body designer Flaminio Bertoni.

Citroen dealers learned the details of the new 7 CV in December, 1933. It was officially unveiled in April, 1934. Here was a car that weighed 1,984 pounds and could reach 56 mph and return gasoline mileage as high as 31.4 mpg.

The engine was a 38-hp 1.3-liter installed behind the final drive with the gearbox in front. The gear-box countershaft carried the pinion for the spiral bevel final drive. The drive shafts had simple Cardan-type inner universal joints. There was a succession of changes in outer joints as more suppliers entered the buiness and f-w-d lost its experimental character completely. The first 7 CV cars used a Weiss constant-velocity ball joint in a leather sleeve and splined shafts. In 1935, less than a year after production started, the 7 CV power unit gave way to the 11 CV of 1,911 cc. The 11 CV car had larger-diameter shafts with Glaenzer-Spicer double-Cardan

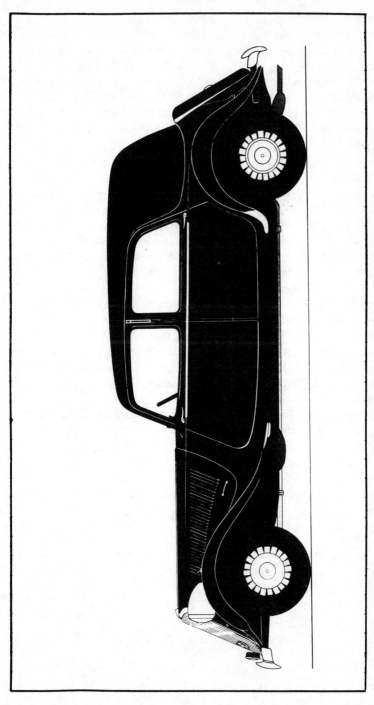

Six-cylinder 2.8-liter f-w-d Citroen went into production in 1939. It had a three-speed gearbox with stickshift on dashboard.

constant-velocity joints. These were retained for the rest of its production life, which lasted till 1955.

The front suspension used transverse control arms, long lower and short upper triangulated links, with longitudinal torsion bars fixed to the lower control arms and anchored in the monocoque structure at the bottom of the cowl. The rear suspension used a simple I-beam axle with trailing arms and transverse torsion bars and a diagonal stabilizer bar. The 1934 cars had a tubular rear axle but a cruciform-profile axle was adopted in 1935.

The 7 CV had a 114.6-inch wheelbase, which was unchanged for the 11 CV Legere. But the 11 CV Normale wheelbase was stretched to 121.6 inches and Citroen added an 11 CV Limousine on a 128.6-inch wheelbase. The 11 CV produced 46 hp and gave the car a top speed of 70-75 mph. In August, 1934, Citroen unveiled a 22 CV f-w-d mode with a 3.8-liter 90-hp V-8 engine (designed as two 11 CV blocks on a common crankcase). It was a showpiece only. Six of them were built but the design never reached production.

Citroen's entire production of f-w-d cars was to use four-cylinder engines exclusively until 1938 when a six was announced. The engine was created by adding two more cylinders to the 11 CV engine, giving 2.9-liters displacement and an output of 76-hp. The 15 CV *Traction Avant* was a fast automobile with a top speed in excess of 80 mph that would cruise effortlessly at 70 all day. It was to prove as surefooted as the smaller models and it became a favorite of big-time gangsters as well as the police! But the 15 CV was heavy on fuel, ate up the universal joints as well as the front tires, and it took a lot of muscle to steer it. Still it remained in production until 1956.

Chapter 18

The Mainstream and Its Twists

The cars that secured the public acceptance of f-w-d as being technically valid were relatively small and light, very modern and thoroughly sensible: DKW, Citroen, Adler. These were the cars that traced out the course which became the mainstream. Their success reverberated across the Atlantic, and the irrepressible E. L. Cord decided to launch another f-w-d model. It was launched in 1935. To European eyes it seemed as much a fantasy as the 22 CV Citroen but it was not its power or size that made it outstanding when viewed by Americans. It was its styling.

The Remarkable Cord 810/812

The coffin-nosed 810 body design by Gordon Buehrig won it more attention than its engineering. In fact, the technical makeup of the car was worthy of more attention than it received. Front suspension was independent with trailing arms forked at their rear end to accommodate the steering swivels. A transverse leaf spring was pleced below the frame and connected to the trailing arms by short vertical rods with rubber bushings top and bottom. The brake drums were conventionally located in the wheel.

When production began, the outer universal joints were Rzeppa-type with four balls but in 1936 Cord switched to a five-ball Weiss-type joint made by Bendix. The gearbox was positioned in front of the final drive unit and was connected to a power-assisted gearshift with a Bendix electro-vacuum mechanism.

The engine was a 4.7-liter V-8 which developed 120 hp and gave the car a top speed of 92 mph. Then Cord introduced the 812—the

V-8 powered Cord 810 from 1936 was noted more for its styling than for its engineering though both deserved great merit. It used trailing-arm front suspension.

same car with a Schwitzer-designed supercharger, boosting power output to 170 hp and top speed to 112 mph.

The 810 and 812 Cords had a 125-inch wheelbase and weighed approximately 4,000 pounds. The steel body was of monocoque construction. Cord production never exceeded 1,500 cars a year and was discontinued altogether when E. L. Cord sold out in 1937.

Herbert C. Snow, formerly chief engineer of Winton and Velie, was vice president in charge of engineering at Auburn, Cord and Duesenberg in the summer of 1934 when design work on the new Cord started but most of the Cord engineering was done under the direction of George H. Kublin who had been chief engineer of Moon during the 1920s and had been connected with the manufacture and assembly of the Ruxton. The Cord V-8 engine was designed especially for the Cord by F. S. Baster, then chief engineer of Lycoming, who built the power unit at Williamsport, Pennsylvania (the Cord was assembled at Connersville, Indiana).

There is a curious postscript to the Cord story for Herbert C. Snow went to Checker in Kalamazoo, Michigan, as chief engineer when the Auburn-Cord-Duesenberg combine was liquidated. Engineering innovation is not what Checker cabs are famous for but Snow built several f-w-d Checkers about 1948. It all came about because Checker president Morris Markin got interested in f-w-d about 1945.

There was a lot of talk at that time about Henry J. Kaiser, who built the World War II Liberty ships, going into the automobile business with f-w-d cars and Markin instructed Snow and his engineers to build an experimental f-w-d Checker. The first one had a four-cylinder engine mounted transversely ahead of the front wheel centers in a standard 1946 Checker chassis. A live front axle was used and an open propeller shaft ran diagonally across the car from the gearbox to the final drive (not unlike the drive train configuration of the rear-engined GMC buses). Later models used a six-cylinder Continental engine. At least one f-w-d Checker was actually placed in service and performed well.

Gregoire via Lindbergh to Kaiser

The rumors about Kaiser were true. It all came about because Kaiser foresaw the need for aluminum in vast quantities in the postwar world and decided to become an aluminum producer. Charles A. Lindbergh, the aviator who made the first solo flight across the North Atlantic in a Ryan monoplane in 1927, had been acting as a consultant to Henry J. Kaiser since 1942.

Towards the end of 1945, Lindbergh met with a Frenchman, J. J. Baron, who was making a study tour of the American industry for his company, Aluminium Francais. Baron told Lindbergh about a little f-w-d car with aluminum frame and body whose construction his firm had sponsored.

Next thing Lindbergh did was fly to Paris to see and drive the car. He was impressed. He was enchanted with it. His report to Kaiser led to an invitation for the car's designer to come to California. This engineer was none other than J.A. Gregoire of Tracta fame

Amilcar Compound from 1938 had all-aluminum chassis and variable-rate rear springs. Drive train was ordinary, with in-line four mounted inside the wheelbase.

Gregoire/Aluminum Francais prototype from 1943 had air-cooled flat-twin carried as front overhang.

who had joined Hotchkiss in 1938 and designed an advanced family car with a cast aluminum frame. This car was named Amilcar Compound (Hotchkiss had taken over Amilcar some time earlier). It did reach production but not many were built because Hotchkiss was busy preparing for war at the time. The engine was an inline water-cooled side-valve four-cylinder unit positioned vertically behind the front wheel axis with a transaxle and Tracta-jointed shafts taking the drive to the front wheels. The front suspension used upper and lower transverse leaf springs.

Radical, Logical, Influential Gregoire

During the war Gregoire devoted himself to refining his ideas, and in 1943 he produced a prototype that maximized the use of light alloy, on order from Jean Dupin, president of Aluminum Francais. Its highly original design showed a logic and clarity of thought that set it apart from any f-w-d cars previously built. It was destined to twist the mainstream. Weighing only 1,190 pounds, it was considerably smaller than the Amilcar Compound but still a four-seater. The engine was an air-cooled flat-twin positioned ahead of the front wheel axis with the gearbox behind the final drive unit. The front suspension was as simple as the DKW's with a lower control arm and an upper transverse leaf spring. Its most unusual feature was the chassis which was a one-piece Duralinox casting incorporating a platform frame, cowl structure, and front stub frame.

292

Gregoire-AF design was destined to be highly influential in post-war f-w-d engineering. It was bought by Panhard who used it as a basis for the Dyna.

Kaiser Adaptation a Failure

Kaiser did not propose to build this minicar in the U.S. but to adapt its design principles on an American-scale car. This task was given to Henry C. McCaslin, formerly assistant chief engineer of

Transverse leaf springs served as control arms on the Gregoire-AF prototype and brake drums were mounted outboard.

Willys and therefore having a strong background in four-wheel-drive systems. Several of the basic ideas in the Gregoire design had to be abandoned, such as the aluminum platform and the horizontally opposed engine.

Kaiser was dependent on existing components to a very great extent for he had no foundry, no forge shop, no machine shops. The f-w-d Kaiser car had to be basically an assembled vehicle using standard components. Two K-85 prototypes were built.

The engine was a Continental flat-head six straddling the front wheel axis, with a three-speed Warner Gear transmission at its rear end. The transmission carried a spur gear train to a transfer case with V-drive to a short propeller shaft running forward to the final drive unit, which was located below a shallower part of the oil pan. It had a spiral bevel pinion and ring gear with constant-velocity universal-jointed drive shafts to each front wheel. The wheel hubs were carried by trailing arms in an arrangement not dissimilar to the Cord design.

The K-85 was hard to steer, lacked stability, and suffered brake-balance problems. By mid-1946 the f-w-d principle was thrown out and McCaslin was fired. The 1947 Kaiser went into production as a perfectly conventional American car. The Aluminium Francais prototype, through no fault of its own, had failed in America. What next? Aluminum Francais took the car to Torino and tried to sell it to Fiat.

Simca Version Dropped but Panhard Succeeded

Fiat's overall technical director, Dante Giacosa, did not want to produce this car as a Fiat but redesigned it for production by Simca at Nanterre. Prototypes were built, tested, and developed, but due to the business politics of the French auto industry at the time, Simca never started production.

Then Paul Panhard got interested in the Aluminium Francais prototype and bought the design. Louis Bionier was given the task of redesigning it for production and simplifying it where necessary. He retained the flat-twin engine and drive train, the monocoque aluminum frame, and the front suspension. The result was the lively little 1947 Dyna Panhard with its 610 cc 30-hp engine.

Gregoire also sold the same design to W. D. Kendall of Grantham, Lincolnshire, who never progressed beyond the experimental stage, and Lawrence J. Hartnett of Melbourne, Australia, who made a small number of cars up to 1951. Belgian rights to the design were sold to Minerva about 1948 but the project was killed. A curious side-light on Minerva and its preoccuption with f-w-d is given by a

1953 announcement that they had acquired the Belgian rights to an Italian f-w-d car called Cemsa-Caproni and planned to start manufacturing, but again, without any results.

Panhard in turn sold a manufacturing license to Ernst Loof, who produced a number of Dyna-Veritas cars in Baden-Baden between 1950 and 1952. In addition, Rene Bonnet and Charles Deutsch found the Dyna Panhard chassis suitable for racing cars and built f-w-d D.B.-Panhards for many years. DB also produced a series of Monomill single-seaters using the Dyna power train and Panhard supplied the Ecurie Monopole with complete power trains for their sports-racing cars. A more modern-looking Panhard came out in 1954, still using a flat-twin engine (which had gone from 610 via 745 to 851 cc). The Dyna 54 was replaced by the PL-17 in 1959, followed by the 24-CT in 1963 and 24 BT in 1964, but the Panhard works (now under Citroen ownership) ceased car production in November, 1967.

Gregoire's Important Flat-four Design

J. A. Gregoire returned to Hotchkiss as chief engineer and started a new f-w-d car project. It was a six-passenger streamliner with a flat-four water-cooled engine using a new front suspension design with variable-rate coil springs located horizontally below the upper control arms. It was a very fast car despite its small (2.2-liter) engine, having a top speed of 95 mph yet giving excellent fuel economy (25 mpg). It was in production as the Hotchkiss-Gregoire from 1952 to 1954. Then Hotchkiss decided to concentrate on trucks. Gregoire continued to develop the car and produced a small number of pure Gregoire cars (in the former Tracta plant) during 1956 and 1957. They remain of vital importance as examples worth following.

Pre-War Citroen Led to 2 CV

However, Gregoire was not the first to combine horizontally opposed engines and front wheel drive though he was certainly responsible for the first production cars built according to this formula. He may not have known about the 1936 Citroen flat-twin prototype when he was working on the Aluminum Francais design.

This Citroen design was the starting point for what was to become the 2 CV. Its development history dates back to 1935 when the new president, and old-time Michelin man named Pierre Boulanger, told his engineers to design "four wheels under an umbrella." In more conventional terms, he wanted low-cost basic transportation, something that could carry four people plus 110

First 2 CV prototype by Citroen ran in 1935. The flat-twin engine was then water-cooled; air-cooling was adopted during World War II. It had crank starting and hand-operated windshield wiper.

pounds of luggage at a speed of 30 mph. Boulanger also wanted some degree of off-road mobility and declared that the suspension must be designed so that if a basket of eggs were put aboard, not one egg must be found broken after crossing a plowed first! The first engine was a water-cooled flat-twin and in 1939 a series of 250 pre-production cars was built at the Levallois works. During the war, the engine was redesigned for air cooling.

Fessia Design Confirmed Advantages

An 1,100-cc water-cooled flat-four powered the 1946 f-w-d prototype built by the Caproni aircraft works in Italy to designs by Antonio Fessia. It was a refined family car that deserved to go into production. But the house of Caproni decided against it, and the prototype was almost forgotten until its designer became technical director of Lancia many years later and revived the Cemsa-Caproni in updated form as the Lancia Flavia.

After the Cemsa-Caproni, Dyna Panhard and Citroen 2 CV, the space savings and architectural freedom offered by mounting small, horizontally opposed engines outside the wheelbase and combined with f-w-d were demonstrated for all to see.

Antonio Fessia, after the Caproni prototype, returned to Fiat where he proposed a new f-w-d model to replace the famous 500 (Topolino) in 1947. Keeping the same four-cylinder in-line engine, he laid it down horizontally and turned it so that the crankshaft ran transversely. The gearbox was located above the crankcase with gearing to a central final drive unit on the front wheel center line. The rest of the power train was carried as front end overhang. This design had the same space advantages as flat-twins and flat-fours and simplified the drive line by replacing the ring gear and pinion with a simple train of spur gears. However, Giacosa designed a still smaller and lighter car with a rear-mounted engine and demonstrably lowered manufacturing cost and this project was chosen for production. Fiat put f-w-d back on the shelf, temporarily.

About 1950 Giacosa toyed with new f-w-d car projects using the Fiat 1100 as a basic. One design, Tipo 123, progressed far along the path to development for production. What really killed it was the opposition of Fiat's director of testing, Carlo Salamano, to any kind of f-w-d vehicle. When the Fiat 124 was being designed, a parallel study for an f-w-d version was conducted and this resulted in the car that went into production as the Autobianchi Primula in 1964.

In the meantime, the Mini-Minor had popularized the transverse-engine f-w-d concept. Despite Fiat's prior start position, it was the little car from Longbridge that twisted the mainstream.

Three-Cylinder From East and West

Of course DKW had been producing f-w-d cars with transverse engines since 1931. But when DKW developed the three-cylinder engine, it was turned around to the car's longitudinal axis. At the same time the power unit was moved from inside the wheelbase to an over-hanging position. This was the work of Fritz Zerbst who had led the development work at DKW since 1936 and had the three-cylinder F-89 prototype ready in 1940. Due to the war, it was not going to be in production for a long time.

It was first produced under another name. The DKW plant in Saxony (East Germany) was nationalized and became part of the IFA

By 1940 DKW had evolved into a three-cylinder car with the engine in the nose of the chassis. Bodies were streamlined.

DKW two-stroke three-in-line ran a shaft straight through from the clutch to the gearbox while the countershaft took the drive to the differential.

organization. And the car that came out in 1950 as the IFA F-9 was none other than Zerbst's pre-war F-89 project. The DKW leaders resettled in the West, revived Auto Union as a corporate entity and set up a plant in Dusseldorf where car production began in 1953. The product, again, was the three-cylinder F-89 renamed 3 = 6 to explain that its two-stroke engine was as smooth as a six.

Wartburg, Trabant and Syrena

The East German IFA was renamed Wartburg in 1955 when the modern-looking P-70 was introduced, first with a two-cylinder 690 cc engine but later equipped with the same 37-hp 900 cc unit used in the F-9. Like DKW, Wartburg aligned the three-cylinder engine longitudinally.

For a "Junior" model, the East Germans decided to go as small as 500 cc. The design was known as the P-50 but when the little f-w-d two-cylinder two-stroke was first shown at the 1957 Leipzig Fair, it was no longer a Wartburg but a Trabant. It was a really new design for the transverse engine was offset to the right with a non-synchromesh four-speed transaxle in the center. The suspension system had lower triangular control arms and an upper transverse leaf spring.

The most recent East German DKW offspring is the Wartburg 1000, in production since 1967 with a 45-hp 991 cc three-cylinder two-stroke engine. As before, the entire power train was positioned ahead of the front wheel centers and the suspension was brought up to date with coil springs and double control arms. The Syrena built in Poland since 1956 is made under a license agreement with the East Germans and its specifications are practically identical with those of the Wartburg P-70.

Auto Union's DKW Led to Audi

Auto Union made fast progress in Dusseldorf. The DKW $3 = 6$ from 1953 evolved into the 1000 and 1000-S by 1958 with 980-cc three-cylinder engines of 44 to 50 hp. A sports coupe, named 1000-Sp and sharing the 1000-S chassis, appeared in 1958 and was in production until 1965. A convertible was added in 1961. A smaller model with a more modern body, the DKW Junior, appeared in 1959. It was equipped with a 741-cc three-cylinder engine.

By 1961 the new Ingolstadt factory built 300 Juniors a day but despite partial redesign, the car ended its life as the F-12 in May, 1965. In the meantime, the resurrected Auto Union firm had become a wholly owned subsidiary of Volkswagen after a period of Mercedes-Benz ownership. Wilhelm Haupt had designed a modern and larger DKW known as the F-102 of which a few were made in 1965 with a three-cylinder 980 cc engine. But the vehicle was really destined for a four-cylinder four-stroke engine designed by Ludwig Kraus in Stuttgart, who was promptly transferred from Mercedes-Benz to Auto Union when production began. And the new car was not called DKW. It was given the venerable name of Audi, as borne by a series of f-w-d cars from Zwickau in Saxony between 1934 and 1940.

Audi had been part of Auto Union since 1932. The first f-w-d Audi appeared in 1933 with a 2-liter six-cylinder Wanderer engine. It

DKW SP-1000 from the mid-Fifties extended reputation of the two-stroke cars but not their production career, which was over by 1965.

Six-cylinder Audi carried Wanderer engine inside wheelbase and used body-work scaled down from Horch designs.

was a design of considerable originality with a backbone frame forked at the front to provide an installation bay for the engine and trans-axle. The front suspension generally followed DKW practice but its transverse leaf spring was used as a lower control arm instead of being mounted on top. This car developed into the Audi 225 of 1936 with a 2.3-liter Wanderer engine. The last pre-war f-w-d Audi was called 920 and was first shown in 1939. It had a Horch 3.2-liter single-overhead-camshaft engine that delivered 82 hp.

Tornax, Tamag, Aero and Jawa

DKW engines and drive units had showed up in some sports cars of the mid-Thirties, notably the 1934 Tornax built in Ernst Wewer's famous motorcycle factory near Wuppertal. The f-w-d 700 cc Tornax was in production until 1936. Another car on similar lines was the Tamag Sepp—but it failed to be built in quantity. DKW engineering practice no doubt influence Ing. Novotny, builder of the Aero f-w-d cars in Czechoslovakia up to 1939, as well as the designers of the contemporary Jawa. When the auto industry was nationalized after 1945, the two were merged and the last f-w-d Aero design was sold as the Jawa Minor, a beetle-shaped little sedan, up to 1950.

Eucort, Gutbrod, Goliath and Lloyd

The Spanish-built Eucort from 1949 was actually made by a license arrangement with Auto Union but several German minicars of the same period followed the DKW school although the cars were even smaller and lighter. Among these were the Hanomag Partner

By 1939 the f-w-d Audi had evolved in looks but chassis design adhered to the in-line six standing aft of the front wheel axis.

of 1951, the Wendax and Staunau from 1951. A new f-w-d Gutbrod also appeared that year, designed by Hans Scherenberg, who took over as technical director of Daimler-Benz A/G in 1966. The Gutbrod had a two-cylinder two-stroke 593 cc engine that delivered 20 hp with fuel injection.

The shadow of DKW practice covered Bremen when Carl F. W. Borgward revived the Goliath and Lloyd marques. The 1950 Goliath 700 was powered by a two-stroke parallel-twin mounted transversely in the chassis. A helical spur-type ring gear was driven from a pinion on the gearbox countershaft and drove both axle shafts via a conventional differential. The Goliath design came from the

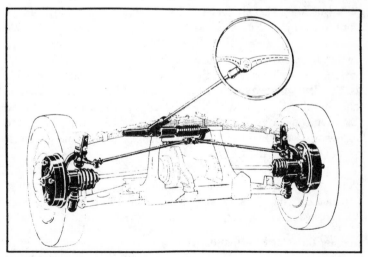

Trabant front suspension was scaled down from the Wartburg's with allowance for the transverse engine installation.

Latest version of the Wartburg will soon be replaced by new f-w-d design using Skoda engines and Citroen drive shafts.

drawing board of August Momberger, who had driven Auto Union racing cars in 1934 and 1935 and came to Borgward in 1949 from a small group of engineering consultants in Hude in Oldenburg known as "Inka."

For the Goliath 1100 of 1957, the company switched to four-stroke engines. Momberger had gone to Ford and Wilhelm Gieschen became responsible for new-product development. He chose the Cemsa-Caproni solution with a water-cooled flat-four ahead of the front wheel axis. Front suspension was assured by lower control arms and an upper transverse leaf spring. This car was renamed Hansa 1100 in 1958.

Borgward also produced an f-w-d minicar named Lloyd. Lloyd cars were smaller than the Goliath. The first one was called LP-300 and was manufactured from 1950 to 1952. The engine was a 293 cc two-cylinder two-stroke unit. Then the 386 cc type LP-400 followed in 1953. A highly refined single-overhead-camshaft four-stroke 596 cc parallel-twin developing 19 hp replaced all two-strokes in 1955 and the Lloyd model designation became LP 600. This led to the Lloyd Alexander in 1957 and a high-performance Alexander TS the following year. On all of these the engines were mounted trans-versely ahead of the front wheel axis.

In 1959 a four-cylinder Lloyd was added using a smaller (897 cc) version of the Hansa flat-four engine and drive train. Regrettably, production of the Hansa and Lloyd cars came to an abrupt end when the Borgward group went bankrupt in 1961.

Another Chrysler Examination

The flat-four engine configuration of f-w-d was rejected (for commercial reasons) by Kaiser but Chrysler pursued it, though

Hotchkiss-Gregoire coupe was powered by a 2-liter flat-four. Wide-track chassis provided seating for six. Aerodynamic body gave high speed and good gasoline mileage.

without any plans for production. In 1949-50, A. Griswold Herreshoff was then in charge of the development design group, with freedom to explore technology in all directions. His team came up with a prototype known as the A-227 which looked like a 1949 Dodge with a lengthened hood and increased front overhang.

Flat-four engine of the Hotchkiss-Gregoire was carried as front overhang. Front suspension shows extremely long upper and lower control arms with variable-rate coil springs in tension.

Gregoire produced small series of sports cars with flat-four engines and Chapron bodies in 1956/57.

Specifically, the idea was to explore the feasibility of moving the entire engine ahead of the front wheel axis by using a flat-six and moving the radiator back against the cowl. Drive shafts initially used simple Cardan joints at both ends but noise and vibration problems led Chrysler to fit Rzeppa joints inboard and Weiss-Bendix joints outboard. The A-227 served simply as a test car and its lessons in f-w-d were noted but it led to no further f-w-d experiments. When Chrysler finally began production of f-w-d cars, it was not in Detroit but in France, and not with a flat-four, but a transverse in-line four.

The flat-four is very much part of the mainstream, however, having been adopted in recent times by Lancia, Subaru, Citroen and Alfasud. The strongest current in the mainstream is the forward disposition of the engine, outside of the wheelbase. This is almost universal for transverse engines and rapidly becoming general for power units carried in the car's longitudinal plane, from two- and four-cylinder engines to Audi's slanting five-in-line and Renault's V-six.

Chapter 19
The Rapids and Backwaters

Long after Harry Miller was out of business, f-w-d cars ran at Indy—and won. Were they proving a point or keeping alive a myth?

The post-World War II generation of American front wheel drive racing cars showed a complete break from the Miller tradition, though they kept their engines well within the wheelbase. The Blue Crown Specials were designed by Norman Timbs and built by Lou Moore, former racing driver turned constructor. The engine was a four-cylinder twin-cam Offenhauser developing 270-hp at 6,000 rpm. A three-speed gearbox was built into the front cover of the transaxle. The chassis had independent front suspension with A-frame control arms and torsion bars. The outer universal joints were Rzeppa-type and the inner joints were simple Cardan-type. The top speed was about 170 mph.

The Novi Governor Special was built around a 500-hp supercharged four-cam V-8, also with a three-speed gearbox combined with the final drive unit. The Novi cars were built by Bud Winfield for Lewis Welch, the actual design work being entrusted to Leo Goossen, chief draftsman of Offenhauser. Front suspension was independent with A-frame control arms and torsion bars. The car was a sensation on its first appearance in 1946 when it averaged 134.499 mph for ten miles around the Indianapolis Speedway.

Blue Crown went to rear wheel drive in 1949 but Novi continued to race f-w-d V-8 powered cars until 1957 (and has been running four-wheel-drive cars since 1964). In 1966 and 1967 Mickey Thompson, builder of racing cars and speed equipment in California,

F-w-d Blue Crown Spark Plug Special won the Indianapolis 500-miles race in 1947 and 1948 and 1949 at average speeds rising from 112 to 119 mph. Indianapolis Motor Speedway Offical Photo.

brought two f-w-d cars to Indianapolis but they proved too slow to qualify.

U.S. Racers and Odd Europeans

By that time, racing car constructors had settled on the midships-mounted engine concept and it proved unbeatable. Yet it's part of the record that American f-w-d racing cars spawned a number of strange offspring in Europe. The first was the Itala Modelle 11 designed by Giulio Cesare Cappa and built in 1925 (but never raced). The engine was a V-12 of 1,500 cc displacement producing 60 hp at 7,000 rpm. Front suspension was independent with equal-length lateral control arms.

Next, Augusto Monaco built an f-w-d single-seater to the designs of Enrico Nardi in 1932. It was called Chichibio and had a -twin 998 cc J.A.P. engine using a motorcycle-type chain drive from the gearbox to the final drive unit. The front wheels were carried by upper and lower transverse leaf springs.

Monaco also built what was perhaps the oddest f-w-d vehicle ever made: A racing prototype from 1935 conceived by racing driver Carlo Felice Trossi. It was powered by an air-cooled 8-cylinder radial aircraft engine installed in the nose of the car (just as engines of that type were fitted in fighter planes of that epoch). Instead of driving a propeller, it drove an output shaft and a transaxle with drive shafts to the front wheels. The drive shafts had dual-Cardan outer joints and single-Cardan inner joints.

Swiss engineer Arnold Zoller was a specialist on supercharged two-stroke engines. In 1934 he had the Rohr company in Over-Ramstadt build an f-w-d single-seater racing car for this latest six-cylinder power unit. It had the engine standing vertically inside the wheelbase and the front suspension used long lower control arms and an upper transverse leaf spring.

A front wheel drive racing single-seater named Derby-Maserati appeared in some events at Brooklands in 1935. It was actually a 1929 Miller with its engine replaced by a straight-eight Maserati. The Fratelli Maserati had also built a front wheel drive monoposto of their own as early as 1932 with an 1100 cc four-cylinder engine. This obscure little Maserati was never raced.

What promised to be the most exquisite f-w-d racing car of all time was called Vesta-Union and was designed in Manchester in 1946 by Arthur C. Whatmough and Fred E. Ellis. The Vesta-Union was a 500 cc Formula 3 project with a four-in-line 16-valve double-overhead-camshaft water-cooled engine calculated to produce 40-hp at 8,000 rpm. All drawings were completed but the car was never actually built.

Paul Emery designed and built a 500 cc Formula 3 racing car in 1950 using a JAP or Norton engine with Norton gearbox and chain drive to each front wheel. The Emeryson performed creditably but was not a consistent winner. Chain drive, hmmm. That's the sort of thing that takes you from the rapids to the backwaters. And Emery wasn't the only one halfway through the 20th Century to use it.

Chain-Driven Bonds and Berkeleys

Lawrence Bond's first front wheel drive was a three-wheeler with a single chain-driven wheel in front (and belongs in the Phanomobil category) but he later designed the four-wheeled Berkeley, also with chain drive. The 1948 Bond carried its front wheel in a trailing arm arrangement with a centrally placed steering fork and a coil spring. Over 20,000 of these had been built by 1957. The

Chrysler test car from 1935 had front wheel drive. The two-door sedan was of compact size and reflected Airflow styling.

Berkeley made its first appearance in 1956 with a 322 cc Anzani engine. It had chain drive from the engine to a gearbox-mounted multi-plate clutch; another chain from the transmission to the final drive unit. Front suspension had short-and-long control arms with a spring strut on top of the upper control arm. Several thousand front wheel drive Berkeley open two-seaters were built up to October, 1960, when the company announced its new rear-wheel-drive Bandit.

In contrast with the three-wheelers equipped with a single driving wheel in front, f-w-d cars with two chain-driven front wheels stem mainly from the studies that the Swiss horologist, automobile engineer and racing driver Charles-Edouard Henriod instigated in 1896. In 1898 he formed a company at Neuilly, suburb of Paris, to build f-w-d cars with a chain transmission and flat-twin alcohol-fuel engines. He was in business there until about 1910 but had no real production of f-w-d cars.

Belts for FWD!

Even more of an anachronism was an attempt that occurred in Leeds, England, in 1919. It was the Stanhope three-wheeler which had *belt drive* to both front whels. It went into production in 1921 with an air-cooled single-cylinder JAP engine. The front wheels were mounted on arms anchored to the final drive casing with a transverse leaf spring. By 1926 the belt drive had been replaced by chains and a V-twin 1,098 cc Blackburne engine was used.

Use of motorcycle engines did not necessarily lead the engineers to use chain drive for f-w-d cars. The B.S.A. (Birmingham Small Arms Company Ltd.) Nine was introduced by a subsidiary, B.S.A. Cycles, Ltd., as a three-wheeler with a single rear wheel in 1930. The designer was F. W. Hulse who copied the Alvis suspension with eight quarter-elliptic front springs. The engine was an air-cooled V-twin coupled to a three-speed gearbox and a worm gear final drive. The counter-shaft was placed high up in the gearbox with its front bearing overlapping the worm gear. In 1932 the V-twin was replaced by a four-cylinder in-line engine while the drive train remained unchanged in principle. A four-wheeled version appeared in 1935, using the name Scout, with a larger engine delivering 32 hp and giving the car a top speed of 70 mph. It remained in production until 1939.

Strange Minicars and Strange Luxury Cars

One of the least-known f-w-d flyweight cars is the Neumann-Neander first built and tested in 1928. It was a small two-seater with tandem seats. The engine was a V-twin mounted transversely in the

Radial five-cylinder tilted up at the nose powered the experimental Chrysler. Entire engine was carried as front overhang. Transverse leaf spring doubled as upper control arm.

car with gearing to the front wheel shafts. Ernst Neumann developed the design over the years and patented a special suspension system with control arms anchored in rubber cushions to provide horizontal compliance. A small series of cars was built in 1935 but Neumann had no actual production line.

An f-w-d Lloyd car made in England was in production from 1936 to 1939. The engines were two-cylinder units of 350 and 650 cc with forced induction by Burt-McCullum sleeve valve charging pumps. The overall design was laid down by F. R. Lloyd and his general manager, G. J. Hannen. The detail design was entrusted to V. Meadows, chief draftsman. Apart from the electrical equipment, the cylinder block casting, the radiator and various small parts, the Lloyd cars were constructed entirely within the small factory in Grimsby.

F-w-d minicars of the Twenties and Thirties were no more weird than some creations at the opposite end of the scale—multicylinder high-performance luxury cars with f-w-d.

The Chaigneau-Braisier was the last design produced under the direction of Henri-Charles Brasier, the man behind the early Mors racers, the great Richard-Brasier cars and a 1902 fore-carriage prototype. The Chaigneau-Brasier appeared in 1928 with a straight-eight 3½-liter single-overhead-camshaft engine and front wheel drive. It used a de Dion front end, not unlike the Ruxton and Gardner design, with an annular end piece to carry the outer jonts and kingpins. The drive shafts were splined to adjust for length on spring deflections. The transmission was split, placing the gearbox ahead of the final drive unit. The Chaigneau-Brasier partnership was alive until 1930 when the firm was taken over by Delahaye, who scrapped the f-w-d designs.

The Imaginative Buccialis

The Bucciali was even more glamorous. The brothers Paul-Albert and Angele Bucciali had been ardent constructors of high-performance cars since 1918 and in 1926 they commissioned the famous designer Edmond Massip, formerly of Latil and Unic, to design an f-w-d Bucciali. The prototype had an unusual transmission system designed by Massip which during development work gave way to another unit designed by Sensaud de Lavaud. The suspension system used parallel links with the upper arm on each side connected to the spring system. The spring elements consisted of two opposed pistons acting against a stack of rubber disks which resisted compression progressively, so as to provide both springing and damping. The shafts as well as the universal joints were completely enclosed.

Early Bucciali models had either 1.7 or 2.4-liter SCAP engines but in 1928 Bucciali went to a six-cylinder Continental. A prototype with a 7-liter straight-eight Mercedes-Benz engine was exhibited in 1929 and this led to the TAV-30, designed for the American market and equipped with a straight-eight Continental engine. A V-16 was announced but never built. The last of the Bucciali cars had V-12 Voisin engines. Once out of manufacturing, the Bucciali brothers continued to work on armored vehicles and even designed a four-wheel-drive sports/racing coupe (but it was never built).

Austrians Rumpler and Barenyi

Next we come to Rumpler, the same Edmund Rumpler who designed a teardrop-shaped sedan with a midships-mounted engine in 1919 and laid out the chassis for the Benz Tropfenwagen in 1922. By 1926 his thinking had turned to f-w-d and he produced a small number of highly original cars with swing-axle type front suspension (Rumpler had taken out the original patent for swing axles while working for Adler in 1903). Clutch, gearbox final drive and differential were together inside one cylindrical housing at the front of the six-cylinder in-line engine and four quarter-elliptic springs on each side located the front wheels. Unfortunately, the talented Austrian-born engineer closed his Berlin-Johannistal workshops in 1928 and his amazing designs were forgotten for many years.

Austrians, from Porsche to Hruska, have made their mark in f-w-d history. One that is often overlooked is Bela Barenyi. Working as an independent engineering consultant in Vienna about 1927 Barenyi devoted himself to studies of high-powered f-w-d luxury cars. He produced, among others, designs for a central-tube chassis where the big six-cylinder engine crankcase formed part of the frame. The gearbox was interposed between the engine and the final drive. Front suspension used upper and lower lateral control arms (single rods as opposed to triangulated arms) and trailing struts on the lower arms.

Another version of Barenyi's chassis had a horizontally opposed engine, also using the crankcase as part of the frame. Unfortunately, these designs were never realized in metal. Barenyi did not long sustain an interest in f-w-d, however. He joined Mercedes-Benz in 1939 and his activity in Stuttgart has been almost entirely within the province of safety engineering.

Laisne, Derby, the Aiglon and Irat

Leon Laisne, the French suspension expert, became interested in f-w-d about 1927 and two years later actually built a f-w-d prototype with all-independent suspension. The front wheels were mounted on trailing arms. The power unit was a small 8 CV in-line four with the gearbox ahead of the final drive.

The 1932 Derby was far more than an experiment. Designed by Etienne Lepicard, it was an f-w-d sports/touring car with a two-liter V-8 engine. The front suspension system was almost a swing-axle design for the drive shafts were enclosed in the upper control arms, and the low-mounted transverse leaf spring was anchored to the control arms. Double-Cardan outer joints were used. In 1933 an economy version powered by an 1100-cc engine was added but production volume was low and the Derby disappeared in 1936.

Chenard-Walcker announced the Aiglon in 1935, a four-cylinder 2.2-liter side-valve medium-size luxury car designed by Henri Toutee, who borrowed much from the Citroen drive train and suspension designs. The original engine was soon replaced by a 2.5-liter overhead-valve engine coupled to a Cotal electromagnetic transmission. The Aiglon was built in small numbers up to 1940. Although Henri Toutee had gone into semi-retirement in 1936, he did not stop designing future models for Chenard-Walcker. But the company went bankrupt and was taken over by Peugeot.

Georges Irat had begun small-scale production of sports cars at Chatou in 1920 and later moved into a larger factory at Neuilly. After seeing the success of the Citroen, Irat went to work on an f-w-d model. It came out in 1936 with a 1,097 cc Ruby engine of 34-hp. Some later models actually used the Citroen 11 CV engine and drive train. Germain Lambert built an f-w-d prototype called Sanchoc in a workshop in Reims in 1934, departing from Citroen influence by using upper and lower transverse leaf springs in the front suspension. Lambert was more prolific on the drawing boards than in actual production but constructed a number of f-w-d cars up to 1953.

Rosengart Ford V-8 & Tracford Ford Four

Also there was Lucien Rosengart, builder of f-w-d Adlers in France. He switched from Adler to Citroen in 1934, introducing the Super-Traction. Also, he wanted a high performance model in his range and decided to build one around the Ford V-8 engine (manufactured in France by Mathis). The head of his engineering staff, Jules Salomon, who had worked for Citroen from 1919 to 1931, designed the Rosengart Supertrahuit. One prototype was built in 1939 using chassis components based on Citroen practice. A few replicas were made and sold in 1946/47 using the 95-hp Mercury V-8.

The f-w-d Tracford sports car exhibited at the Paris Salon d l'Automobile in 1935 had a Ford engine but it was a British-built in-line four, not the Matford V-8. It was a Y-type Ford chassis converted by a company at Gennevilliers that turned the engine around and installed a transaxle ahead of the flywheel. It was in production up to 1939.

Germany's Juwel and Stoewer Designs

On the other side of the Rhine, Brennabor produced its first front wheel drive car shortly after DKW and Stoewer had made the plunge. It was given the model designation Juwel and was a light car with a six-cylinder engine. The radiator was set back, close to the engine on top of the gearbox, which separated the power unit from the final drive. Fully independent front suspension was used with X-shaped lower control arms and an upper transverse leaf spring. However, Brennabor discontinued all car manufacture in 1933 and few Juwels were sold.

Bernhard Stoewer, a constructor of conventional cars since 1898, became interested in f-w-d about 1927. The first f-w-d Stoewer came on the market in 1931. It was called the V-5 and was powered by a 25-hp 1.2 liter V-4 cylinder engine. The gearbox was positioned between engine and final drive and the front suspension used a transverse leaf spring.

Tracford built in France used British Ford chassis and engine with special transaxle for f-w-d conversion. Only about 20 cars were built and a Tracford raced at Le Mans in 1935.

The car was renamed R-140 in 1932 and was equipped with a 30-hp 1.4-liter V-4. One year later, it became R-150 with a 1½-liter 32-hp engine. Bernhard Stoewer had designed the straight-eight rear wheel drive Gigant and Marschall models in the late Twenties but his first eight-cylinder f-w-d creation had a V-8. It came out in 1934 and was called Greif. The 2,488 cc V-8 delivered 55 hp. Drive train configuration was based on the smaller models. But the mainstay of Stoewer passenger car production on the Thirties were the rear-drive Greif Junior (built under Tatra license), Sedina and Arkona.

Japan's Roland and Suzuki Attempts

Japan's first front wheel drive car was designed and built in 1930/31 by Kazuo Kawamata who named it Roland. It was a small sports two-seater powered by an 18-hp V-twin with its crankshaft running in the fore-and-aft plane. The drive went through a three-speed transaxle located in front of the engine, then via-double-jointed shafts to the front wheels. Front suspension was made up of upper control arms and twin lower quarter-elliptic transverse leaf springs on each side. About ten were made. The same designer prepared a V-4-powered f-w-d car in 1935 which was produced in small numbers under the name Tsukuba up to 1939.

Many years later the Suzuki Motor Co., makers of the Suzuki motorcycles and minicars with two-stroke rear-mounted engines, had a brief flirtation with f-w-d cars. The Suzuki Fronte 800 was produced from 1964 through 1968 powered by a 3-cylinder two-stroke engine mounted in line ahead of the front wheel axis. A two-door four-seater sedan with a curb weight of 1,655 pounds, it was nose-heavy, carrying 63 percent of the weight on the front wheels. It was built on an 86.6-inch wheelbase and 152.35 inches long.

Torsion bar front suspension was used with upper and lower A-frame control arms. Rear suspension was independent with trailing arms and transverse torsion bars. The engine delivered 41 hp from 785 cc and was combined with a four-speed transaxle and a final drive ratio of 4.385:1. It ran at a road speed of 14.3 mph per 1,000 rpm in top gear but could only reach 71.5 mph—far below DKW performance levels.

Californian Lewis and War-Time Ford Designs

In 1937 a Californian, Paul Lewis, designed a three-wheeled streamliner, two wheels in front and one in rear, with f-w-d. It was powered by an air-cooled flat-four Doman-Marks engine located in the nose of the chassis with a three-speed transaxle behind it. The gearbox followed right behind the clutch and a set of V-drive skew gears took the power to the final drive unit below the gearbox. Drive shafts had Rzeppa joints at the outer ends, Spicer joints at the inner ends. Lewis wanted to get production started but only one prototype was built.

Ford's first contact with f-w-d was the ill-fated V-8-powered Millers of 1935. But the idea was taken up again when post-war products were being planned. Ford began work on a small f-w-d car in August, 1942. The design included a four-cylinder transverse engine with outrigger clutch and chain drive to the three-speed gearbox lying next to the crankcase. The final drive unit was nearly centrally located, giving drive shafts of practically equal length. Rzeppa joints were used at the outer ends and possibly also at the inner ends.

By 1945 the four-cylinder engine idea had been given up and the sixes and small V-8s that took its place were positioned lengthwise. As a result, the chassis was converted to rear axle drive. In this form, the project evolved into a car that went into production in France in 1948 as the Ford Vedette.

Post-War European Tries

The end of the war in Europe brought many a dream to fruition but not always for the inventors of new f-w-d cars. Marc Birkigt, technical director of Hispano-Suiza, was reportedly toying with a design for a high-powered f-w-d car in 1946-47 but no details are

314

known except that the power unit was to have been a V-8. Birkigt was close to retirement and the project was shelved when he left the company and settled in Geneva where he died in 1950.

Mathis of Strasbourg engaged Jean Andreau to design a range of post-war models and two prototypes were exhibited in 1947. One was a three-wheel egg-shaped vehicle known as the VL-333. The two front wheels both drove and steered. The larger vehicle was a highly aerodynamic design with four-wheel independent suspension and a horizontally opposed six-cylinder engine driving the front wheels. This car was called 666. But neither ever reached production.

Another French experimental f-w-d car was the Dechaux appearing in 1949. It was powered by an air-cooled four-cylinder engine mounted transversely in the chassis and featured all-independent suspension. F-w-d ultra-minicars such as the Dolo, Deshais, Julien, and Bernardet appeared—and disappeared—about the same time in Paris.

Apart from the Cemsa-Caproni, one of the first to appear in Italy was the O.P.E.S. Ninfea, a small f-w-d sedan built in Torino in 1947. It was powered by a three-cylinder air-cooled engine of 784 cc. The project was kept alive until 1950. Benelli, motorcycle manufacturer of Pesaro, considered adding a car to its program and in 1950 built an experimental V-twin 500 cc f-w-d mini-car. The project was shelved before any serious development had got under way.

Olds Toronado from a T-bird?

Some recent f-w-d car projects may seem abortive in the absence of any direct connection with vehicles that are in production today. As an example, a Ford engineer of unconventional bent, Frederick J. Hooven, designed an experimental f-w-d Thunderbird, and the first such test car was built in 1958.

The engine was installed on the front wheel axis with chain drive from the flywheel to an adjacent hydraulic torque converter, with the usual three-speed planetary gear sets and final drive unit alongside the crankcase on the left side. The right-side drive shaft ran through the lower part of the crankcase. Hooven applied for a patent on this design in 1959 and it was granted in 1962.

Several cars were built after the first one but the test program led to negative conclusions and the f-w-d investigation was halted in the summer of 1962. But when Oldsmobile built its Toronado, it was almost as if the Ford patent drawings had been used. GM asked politely for permission to use this layout and Ford happily conceded the rights.

NSU Ro-80 from 1967 was a completely original and very refreshing design. Due to high production cost, it had to compete against BMW and Mercedes-Benz and lost.

Influential NSU Ro-80

NSU built rear-engined small cars exclusively from 1957 to 1967 and then announced a fast, roomy, high-quality f-w-d sedan designed by Ewald Praxl. It was called the Ro-80 and is powered by a twin-rotor Wankel engine. The engine rested in front of the front wheel centers with its semi-automatic transmission behind the final drive. Front suspension was of the MacPherson type and front disc brakes were placed inboard. Both inner and outer joints were of the constant-velocity type.

It was produced in limited numbers from 1967 to 1977. A dead end? No, because Praxl used a lot of Ro-80 design elements in another project, a smaller car called the K-70, which became the first f-w-d Volkswagen. And one day the Ro-80's place will be taken by a new rotary-powered Audi.

Impressive 1969 Mazda R-130

NSU/Wankel's licensee in Japan, Toyo Kogyo Co., makers of Mazda cars and trucks, has remained faithful to the live rear axle for

Twin-rotor Wankel engine mounted as front overhang, inboard disc brakes, and all-independent suspension with coil springs were major features of the NSU Ro-80.

Mazda R-130 was limited-production model with f-w-d and twin-rotor Wankel engine located in the longitudinal plane ahead of the front wheel axis. Body design came from Bertone in Italy.

all its volume-production cars. But the company did have an f-w-d model in limited production in 1969-70, the R-130. It was developed from a prototype known as the RX-87, first shown in November, 1968. The twin-rotor engine rested lengthwise ahead of the front wheel axis as in the NSU Ro-80 with a four-speed transaxle and a 3.90:1 final drive ratio. The drive shafts had constant-velocity universal joints at both ends. Front suspension used unequal-length A-arms and longitudinal torsion bars.

The R-130 coupe was built on a 102-inch wheelbase and had an overall length of 185 inches. It weighed 2,767 pounds and the 126-hp engine gave it a top speed of 118 mph. The car was built in very small numbers and soon withdrawn from the market. A failure? Not at all.

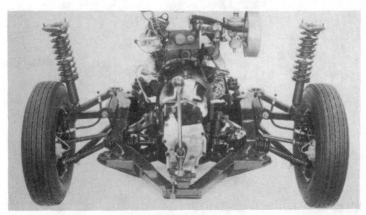

Triumph 1300 engine was mounted longitudinally with geared transfer to gearbox and differential located below. This installation made for convenient shift linkage.

Toyo Kogyo decided it was not marketable concept for its time. But now? It may never be revived in its original specification but the technical director of Toyo Kogyo, Kenichi Yamamoto, told me when I visited him in Hiroshima in 1978 that he was very interested in f-w-d and had every intention of producing f-w-d cars in future.

Rover Experiment and Triumph Failure

If rotary engines lent themselves beautifully to f-w-d installations, that is no less true for gas turbines. Rover built an f-w-d turbine-powered prototype in 1962. It was an experimental ramification of the P-6 project which led to the Rover 2000. The production car of 1963 ended up with an in-line four and rear wheel drive, as planned since 1956 by chief engineer Robert Boyle. But his assistant Spencer Wilks suggested a 2-liter flat-four—more suitable for f-w-d—and chose to drive the front wheels on the T-4 gas turbine car whose body shell was identical with that used for the 2000, a four door sedan. The car was flown to New York for the 1962 auto show and I drove it at Idlewild airport. Rover is now grouped with Triumph and Jaguar in the British Leyland organization. Jaguar has no f-w-d experience but Triumph had a fine little f-w-d car in regular production, and then gave it up!

Triumph's first front wheel drive production car placed the engine longitudinally in the chassis but almost directly on the front

AiResearch Division of Garrett Corporation proposed its small automotive gas turbine for f-w-d cars in 1972/73 with total disregard of need for constant-velocity universal joints.

wheel center line with the gearbox and final drive below the crankcase. The outer universal joints were Birfield-Rzeppa and the front suspension used short-and-long control arms with coil springs on top of the upper control arms. This vehicle was called the Triumph 1300 and was introduced in October, 1965. It was designed under the direction of Harry Webster, director of engineering at Standard-Triumph since 1957. Triumph's experience with f-w-d goes back to 1943 when they designed and built an experimental vehicle in conjunction with the Ministry of Supply. It was nicknamed "The Bug" and never reached production.

The 1300 looked like a little brother to the Rover 2000 and evolved into the 1500 when its engine was enlarged in 1970. At the same time Triumph introduced the Toledo which was the same body shell with the same engine but the drive train converted to rear axle drive, with corresponding modification of the suspension system. The Toledo evolved into the Dolomite in 1972 and the f-w-d 1500 was then discontinued.

Future FWD Ultra-Minis?

To end on a more upbeat note, we should consider the potential of f-w-d for the next generation of extremely light vehicles—successors to the "bubble cars" of the mid-Fifties. The Valentine 78 is an Italian prototype that makes excellent sense. It exists as a three-wheeler and a four-wheeler and the two are identical ahead of the rear suspension.

Power comes from a 251-cc parallel-twin air-cooled motorcycle engine positioned transversely and tilted forward. The transmission is a Salsbury torque converter (as commonly used on snowmobiles) that incorporates the final drive. Drive shafts have Rzeppa-type outer joints and Delta-type inner joints. A MacPherson suspension system is used with a lower control arm made up of long small-diameter rods serving as drag and compression struts and spring legs mounted on top of the hub carriers. Trailing-arm suspension is used at the rear end, so designed that for the three-wheeler, the left rear wheel is eliminated and the right-hand suspension moved to a central location. A steel tube cage serves as both frame and support structure for a plastic body with two-or three-passenger accommodation.

Valentine 78 was designed by Studio Paolo Pasquini in Bologna and first shown in Torino in April, 1978. It is 122 inches long overall and has a curb weight of 705 pounds. Pasquini claims a top speed of 53 mph and a 50-plus mpg fuel economy. It deserves to go into production.

Index

320